Effective Meetings

Each book is carefully co-ordinated to complement *The Sunday Times* 'Business Skills' video training package of the same name, produced by Taylor Made Films Ltd.

Effective Meetings

By

Philip Hodgson and Jane Hodgson

C
CENTURY
BUSINESS

To Joanna and Peter who helped a lot.

This paperback edition first published in the UK 1993
by Century Business
An imprint of Random House UK Ltd
20 Vauxhall Bridge Road, London SW1V 2SA

Random House Australia (Pty) Ltd
20 Alfred Street, Milsons Point
Sydney, NSW 2061, Australia

Random House New Zealand Ltd
18 Poland Road, Glenfield
Auckland 10, New Zealand

Random House South Africa (Pty) Ltd
PO Box 337, Bergvlei, South Africa

First published by Century Business in 1992

Typeset by Servis Filmsetting Ltd, Manchester
Printed and bound in Great Britain by
Mackays of Chatham PLC, Chatham, Kent

A catalogue record for this book is available from the British Library.

ISBN 0–7126–5662–6

Contents

Acknowledgements

We would like to thank a number of people who helped us in the writing of this book. Firstly Edgar Wille and Lucy Shankleman who got us into the project in the first place. Glynis Allen, Harry Hill, Deirdre Tidy and Linda Tranter who read early drafts and commented on them. Gill Chatto and Helen Stewart who did a lot of the typing. Caroline Lewis and Catherine Trew who did sterling work on the illustrations at short notice. Elizabeth Hennessy and Martin Liu who were models of publishing patience and support. Most especially our children, Joanna and Peter who patiently put up with parents chained to the word processor.

1. Meetings are a Problem

A number of very rude comments have been made about meetings:

> *'The length of a meeting rises with the square of the number of people present'.*
> *'A meeting is a group of people that keeps the minutes and loses the hours'.*
> *'What is a committee? A group of the unwilling, picked from the unfit to do the unnecessary'.*

Many millions of meetings are held every day in organisations all over the world. We estimate that in the UK alone, more than four million hours are spent each day in meetings. That means many thousands of people sitting listening, making suggestions, solving problems and making decisions. And many engaging in less useful behaviour – doodling, picking their nails, looking out of the window, or wondering when the coffee will arrive.

In the course of running numerous training courses and being involved in many consultancy projects, we can both put hand on heart and say that whenever the subject of meetings is raised, it is always expressed as a problem.

Sometimes the problem is that the people raising the problem feel that they are not as effective as they could be in contributing to, or chairing, meetings. More often, they feel that the problems arise from other people at the meeting. Perhaps they don't chair the meeting firmly enough – or they do so too firmly. They talk too much – or don't say enough. The meeting doesn't have an agenda –

or it has one in theory but not in practice. Perhaps the chairperson will not allow any diversion from the agenda – even if the diversion would mean dealing with the subject more efficiently.

Time is wasted, is the recurring theme. People feel they go to too many meetings, or that they go to unnecessary meetings, or that they go unnecessarily to some meetings (different from unnecessary meetings), or that the meetings themselves don't make use of time efficiently.

Subjects are dealt with at too great a length, or they are glossed over and might just as well not have been on the agenda, so quickly are they brushed out of the way. People chat – yes, people *are* supposed to talk at meetings – but they chat about other things, not the business in hand.

The complaints vary, but they have a consistent theme in that even those people who ask for help to improve their own meetings contributions also tend to blame others for some of the problems they perceive.

So who is to blame? Who are these people who stalk the corridors of businesses and organisations waiting to get into meetings and cause problems? Whoever they are, they are pervasive and persistent. They get everywhere.

Everyone could help to improve the quality of meetings they attend. Before you go further, take a moment to think about the meetings you go to and the problems you notice. Ask yourself the following questions: What are the problems I encounter at meetings? Who causes them? Is it me or the other participants? Or a combination of both? Most crucially, ask yourself if there is anything you can do about it, and whether you are motivated to do so. We will analyse problems in more detail in Chapters 2 and 3.

Many people cannot only identify that problems exist, but have a clear idea of how meetings can be improved. Green and Lazarus, in a survey of American managers found that the eight elements which people thought made a productive meeting were:

- adequate preparation
- agreement on follow-up action
- staying on the subject

- clearly set objectives
- beginning on time
- physical environment
- ending on time
- having a written agenda

In this book, we aim to identify the problems which arise at, and around, meetings. There are problems concerning structural aspects such as time, agendas, objectives and so on. There are also problems concerned with how the people at the meeting use their talents and skills to help or hinder the meeting to achieve a positive outcome.

We aim to show how meetings can be a positive force for change, and why good productive meetings are so important for organisations. Another supposedly derogatory comment made about meetings is: 'A camel is a horse designed by a committee'. Yet if you were trying to design a horse which could walk over sand without sinking, carry at least twice as much the average equine and go for days without eating and drinking, then a camel would be a good solution – they aren't as friendly though!

Meetings can be frustrating and unnecessary (and, unfortunately, these are the ones all too often remembered and discussed). But meetings can also be stimulating and exciting, creating ideas, generating enthusiasm, motivating teams and giving the satisfying feeling of a job well done. Without meetings the process of communication would be much lengthier, creativity would be stifled and poorer decisions would almost certainly be made. Those of you who regard meetings as the biggest waste of time in working life may disagree, but imagine trying to do your work without meetings. In order for more than one person to be involved in a decision, vast quantities of paper would need to be sent out for comment, sent back with comments, then sent out again to confirm the revisions and so on, in an awful organisational paper-chase.

Use this book to help you get more out of the meetings you organise, and to contribute effectively to the meetings you are invited to attend.

How to use this book

This book is intended for managers and others who chair and/or attend meetings. We have tried to make our examples as widely representative as possible as we anticipate that the organisations readers represent might be in the public sector, the private sector, charities, societies and amateur organisations. We have assumed that our readers will probably not have very much time to devote to the understanding and improving of their meeting skills, so we have tried to provide a format that gives quick and easy reference to examples and checklists.

Structure
We have written each of the 16 chapters to stand on its own and be read, or dipped into, without the need to refer to other chapters. This means that some subjects are referred to several times. Where we do mention a subject more than once, we refer to the chapter in which the most detailed treatment occurs. By so doing, we hope to meet the needs of both the reader who wishes to skim and the reader who wants greater detail.

The book progresses logically through the sequence of events involved in a meeting. We have conceived it in three broad stages:

Stage One **Before the meeting** deals with diagnosis of meeting type, symptoms of problems, likely areas of failure, and preparation for the meeting.

Stage Two **During the meeting** deals with two components: the major skills and tasks to be achieved during the meeting, ie. opening the meeting, ensuring the agenda is appropriate and clear, maintaining control over the meeting, ensuring that decisions are reached and identified. The second component concerns the extra skills that can further enhance a meeting. Here we discuss influencing skills, politics and power as they apply to meetings, and give tips for making presentations.

Stage Three **After the meeting** deals with the follow-up and implementation of agreements and decisions arising from the meeting, ensuring that whatever was decided actually gets put into practice. We also look at longer term development of effectiveness in meetings and examine some of the many other kinds of meetings in which people are sometimes asked to participate.

We give practical examples throughout the book of how to operate during the various stages of the meeting. However, sometimes we review the theory behind the practical advice we give in other chapters. We appreciate that many managers are allergic to theory, but in order to improve or develop a meeting, it is necessary to understand the principles that govern its operation. We have tried to make as many links as possible between theory and practical application.

The early chapters are about the essentials that everyone must know and do to make a meeting effective. Later chapters contain more detail and advanced ideas relating to some of the more subtle and complex problems that can cause difficulties in meetings. Our assumption is that everyone can improve their own contribution to a meeting, and can probably help their colleagues to improve their contributions. The danger comes when people start to believe that they cannot improve their own meeting performance further.

Chairperson and contributor

Although the role and skills of the chairperson are enormously important in any meeting we do not subscribe to the view that the outcome of the meeting depends purely on the chairperson. Most of the people who attend meetings will by definition not be the chairperson. We feel they have a major contribution to make which is often unrecognised. Participants in a meeting need to prepare and can exercise just as much skill as the chairperson. Effective participants can even make up for ineffectiveness on the part of the chairperson. We therefore pay a lot of attention in this book to participant contributions and skills.

Chapter layout

Because we anticipate that most readers will want to dip into selected chapters we have tried to give each chapter approximately the same structure. For most chapters this is:

- an opening example
- what to expect from the chapter
- the main content with illustrative examples
- a summary of the chapter
- a checklist for applying the main principles

In some cases it has not been possible to follow this format exactly, although with the exception of this and the last chapter the other fourteen have summaries and checklists.

SEX AND PRONOUNS

Since both women and men go to meetings, we have used female and male examples and their attendant pronouns. We have tried to mix them up as much as possible. It has not been our intention to typecast or stereotype.

2. Making Meetings Pay

Amy, aged six, is talking to her father at breakfast. He has just said that he hasn't got time to fix her dolls' pram this morning because he is late for a meeting and has to rush (he often has to rush because of meetings).

'Dad, why do you go to so many meetings?'

'Because it is part of my work. I have important things to talk about to other people at the meetings.'

'So does the work get done at the meeting itself?'

'Oh no of course not, the real work happens after the meeting has taken place.'

'So why bother with the meeting? Why not save time and just do the work anyway?'

'If only I could . . .'

Many people wonder whether all the meetings they go to are worthwhile, and whether meetings constitute real work. It is very easy to confuse being busy with working effectively. But 'busyness' is not the same as business, although the derivation looks depressingly obvious. It is certainly easy to be busy attending meetings, people fill up their diaries with meetings and stride around looking important. But, as Amy asks, when does the work actually get done? And what value does attendance at meetings bring?

In this chapter we examine how to assess whether your meetings are giving value for the time and money invested. To do this we first review the many different kinds of meeting and provide frameworks to distinguish between the major types. We then move on to counting the costs of meetings, and finally show you how to carry-out an audit on your meetings to enable you to discover how well or badly they are serving your organisation.

KINDS OF MEETINGS

We asked colleagues and clients for examples of different kinds of meetings and from their answers compiled this list of well over 60:

To make decisions
to analyse a problem
to solve a problem
to inform others
to gather data
to listen to input (complaints, hearings, proposals)
to negotiate
to resolve a dispute
to plan for the future
to generate ideas
to review progress
to record data
to allocate blame
to sell
to persuade
to educate or develop
to argue
to observe a ritual or ceremony (wedding, funeral, speech day)
breakfast meetings
lunch meetings
dinner meetings
meetings with drinks
meetings with experts and specialists
meetings amongst equals
meetings between unequals
meetings to launch something
meetings to stop something
meetings at the end of something
meetings to measure something

meetings to support something
meetings with other nationalities
meetings in other countries
meetings by telephone
meetings by video
meetings with translation
meetings in corridors
meetings in car parks
meetings in toilets
surprise meetings
formal meetings
informal meetings
hurried meetings
meetings under pressure
meetings with your accountant
meetings with your lawyer
meetings with your bank manager
public meetings
short-term meetings
long-term meetings
boring meetings
regular meetings
meetings in cars
meetings in aeroplanes and trains
coaching meetings
mentor meetings
counselling meetings
therapy meetings
T-Group meetings
covert meetings
plotter's meetings
fun meetings.

No doubt you could add more. We print this list to illustrate the variety of meetings you may attend every year. Each meeting type requires different skills and methods to make it work best.

Before we go on to draw up some categories of meetings take a piece of paper and using our list, jot down three things.

1. which meetings you go to most frequently
2. which meetings you find hardest to work in effectively
3. which meetings you feel are giving you or your organisation least value

The next section may show common characteristics between your answers to the three questions.

For the rest of this chapter we will assume that you have identified one particular meeting that you wish to improve. The frameworks and audit techniques are directed at one meeting, or a series of similar meetings. The costing technique can apply to a mixture of meetings.

FRAMEWORKS FOR MEETINGS

We look at the major building blocks for meetings and identify some significant dimensions that are applicable to most meetings.

Building blocks for meetings

Purpose
Identifying the purpose of a meeting is most important. Some meetings have a single purpose, others have a mixture of purposes. Sometimes the purpose or purposes of the meeting are clear and above board. At other times there may be one stated purpose and a number of other covert ones. So the first question to ask is: what is the main purpose of the meeting? Is it to give and receive information or to make decisions and resolve issues?

Once you have established the purpose consider whether you really need a meeting at all. Sometimes, meetings are called for the purpose of spreading the blame. Joe decides on a course of action, then tells a meeting about it, thus making him feel that he is no longer solely responsible. Spreading the blame is not a good reason for holding a meeting.

Time-frame
The time-frame refers to the time with which the meeting is concerned. Some meetings are to do with past events, others with

things that are happening now, and others with events planned for the future. The time-frame will have an effect on the tone and urgency of matters discussed at the meeting.

In what tense are most people speaking at the meeting? Past? Present? Future?

Style
There are many components to style, but these are a few:

Controlled	v	Uncontrolled
Information available	v	Information not available
Formal	v	Informal
Urgent	v	Important
One-off	v	Regular

Choosing and setting the appropriate style for a meeting can go a long way to producing a good and timely outcome, whereas the wrong style can delay decisions and prevent the meeting achieving its objective.

Dimensions of meetings
Using the first three dimensions listed above, it is possible to plot some diagrams which can be helpful in identifying what kind of meeting you are dealing with.

Figure 2.1 overleaf compares the amount of control brought to the meeting and the amount of useful information available at the meeting.

Quadrant A represents meetings that are controlled and have the information they need. Well prepared, and well chaired business meetings fall into this category.

But in quadrant B insufficient information is available. Military organisations, the emergency services, companies facing a hostile takeover bid are examples of people in the position of not having all the information they would like. If there is a strong leader in the group then their meetings are likely to fall into this quadrant.

Quadrant C indicates chaos – no information and no control. However, it can be a useful way of operating when a lot of creativity is needed. Brain-storming, and other creative techniques fall into this category, otherwise, most people find it uncomfortable.

Figure 2.1 Control and information

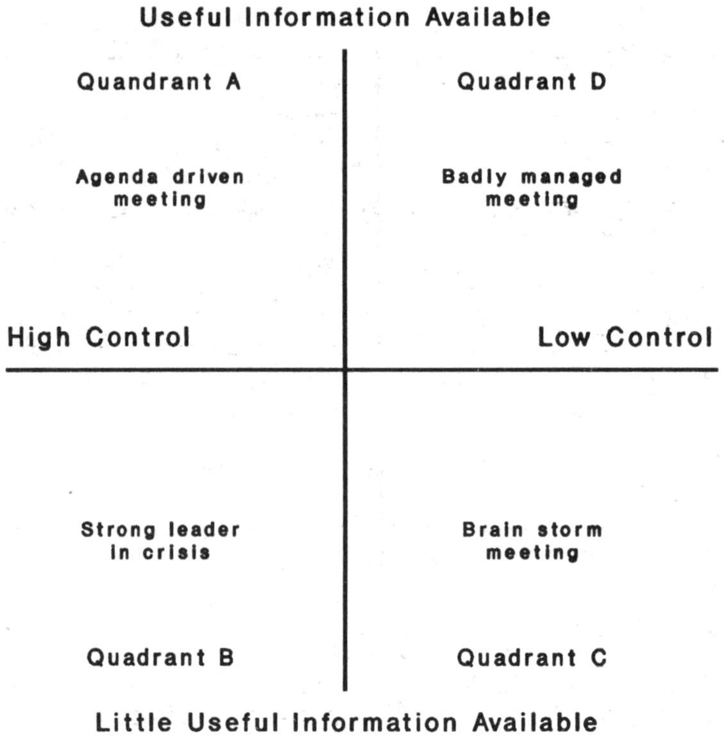

Useful Information Available

Quandrant A	Quadrant D
Agenda driven meeting	Badly managed meeting
High Control	**Low Control**
Strong leader in crisis	Brain storm meeting
Quadrant B	Quadrant C

Little Useful Information Available

Quadrant D is to be avoided at all costs. If you do have the information needed to make a decision, then a certain degree of control is necessary to ensure that the information is used wisely. Meetings that fall into quadrant D are likely, at the very least, to be wasting time and probably making bad decisions too.

In Figure 2.2 control is compared with the level of formality.

Quadrant A shows meetings that are formal and controlled. AGM's, board meetings, courts of law and many public meetings fall into this category. Their role is to be clear and accountable, but seldom creative.

Quadrant B represents the majority of everyday business meetings that are reasonably well chaired and keep to an agenda.

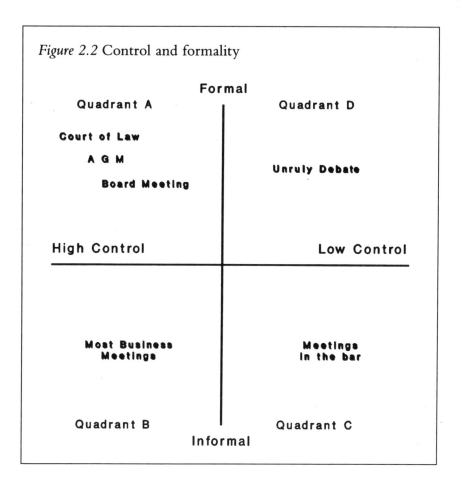

Figure 2.2 Control and formality

Depending on the level of control, they may become heated, and stray from the point.

Quadrant C represents meetings that occur in the bar, chance meetings, some kinds of therapy meetings, and business meetings that have lost their way. Sadly, many people think their business meetings fall into quadrant C too often.

Quadrant D represents formal meetings that have got out of hand. A badly managed debate, unruly political meetings, even the House of Commons when feelings run high. Characterised by a lot of hot air, and not much progress, they are guaranteed to be lengthy, noisy – but possibly entertaining, if you are not too emotionally involved.

Plotting the quadrant position of meetings you attend regularly can be illuminating – it's rather like doing a 12,000 mile inspection on your car in that it allows you to decide whether a further overhaul with more detailed work is necessary.

THE COSTS OF MEETINGS

Estimates, of course, are always difficult because they involve so much generalisation, but suppose it costs your organisation something like £40,000 per year for your services, i.e., to pay you, to accommodate you and to pension you. Dividing that by 200 working days in the year, and eight hours in the day we arrive at a figure of £25 per hour.

Having decided your approximate cost per hour you can put a cost on the meetings you attend. Estimate how much time – and therefore money – you spend at meetings each week and each year.

If you have difficulty in estimating, set up a meetings log, and record over, say, a month the different types of meetings and how much time was spent on each.

Wasted money, wasted time

Suppose that not all the meetings you attend are as efficient or effective as they could be. Assume that you and each of your colleagues could save just one hour each week because of the greater skill you employ chairing and participating in meetings. What would be the saving?

If there are 100 people in the organisation to whom these savings of one hour per week apply, then:

Number of people	100
Total hours saved per week	100
Total hours saved per year	5,000
Annual saving @ £25 per hour	£125,000

For 100 people a saving of one eighth of a million pounds seems worthwhile, but we have ignored opportunity cost. Because if those 100 people put their newly liberated 5,000 hours to useful work,

14

what else could they generate? Who knows, but it is reasonable to expect that it is probably worth £25 per hour, which is another £125,000.

So the final cost saving could amount to something like £250,000 for 100 people, as the result of shortening meetings by as little as one hour per week.

How do you do it? Read on – this book could prove to be worth quite a lot more than you paid for it!

MEETINGS AUDIT

Financial audits, training audits and safety audits are all ways of checking to see if the money, time and effort invested is giving value. A meetings audit works the same way.

There are four parts:

Part One The kinds of meetings you hold.

Part Two The aims, objectives and outcomes you expect from these meetings.

Part Three How effectively these meetings will be able to meet their objectives, and the improvements you believe possible.

Part Four What you can do to bring about those improvements, and ensure they continue.

Part One – What kinds of meetings?

This has largely been covered in the previous section. Is there a particular kind of meeting, i.e. 'the Monday meeting' that seems to be in need of attention? Are there skills or styles that are lacking? Pareto's 80:20 law is useful here. Probably 80 per cent of the savings can come from adjustments to 20 per cent of the meetings. When identifying the different kinds of meetings, look particularly for those that will generate savings.

Part Two – Aims, objectives, outcomes

Why was the meeting called? Was it necessary to have a meeting, or would some other method of communication be better? What was its purpose? What targets were set? Did every member of the meeting agree and support the purpose and objectives of the meeting in question?

How clearly were the objectives set and communicated to every-one concerned? Were they the right objectives? Did the objectives of the meeting address the original need?

Part Three – How effective, and how to improve?

If you know the objectives then you can compare the outcome of the meeting with the objectives to see if they match. You may find that different people were expecting different outcomes from the meeting, so there are different success criteria, depending on who you talk to. This, though, is likely to mean that there wasn't complete agreement on the purpose of the meeting in the first place.

Did the right people go to the meeting? If not who was left out, or who should have been left out? What skills were required to progress the meeting and ensure that it met its objectives? Have those skills been developed within the organisation?

In order to improve a meeting you need to know:

- what is wrong
- what needs to change

What is wrong

In the next chapter we describe the six causes of failure in meetings. Use this list to identify the failure and its likely cause, then assess what needs to change.

What needs to change

Only when you have worked out what needs to change can you start to plan for the implementation of that change. The likely targets for change usually boil down to one or more of three possibilities:

1. The circumstances of the meeting, its physical location, its tim-ing, its preparation, etc.
2. The other people at the meeting, whether they are the chairper-son or the participants. It might be aspects of their behaviour, their expectations, their knowledge, the leadership shown or not shown, etc.

3. Or it might be *you*! You may be doing, or failing to do, things that inhibit the other participants. You as chairperson may be failing to control the meeting, etc.

Our experience suggests that it is often enough for participants to become aware of what they are doing wrong for them to be able to change their approach. Sometimes rather more direct feedback is necessary, and in Chapter 14 we suggest the use of a meetings coach as a way of gathering and making use of that feedback.

If you wish to carry out a meetings audit, then use our frameworks and dimensions as a way of identifying the kinds of meetings you hold or attend. Then decide which meetings you wish to work on in more detail, and use the four-stage method to review how efficiently and effectively the meeting is working. Depending on the exact nature and objectives of the meeting you are reviewing, you will need to draw up your own checklist. If you prefer to use a pre-written checklist then use the one at the end of this chapter.

SUMMARY

How many different kinds of meetings do you attend? The chances are that you attend a considerable variety of meetings during the year. Meetings fall into two broad categories defined by purpose: to give and receive information, or to make decisions and resolve issues. It is useful to categorise your meetings to decide whether they are giving you value for money, time and effort. Use dimensions such as *control versus lack of control*, or *formal versus informal*. Use figures 2.1 and 2.2 (on pages 12 and 13) to plot the position of your meetings. Are your meetings delivering their expected results, or are they wasting time?

Estimate the costs of each of the meetings in which you are involved. Simple estimates, given in this chapter, offer the prospect of saving considerable sums of money. Can you take advantage of this?

Having identified meetings that need some attention, conduct a detailed meetings audit. Use our four-part method of analysis, draw up your own checklist, or use the following checklist.

CHECKLIST – MAKING MEETINGS PAY

1. How many different kinds of meeting do you get involved with each year?
2. How many different kinds of meetings do you regularly attend?
3. Which meetings do you go to most frequently?
4. Which meetings do you find hardest to work in effectively?
5. Which meetings do you feel are giving you or your organisation least value?
6. Which meetings do you feel are giving you or your organisation most value?
7. What do you feel is the main difference between the previous two kinds of meetings?
8. How much money do you spend on meetings each month, each year?
9. Choosing a particular meeting, what is its main purpose?
10. What is the time-frame for the meeting?
11. What are the major style components?
12. What quadrants does this meeting fall into according to figures 2.1 and 2.2?
13. How much do you spend on running this meeting?
14. If you could shorten it and still make it effective how much time and therefore money could you save?
15. When reviewing the purpose of the meeting, what targets were set for it and did every member of the meeting agree and support those targets?
16. How clearly were the objectives communicated to everyone concerned?
17. Were the objectives the right objectives, and did they meet the original need?
18. How efficient is the meeting? Does it take up too much time, or involve too many people?
19. Is there an alternative to having a meeting?
20. Could the meeting occur less frequently, or could it leave out some components?
21. Are the skills needed at the meeting available, or are there skill deficiencies?

22. Have changed needs been identified for the meeting?
23. Is the problem the circumstances, the people, or you?
24. Is appropriate feedback reaching the right people?
25. Is a coach or mentor available?
26. What time-scale have you set for improving the meeting and how will you measure the improvement?

3. Why Meetings Fail

Two men are walking down the corridor towards each other. George is carrying a coffee, Mike is carrying a lot of papers.

'See you at the meeting George.'

'What meeting, I don't know about any meeting' George says curtly.

'But didn't you know that we are going to have an emergency meeting to discuss our budgets?' replies Mike, 'that's why I have all these papers. 'Haven't you prepared?'

From George's point of view, this meeting already looks doomed to failure, simply because he did not know about it. Because he didn't know he was not able to prepare, so even if he rushes into the meeting now, he is unlikely to contribute as much or as well as he might. Failure of preparation, and quite probably failure of purpose have reduced George's chances of performing effectively. This may not be George's fault but somehow the meeting has let him down.

In this chapter we look at the reasons why meetings fail. Although there are many more, we have picked out six major causes. They are:

1. failure of preparation
2. failure of purpose
3. failure of communication
4. failure of resource utilisation
5. failure of decision
6. failure of implementation

A meeting can fail, of course, for more than one reason, and often a failure at one level triggers further failures along the line.

This chapter is concerned with diagnosis. You can use it to help you assess and evaluate meetings as part of a meetings audit (see Chapter 2). In the next chapter we look at what you can do to prevent failure in the meetings you run and attend.

FAILURE OF PREPARATION

'Now will you brief us on the details of our launch of product X into Germany?' said the chairman to George. George looked ashen. 'I am sorry, I didn't know I was supposed to present my ideas at this meeting,' he replied meekly.

'I would like to discuss this point further,' said the chairman, 'but I didn't realise that the meeting would take this long. I am very sorry but I have to leave now to catch a plane.'

These two examples, together with the example at the beginning of the chapter, are symptoms of lack of preparation. Either the details and requirements of the meeting were not circulated beforehand, or the people who were going to attend didn't take the trouble to find out what the meeting was supposed to cover and how long it was likely to last. It is unfortunate that most people assume that attending the meeting is all they are required to do. In fact the meeting itself may be the least significant part of a much longer process. Any meeting requires the allocation of at least two, and often three or more, blocks of time:

1) the time to prepare for the meeting
2) the time for the meeting itself
3) the time to follow up and take action after the meeting

If you were setting off for a picnic, to climb Mount Everest, rob a bank or run a relay race, it would be normal to set aside time in order to get things ready and prepare yourself. Why, then, don't we take the same view with meetings since in the long-term they may have just as dramatic an effect on our lives and those of others?

FAILURE OF PURPOSE

There are three broad categories in which purpose can be the reason for the failure of a meeting. They are:

1. failure to have a purpose
2. failure to communicate and clarify the purpose
3. failure to adapt the purpose

Failure to have a purpose

> *'Why are we meeting today?'* asked Gill,
> *'Because it's Monday and we always have a meeting on a Monday. That's when the supervisors get together,'* said Mike.
> *'But we had an exhaustive session on Friday when we reviewed all our work as part of the preparation for annual appraisals,'* replied Gill.
> *'Yes, you're right'* said Mike ruefully, *'why then are we meeting?'*

Some meetings take on a life of their own and their original purpose is lost in the mists of time. We remember working for a manager who held a weekly meeting with a pre-printed agenda on which the first 12 items were constant. Since nothing much changed from week to week on some of these items most members of the meeting didn't understand why they were there at all. The chairman, when challenged, said it was important for the people to get together, but never managed to explain the purpose for which they were doing so.

It is thus important that everyone attending the meeting understands its purpose and can answer the question: 'Why are we having this meeting?'

Failure to communicate and clarify the purpose

When a manager has done a lot of preparation for a meeting and none of it is used, that individual will not unreasonably feel less motivated to come to meetings in future. The likelihood is that he worked very hard preparing materials, figures and data in the mistaken belief that he understood the purpose of the meeting. If the chairperson of the meeting was just looking for a quick review, rather than a detailed assessment, he should have said so at the outset.

Some people come to meetings expecting to hear others' views, not to make decisions. Other people expect that decisions will be made and they can move on from that point. If the meeting is purely to inform and debate, then participants will approach it in a different way than if they are being asked to commit themselves to a final decision.

Failure to adapt the purpose

The purpose of a meeting may alter with time. People meet regularly to further various projects and schemes, and quite often the objective of these projects shifts for all sorts of reasons. It is important therefore to sustain purpose where it needs sustaining, but not to be blind to the need to adapt the purpose when circumstances change. One meeting spent three hours analysing the impact of a competitor's product in the marketplace, only to discover at the end that one of the quieter participants knew that the product was about to be withdrawn. She wasn't able to say so because she wasn't asked and couldn't get a word in anyhow, so the meeting became an exorbitant waste of time.

FAILURE OF COMMUNICATION

Before the meeting

Failure to communicate the purpose of the meeting beforehand, as has already been mentioned, can lead to people being wrongly prepared or unprepared to contribute appropriately. However, it is also possible to fail to communicate the importance of the subject matter, or its urgency. If people are simply told that they must attend a meeting, without any understanding of its level of urgency or importance, then they may fail to come prepared, may fail to come in time, or fail to come at all.

During the meeting

Communication can break down for a number of reasons while a meeting is in progress. Most significant is the failure to recognise that people respond to the perception of what is said or done, rather than what was actually said or done. People then act on those perceptions. A failure to confirm exactly what was meant and what was perceived will lead inevitably to wrong applications of poorly understood solutions. Sometimes, though, the style and atmosphere of the meeting can make it hard for individuals to confirm their perceptions.

Poor listening causes a frequent communication failure in meetings. Some people believe listening is merely waiting for the other person to finish talking before they have their turn. If people spend most of their time talking *at* each other, rather than listening *to* each other, it is not surprising if the meeting produces poor quality results. Effective and active listening (discussed in Chapter 8) will normally lead to an increase in trust between participants. Trust is like a lubricant: if there is a high degree of trust between participants, then even if their skills are not great, they will work together more effectively and are likely to produce better results. Where trust is missing, the whole meeting is required to work harder to ensure that communication is not misrepresented or misunderstood.

Trust takes time to build but can be lost in a moment. The same is true of honesty. Honesty in communication gives strength to the meeting but a lack of honesty reduces its performance and effectiveness. It is tempting to ignore painful truths, but effective participants at meetings go out of their way to encourage colleagues to be honest, however uncomfortable this is.

After the meeting

The writing and distribution of meeting minutes is often a very political affair. Minutes can sometimes take on a life of their own and exist almost in spite of the meeting that generated them.

People who did not go to the meeting need to know what was discussed and what decisions were reached. If they are presented with meaningless information, it is unlikely that effective action will result.

FAILURE OF RESOURCE UTILISATION

Use of experts

Some time ago NASA was required to test part of the USA Star Wars Initiative. NASA mounted a mirror on one of the space shuttles as part of an experimental test of a laser system where the laser would be fired from Earth to bounce off the mirror. When the laser was fired from Earth, the mirror on the space shuttle was pointing in the wrong direction and the whole experiment was wasted at a cost of several million dollars.

*The reason: the radar which aligned the mirror on the shuttle was due to lock on to a mountain in Hawaii. The mountain was 13 thousand feet high. Unfortunately the radar on the space shuttle was calibrated in kilometres. So when it failed to find a mountain 13 thousand **kilometres** high, and indeed to find such a phenomenon on Earth, it selected the Moon as the next best thing. Thus when the laser fired, the mirror was aligned in the opposite direction.*

One can imagine that a year or two previously at a meeting between the various contractors supplying NASA, two experts had sat on either side of a table. One of them assumed that all calibrations were in feet, the other that all calibrations were in kilometres. Unfortunately neither managed to speak to the other and the final result was a huge and very public waste of money.

'Experts' are one of the resources available to meetings. These people fall into three categories:

1. Those who believe they are experts even though other people have doubts about this. They will tend to lead the meeting down a route defined by their own perceived expertise. Often these routes are dead ends, or lead to ineffective solutions. Competent questioning (see Chapter 9) will expose these people and demonstrate their true level of expertise.

2. There is the quiet expert, who needs to be encouraged and brought out. He may have facts and may have opinions, and both may be useful subject material in the meeting. The chairperson will

need to work hard to ensure that the maximum benefit is gained from the quiet expert.

3. There is the loud expert who will tend to push the meeting towards her own opinion. If no-one else in the meeting is prepared to challenge or question, then the loud expert will deny any other possible solutions than the one she is pushing. A loud expert can produce a good solution, and a quick solution, but only if their expertise covers all of the problem areas being discussed at the meeting.

Use of time

Time is a resource which is frequently wasted at meetings. One of C. Northcote Parkinson's 'laws' demonstrates that time spent at a meeting is inversely proportional to the importance of the subject. Meetings frequently fail by not allocating time in proportion to the importance of the subject under discussion. Failure to link time with importance also encourages self-declared experts to spend time lavishly on their own particular hobby horses.

Use of physical resources

The physical resources that are available may be reviewed and used in innovative ways. There is a story of the flight crew of a commercial airliner which suffered severe failure of its control mechanisms, and so became very difficult to control. The flight crew invented a new way of using the subsidiary controls (trim tabs) and the thrust from the tail-mounted high-level jet to control the aeroplane and make a safe, if bumpy, landing. If they had not invented this entirely original approach, the aeroplane almost certainly would have crashed, causing much loss of life. The solution came not from one individual, but from all three flight crew members working together rapidly and under immense pressure to build on each other's ideas about innovative ways to control the pitch of aircraft.

Many meetings face problems which require original and innovative solutions such as creative ways of using physical resources. An effective meeting which builds and develops ideas as it goes along is much more likely to produce appropriate solutions. Failure to listen and to build on solutions will result in a failure of the meeting's output.

FAILURE OF DECISION

Failure to distinguish discussion from decision

> *'We had a long meeting at which everyone got very heated. We all said our piece, some repeating themselves. At the end, the chairman heaved a sigh of relief and said 'thank God that's settled', looked at his watch and with a muffled apology that he was late for lunch with a major shareholder, rushed out. Actually we hadn't decided anything and the whole argument broke out again for another hour.'*

This observation comes from a senior manager of a company going through much change. The failure here is to confuse discussion of the problem with making a decision, and to confuse having the meeting with finding the solution. Some meetings are called to dispense information and data and to discuss things, but many are also called to decide matters. The agenda can be useful to explain why the meeting is called and to agree what has to be decided and in what time-scale.

Communiques from world leaders often reveal if a decision has actually been taken. If nothing much has occurred, the communique will talk about what happened at the meeting and what needs to happen next (we are all used to 'full and frank discussions about the need for peace, improved relationships' etc.) If something *did* actually get decided, the communique will be much shorter as it will deal simply with the outcome and not the activity which led up to it.

Failure to confront hidden agendas

Some meetings fail because of underlying problems between participants. It will be obvious to meeting participants if, whenever the production director says something, he is always contradicted by the marketing director. The question is: does this natural disagreement relate to this meeting only, or does it refer back to previous discussions? Does the marketing director have a hidden agenda concerning production? Will he obstruct a useful decision because the hidden conflict between the two departments is neither acknowledged nor resolved at the meeting? Hidden agendas (see Chapter 12) get in the way of good decisions.

Failure to recognise reality

Some years ago the newly-appointed director of a faded, but once highly successful, hotel company was being shown round the flagship hotel by the head housekeeper. They arrived at a magnificent room covered in dust sheets. The director asked why the room wasn't available for guests. It was explained that the room was kept only for 'special' guests, and unfortunately there had not been many of those recently. The director asked if they could let the room to anyone else and was told that there were many people who could afford it but if they were allowed to occupy it, the room would no longer be available for the 'special' people! That hotel almost went bankrupt before people like the director, who lived in the real world, were able to recognise what was wrong and do something about it.

Many meetings fail to make decisions because they avoid the reality of their situation. The head housekeeper was living in a world which had disappeared 10 or 15 years earlier, nevertheless she still clung to the notion that 'special' guests were going to be as plentiful in future as they had been in the past.

Failure of courage

It was probably the British television series 'Yes Minister' that highlighted the awfulness of asking a politican to make a 'courageous' decision. Yet sometimes in meetings it is clear that a decision has to be made, and it is also clear that there will be unpleasant consequences following that decision. Many organisations have deferred the need to face up to staff cuts, make an individual redundant, demote people etc. because they were afraid of the consequences. Sometimes the joint responsibility shared by members of a meeting can go some way to supporting difficult decisions.

FAILURE OF IMPLEMENTATION

New Years resolution syndrome

Around the beginning of each year a lot of people make decisions about giving up smoking, losing weight and changing their lives in all kinds of impressive and dramatic ways. Generally speaking, the resolve wears off after a few weeks, and people go about their business as before. There is a kind of similarity where a failure to implement the decisions of a meeting occurs.

Sometime ago in a household not a million miles from the authors, a happy Saturday morning was spent looking for a favourite, but mislaid, shirt, belonging to a young man. The shirt was finally found, in a corner under a bed. A need for improved storage space was identified and an expedition to the local DIY store produced an attractive set of baskets. Surely now the bedroom would be tidier? You've guessed the answer. It didn't happen because the will to change was in the parents' minds, not their son's. The mechanism for implementation was there, but there was no desire to use it.

The same often happens after meetings. Minutes are circulated, notes are drafted, but unless there is a will to implement the decisions taken by the meeting nothing will get done.

Failure to install a mechanism

The chairman of a financial services organisation was having dinner with a colleague. The subject of health and safety at work came up and it became clear that the chairman's organisation had no health and safety representatives. He called a meeting of his directors and they agreed that they must have some health and safety representatives. A memo was drafted, representatives were appointed, but given no budget, no extra time in which to do the work, no training and no briefing on what they were supposed to do. As a result, no health and safety actions were implemented and, although the chairman had set up the process with the best of intentions, the result was seen as a pointless and frustrating failure by the other members of the organisation.

SUMMARY

This chapter has looked at the failures of the meeting as distinct from individual skill or task deficiencies. Failure of preparation usually means that the meeting does not start with all the people or information it requires. Failure of purpose and failure to adapt the purpose implies that participants don't know why they are meeting, or believe they are meeting for a different purpose. Failure of communication can occur before, during and after the meeting, and is often due to the fact that people act on their perceptions of what was said or done, rather than what was actually said or done.

Failure of resource utilisation means that experts and expertise, time and timeliness, and the physical resources available are not used as effectively as they could be. Failure of decision may occur because of the inability to distinguish between decision and discussion, a failure to confront hidden agendas and unresolved issues, or a failure to recognise reality and to work accordingly. Finally, failure of implementation can occur because there is no mechanism to implement, or because there is no will to use that mechanism.

CHECKLIST – WHY MEETINGS FAIL

1. Were the details and requirements of the meeting circulated beforehand?
2. Were time, location, other participants' names also circulated?
3. Were timings indicated?
4. Was time allocated for preparation, for the meeting itself, and for follow-up action?
5. Does everyone know what the purpose of the meeting is?
6. Can everyone answer this question: Why are we having this meeting?
7. Does everyone understand what the output from the meeting will be, a discussion, a decision, or what?
8. Does the purpose of the meeting still match the original need?
9. Has the purpose been adapted according to circumstances?
10 Has the importance or the urgency of the subject matter been communicated?
11. Are people listening during the meeting?
12. Are people confirming their perceptions, and the perceptions of others, during the meeting?
13. Is the style and atmosphere of the meeting appropriate to its subject?
14. Are there good levels of trust between participants?
15. How much honesty is being demonstrated?
16. Are the notes of the meeting written clearly and distributed after the meeting?
17. Are the experts used effectively and allowed to talk?
18. Are self-declared experts challenged,. loud experts quietened, and quiet experts encouraged?
19. Does the time spent relate to the importance of the subject?
20. Is the best use made of physical resources?
21. Are creative uses of resources encouraged?
22. Is discussion allowed to get in the way of decision?
23. Are hidden agendas confronted?
24. Are people realistic at meetings?
25 Are mechanisms in place to implement decisions?
26. Is there a will to utilise those mechanisms?

4. Planning the Meeting

'How are you Mike?'

'Terrible. I've just come back from one of Paul's meetings. As usual it was a total disaster, nothing was decided, everyone got ratty with each other because we all wanted to talk about something different. I've got a splitting headache and you wouldn't believe the amount of passive smoking I've done in the last two hours. The thing that gets me is that we do actually need to meet to discuss lots of issues. If only Paul put a bit of thought beforehand into what was going to happen, we could have a really productive and useful meeting instead of a total waste of time.'

All meetings need to be planned. The amount of planning required can vary from a few scribbles on the back of an envelope, to the formal and fairly lengthy preparations needed for something like an annual general meeting. The planning for an average office meeting may be no more than fifteen minutes-worth of jottings and telephone calls, but those fifteen minutes may be the most important minutes of the whole meeting.

The person who calls the meeting has the responsibility for ensuring the meeting runs smoothly, and for its tone or climate. Let us look for a moment at a blueprint for disaster.

Half the people needed were either not invited or haven't turned up. The agenda is not clear, or non-existent. People have not had the opportunity to formulate their thoughts or familiarise themselves with essential documents beforehand. The room is small, hot and stuffy. The chairs are hard and jammed close together. There are constant interruptions.

Perhaps this is an exaggeration, and there are no meetings quite like that, but I wonder how many people have never attended a meeting with at least one or two of these features. Meetings can fall apart if some essential person is not there, or if another person has failed to bring vital information because they did not know it would be needed. The effectiveness of meetings can be greatly reduced by the physical discomfort of the people attending them.

In this chapter we look at the preparations you can make to ensure that the meetings you call are as effective as possible. Although there may be times occasionally when you arrive in someone's office, see someone you've been meaning to talk to and grab the opportunity to convene a meeting on the spot, you will usually know beforehand that a meeting involving you is going to happen.

Good preparation gets you a long way towards holding a successful meeting. This need not necessarily take much time; the four essential steps of good planning can be done in about fifteen minutes. Of course, it may take you longer than that to prepare your own contribution to the meeting. What we will be talking about here are the nuts and bolts of pre-meeting planning which are nothing to do with what is said at the meeting, but which nonetheless can have a tremendous impact on its success.

This is the simple four stage approach to planning a successful meeting.

1. **Know your objective**
2. **Decide who should be there**
3. **Prepare an agenda**
4. **Arrange the time and place**

These four stages sound very simple, and in fact *are* very simple. For some meetings they will take very little time. Larger meetings may take longer and need the help of administrative staff.

KNOW YOUR OBJECTIVE

If you are the person instigating the meeting, the first question you should ask yourself is:

'What would happen if the meeting wasn't held?'

This will help you to decide:

- What is the purpose or objective of this meeting?
- Does it really need to happen?
- Why?

One of the classic examples of a meeting without a purpose is the 'Monday Meeting', the sort of meeting that has been held at the same time, with the same group of people, for as long as anyone can remember. The meeting happens because it has always happened. It becomes a reason for existing in itself. Often people exchange information at the meeting about things that are going on within the department, but without stopping to wonder if this information really needs to be discussed in a meeting, or whether there isn't some other equally effective and less time-consuming way of passing it on.

So why is it important that everyone who attends a meeting should have a clear idea of what that meeting is aiming to achieve?

- If you are the person calling the meeting, it is important that *you* are clear about its purpose because this is one of the key facts you need to pass on to the other people who are to attend.
- Meetings without a clear purpose become demotivating and frustrating for those attending them.
- If meetings are held regularly without clear objectives, people begin coming to them with the expectation that they will be useless and boring, which makes people less likely to contribute or listen. This will almost certainly lead them to think that the meeting *is* useless and boring.
- If people *are* clear about the objectives, they are aware of the importance of the meeting and the contribution they can make to it.
- Clarity of purpose leads to individuals making greater efforts and being more motivated to do what is expected of them.

Meetings can be divided into two types, depending on the objective:

1. Meetings concerned with the giving and receiving of information:

- providing information about a product or service
- presenting an idea or report
- exchanging information
- encouraging creativity
- consulting a group about something
- informing a group about a decision

2. Meetings concerned with decision-making, where an outcome is required:

- problem-solving
- negotiating
- making decisions

In reality, many meetings have a mixture of objectives. In the same meeting you may wish to gain information about how the new software is helping to sort out the invoicing problem, and also make a decision about the level of sales targets for the following year. This is fine. As long as you are clear beforehand what you are aiming to achieve, then the rest of the planning and preparation for the meeting follows on naturally.

DECIDE WHO SHOULD BE THERE

Once you know the purpose of the meeting, you should have a fair idea of who should attend. If you are clear about the kinds of decisions required, you can invite people with the appropriate expertise and from the appropriate level in the organisation to make that sort of decision. If you need to have a meeting to discuss the fact that too many bottles are being broken by the bottle-washers, and to find a way to reduce the percentage of breakages, then the board of directors, though no doubt experts in their own fields, are unlikely to be as effective at solving the problem as a group of bottle-washer-supervisors.

There are a number of reasons why people are invited to meetings. Some are valid, and some are not. The golden rule of inviting people to meetings is:

Only invite those who really need to be there

These are some of the valid reasons for inviting people to a meeting:

1. *They may have information to communicate*
   A person might need to be invited to a meeting because they have something in particular to communicate. Maybe they have been working on a project or need to put their department's view to the meeting.

2. *They may need to be given information*
   Sometimes, the most effective way of distributing information is to invite people to a meeting. It means that they are able to ask questions and clarify areas which are unclear. Sometimes meetings are held specifically to give certain information to a number of people. At other times, part of a meeting might be concerned with giving information, which may then need to be discussed and acted upon. Certain people may need to be there to be informed of the thinking around a particular subject.

3. *They may be an expert in a particular subject for discussion*
   There are a number of good reasons for inviting the right experts to your meeting. Sometimes, you will need specific expert advice as to whether X is possible, or what effect Y will have on Z. If your project or problem requires a number of specialist inputs, make sure they are all present. You not only need their advice, but, if the item you are discussing will have an impact on the workload of their team or department, you are much more likely to have their commitment to implementing their part of the plan if they are involved in it from the beginning.

4. *They may have executive responsibility for an area under discussion*
   If a person has the executive responsibility for an area, they may need to be invited to the meeting for any one of a number of

different reasons – the authority they have, to inform them of what is going on, or to gain their support.

5. *They will be annoyed if they are not invited*
This is not always a valid reason for inviting someone to a meeting – indeed it may be a totally invalid reason. It becomes valid when there is a good political reason for not annoying someone. You may well find that you can avoid having some people whom you don't want but who think they ought to be there, by explaining the purpose and content of the meeting and the reasons why it doesn't concern them. But there may still be occasions when it is more politically astute to invite someone you don't want rather than exclude them altogether.

There are also a number of totally invalid reasons for inviting people to meetings.

- He's always come in the past
- She always offers to take the work on even though it's not her job
- I want to ask his advice on something else after the meeting
- I'm scared of her
- I like them and they are nice to me

Problem-solving meetings
When you are holding a meeting which involves some aspect of problem solving, there are a few other criteria to take into account when inviting the participants:

1. They should have a knowledge of the subject, commitment to solving the problem, and time to participate.
2. Try to invite people with a diversity of viewpoints. When a number of people get together to solve a problem, the more people there are with different views, the longer it takes. However, research has established that a better decision is made by a group than by an individual. This can easily be seen by the various group exercises run on training courses where partici-

pants are told that they are stranded in the middle of a desert, on the moon, or on a desert island. They have to make decisions about the usefulness of a list of objects, first individually, then as a group. The group takes much longer than individuals to come to a decision but, with very few exceptions, the group score is better than the individual scores, when compared with the answers of a panel of experts. This is discussed in more detail in Chapter 7.

3. Invite people who are able to be open-minded about a subject. Most problem solving involves a stage of creativity and divergent thinking. People who operate within narrow tracks are generally poor at allowing their ideas to diverge, they naturally want to converge. These people may also have great difficulty in giving proper consideration to ideas that differ from their own (strongly) held beliefs.

4. Be clear about the kinds of decisions which need to be made and invite people who are at the right level to make those kind of decisions. It is infuriating to convene a meeting, which after heated discussion comes up with a useful answer, to find that the people involved do not have the authority or power to implement the decision. Of course some meetings are called to make recommendations to a Board, or other higher power, but even these should have participants who can speak with authority on the probability of being able to implement the proposals.

5. Try to ensure that the people you invite are as near as possible the same status within the organisation. In meetings where one or two people are at a higher level than the others, remarks are often addressed to them, rather than to the meeting as a whole. When people of high status are at a meeting, with others of lower status, it can be counterproductive in that they tend to dominate the discussion. Often their ideas are accepted even though they are not the best ideas.

How many people should you invite?

The size of the meeting will depend to a great extent on its purpose. It will also depend on the number of people who absolutely have to be there. Meetings with the purpose of presenting something to a number of people have the potential for being very large. Meetings which have to make a decision or solve a problem must be limited in size if they are going to achieve their purpose in a reasonable length of time.

If a decision has to be made or a problem solved, then the fewer people involved the quicker it will be. So if you want a really quick decision, make it yourself, without the benefit of a meeting. However, as we establish in Chapter 7, this is not always the best or most acceptable way of making a decision.

The principle, however, remains. If you have a small number of people making a decision, they are likely to come up with the answer sooner than would a large number of people. One of the problems with having only a few decision-takers, though, is that there will be less scope for ideas and creativity within the group. There will be fewer options suggested, and more likelihood of groupthink – people becoming such a cosy and coherent group that they are less detached, and more likely to make decisions that in the long term will be seen as unwise.

Large meetings are potentially more effective for making decisions because more resources are available – more expertise, more knowledge, more ideas. However there are a number of problems with having large numbers of people at meetings where everyone or nearly everyone needs to make a contribution. Some of these are:

Non-participation
If a lot of people attend a meeting, there is a higher chance that some of them will not contribute. The danger is that the active contributors may be the loudest members of the group, rather than the ones with the most insight or knowledge of the problem. While they hold the floor, they may be preventing the quieter person, with perhaps the idea that would have made the difference from speaking.

Lack of control
Large meetings where lots of people have much to say, are more difficult to control than smaller ones. The task of the chairperson, which is to ensure that as many people who want to have their say,

while keeping the meeting to the point, can become almost impossible. Very quickly a meeting can degenerate into a shouting match.

Poor use of time

This point is linked with the previous one. When a lot of people
need to have their say, even though the chairperson does his or her
best to keep to the agenda, much time is often spent discussing early
subjects on the agenda. This can leave too little time for later items
which may be rushed out of the way without proper consideration.

Difficulty in reaching agreement

We mentioned earlier that groups made better decisions than individuals even though it took longer. However, you may not have very
much time. Sometimes a large group of people can find it difficult to
reach consensus. Of course it would be possible to sit there all night
until a decision was made, but all too often the problem of non-
agreement is solved by postponing that item on the agenda until a
later date when Bob and Mary will have done some fact-finding.
This is just postponing the argument until next time.

The answer with problem-solving and decision-making meetings
seems to be to make them large enough to have a variety of talent
and expertise, but small enough to allow everyone to put in their
two penn'orth. Dependent on the circumstances the ideal number is
probably between three and twelve people.

Meetings to present information

If the purpose of your meeting is to present information to people,
then in theory there is no limit to the number of people you could
invite. In reality you probably will want to limit the size. Usually,
presentations are made to people when the information is too complex, new, important or startling to be distributed by paper. This
will usually mean that the people attending the presentation will be
allowed or even encouraged to ask questions.

So the size of your meeting should be limited by the sort of
information which is to be presented and the extent to which you
want people to be able to ask questions. If a very large number of
people are present, then only a few of them are going to be able to

have their concerns addressed and their confusions clarified. If the information is of a relatively simple nature, then large meetings may well be adequate. Where the information being presented affects individuals personally, or is complex, they will want the opportunity to clarify issues for themselves, so smaller meetings will be more effective.

If it is important that the information you are presenting gets through to everyone present, then relatively small meetings also have an advantage in that it is more difficult for members of a small audience to sleep, dream, or plan their holiday in Istanbul. Large audiences give anonymity, it is easier to feel concealed. If the meeting consists of fewer people, there is a more personal feel to the event. Individuals perceive that the information is addressed to them more directly than if they are part of a very large group.

Here are two examples of how different organisations tackled the problems of presenting to staff information which would have a direct impact on their working lives.

Some years ago an organisation in the public sector decided to adopt Management By Objectives. The staff of each department (consisting of 70–100 people) were informed by letter that this was the intention, and that an important meeting to explain Management By Objectives (which after the initial introduction was referred to as MBO) would be held on a certain date. All staff were urged to be there, on pain of all sorts of terrible threats. The day came and they all attended.

The meeting lasted all afternoon and went into some detail. At its conclusion the staff were encouraged to ask questions. All this might seem very reasonable, except that the organisers had not appreciated that half the staff had not understood what was going on for the last half hour and had switched off completely. They were wondering what they were going to have for supper or how late the trains would be. Others, more on the ball, asked questions which ranged from the very first point made, to the very last. Questions tended to be very personal in that they tended to address how particular aspects of the scheme affected the way they currently did ABC or XYZ.

The interest taken in the answers to these questions by the half of the audience which had switched off was restricted to how soon they would be over, so that they could go home/ finish that report/ make a phonecall etc. A good proportion of that audience went away unsure what the letters MBO stood for, let alone how it would affect them.

In the late 1980s, a large financial institution decided to adopt a new appraisal scheme. All departments were told that there would be a series of meetings, (called briefings) to explain the scheme. The maximum number of people at any briefing was 25. The presenter stopped at regular intervals to allow questions about various parts of the scheme. This gave ample opportunity for everyone to ask questions before they forgot what it was they had been puzzled about. As relatively few people were present, those who wished to sleep or dream had to be very circumspect about it.

The second example demonstrates a good way of presenting complex information which is going to have a direct effect on the individuals concerned. Inevitably there would still be one or two people planning their holiday or thinking about a piece of work, but because the meetings were relatively small, it seemed as if the information was being directed at individuals, rather than at 'the group'. Each individual was therefore much more likely to listen and to absorb.

PREPARING THE PRE-MEETING PAPERS

The third stage of effective pre-meeting preparation is deciding what is needed in the way of pre-meeting papers, preparing and sending them out. The paperwork you may need includes a note or memo giving notice of the meeting, the agenda and any documents relating to agenda items.

Notice of the meeting
If there is time to do so before the meeting, a note or memo giving notice of it means that it is more likely to be logged in the diary and focused in the mind – and gives people few excuses for getting wrong the date, time, place etc.

The notice of the meeting should include:

- the purpose of the meeting
- the topics to be covered (with an attached agenda or a note asking for items to go on the agenda)
- the date, time and place
- the probable duration
- a list of participants

For some individuals it may also include a request to present some information at the meeting, or to provide the other participants with information before the meeting.

For informal meetings the notice need not be long or formal. See Figure 4.1 for an example.

Figure 4.1 Memorandum

To

Mary, Fred, Peter, Joan

PB3   Netherlands Trade Fair

When we meet on 23rd Feb at 10.30am in my office, please can you all bring ideas for brochure revisions. I will also want to agree

a) Budgets by departments
b) Timescales till end June.

Please let me know by 17/2 any other items you want to discuss and I will circulate. I'm hopeful we can finish by 12.30.

Janet
12/2

Figure 4.2 Notice of formal meeting

From: Regional Director

To: V. Crowe, A. Sinclair, P. Chalmers, S. Croft, B. Clowne, Z. Turner, M. Francis, P. Terry.

21st March

Heads of Departments Quarterly Meeting

The quarterly meeting of Heads of Departments is to be held on Tuesday 6 April at 10.00 in Meeting room 3. I have made arrangements for a sandwich lunch and anticipate that we should finish by 15.30.

I shall be circulating the agenda on 31st March. If you have any items which you wish to be included on the agenda, please send them to me by 28th March at the latest.

I would like to spend the second half of the meeting looking at ways of cutting costs in the second and third quarters. I would particularly like to focus on savings which are environmentally friendly.

B. Hazim

Figure 4.2 gives an example of a notice of a more formal meeting.

The agenda
The agenda is the backbone of a meeting and it is vital to have one. If a meeting is called on the spur of the moment, an agenda can be jotted down on the back of an envelope for immediate use. If a meeting is pre-planned, the agenda is perhaps the most important item to consider.

If it is possible to send participants the agenda before the meeting, then do so. It tells them what is to be discussed so they know what to prepare. It gives them a good idea of how long the meeting should last so that they can plan the rest of their day. If there is no time or opportunity to send out the agenda beforehand, at the very least there should be a copy for everyone when they arrive. We will deal with agendas at greater length in the next chapter.

Documents relating to agenda items

If the participants need to have absorbed certain specific information before they can discuss it, such as budgets, plans, proposals, then send the information out before the meeting. Sometimes several items on an agenda have bits of background which can be explained more easily by written information beforehand than at the meeting. Written documents also mean that people can use them as checklists to make sure they have understood everything they need to.

Providing the information at the meeting is a poor substitute because time is wasted while each individual reads and digests the information at a varying pace.

Circulating data beforehand has one other advantage which is that any mistakes, typing errors, or ambiguities have a better chance of being spotted before they are released to a wider public. One disadvantage might be that sometimes the participants don't read the material, perhaps because there is too much of it. They then spend the first part of the meeting surreptitiously 'glancing through' the papers desperately trying to catch up. This can never entirely be avoided, but can be kept to a minimum by sending out the information in good time and keeping it as readable as possible.

ARRANGE TIME AND PLACE

The time, place, duration, heating, seating, lighting and refreshments can make a lot of difference, positively or negatively, to how well people perform at meetings.

Timing the meeting

When should the meeting be? How long should it take? What time of day is best?

Many meetings answer such questions for themselves. Sometimes

45

a decision needs to be made now and not next week. Sometimes the only time when the meeting room is available is at 3pm on Wednesday. On the occasions when you do have some say in the matter and are able to make these decisions for yourself, these are the things to bear in mind.

What date?

In an ideal world, the meeting date would be set far enough in advance for everyone to be able to do the necessary preparation, but soon enough that the subject matter is dealt with promptly. This may not always be possible in this far from ideal world where you are at the mercy of the urgency of the subject matter, the availability of people who need to be there, the availability of rooms and many other criteria peculiar to your organisation.

What time?

The time of day when a meeting is held can have an effect on its dynamics. We are all familiar with the full, sleepy sensation that is the aftermath of a good lunch – a pleasant sensation when the opportunity arises to have a quiet snooze, not such a pleasant sensation when someone is speaking at a meeting and you really need to pay attention. There are few things worse when at a meeting than having to prop open your eyelids with willpower.

However poor the timing of a 2pm meeting may seem, there are worse times. Commonsense would indicate that 4pm on a Friday afternoon might not be a time when many people would be highly motivated to attend, but there are other reasons for avoiding the end of the day if you can. Ergonomic research has established that performance and alertness fall off rapidly during the latter part of the day. So if you plan to hold a meeting in the later afternoon, be aware that your contributors might not be operating at the peak of their capacity. However, they will want to despatch the meeting quickly since many of them will want to go home.

The meeting place

You may think that the location of a meeting is the least consideration when planning it. As long as there is a room where all the participants can squeeze in, and it's convenient and available, go for it. Not so. The place where the meeting is held can have a great effect on the climate of the meeting. It can set the scene for a useful productive session or encourage the meeting to be uncomfortable in one way or another.

The place where the meeting is held will depend a lot on its size and formality. Many day-to-day informal meetings are held in a manager's office, with chairs drawn up around the desk or around a coffee table at one end of the room. At the other end of the scale, big presentations need a large room, usually with audio visual facilities available.

Let's look at the considerations which can make all the difference to the comfort of a meeting.

Room size

It's important that the room should be big enough for the number of people invited to be comfortable. Sitting around a table squashed knee to knee and elbow to elbow is not conducive to getting the best performance from people. Everyone has a concept of their own personal space surrounding them, like an invisible bubble. The size of this bubble depends on who you are with – you may be very happy to sit shoulder to shoulder with your family or friends, but not so happy to be so intimately pressed against your managing director. If your personal space is unavoidably invaded, for example in a crowded lift or train, you will probably deal with this by avoiding eye contact with the other people around you – looking at your shoes, or gazing unseeingly into space. A meeting full of people who are avoiding looking at their immediate neighbours may not be the most effective way of achieving the optimum outcome. One study found that when people felt crowded, the level of interaction between them dropped.

An extremely large room for a small number of people can also have a dampening effect on the mood of a meeting. Research has established that social groupings develop more rapidly in small spaces. A few people in a very large room can give a cold and formal feel to the gathering. It may be possible to lessen this effect by meeting in the corner of the room, or blocking part of it off with screens, or having a focal point around which the meeting is gathered.

Where to hold the meeting

You may not have much choice as to where you hold your meeting. Given that you need a room of the appropriate size, you may be constrained by where a room of that size is available. The modern trend of open plan offices often means that meeting rooms are at a premium, especially at certain times of the year such as annual appraisal time when you find earnest discussions going on in the most unlikely places such as staff canteens.

If you are in the fortunate position of being able to choose the most appropriate place for your meeting, take the following considerations into account.

1. *Where is the most convenient place for all the people you have invited to attend?* If people are coming from a number of different places, it might be better to hold the meeting in a central location, thus saving the time of all concerned, rather than bringing everyone to your office or headquarters.

   A meeting which one of the authors attends as an associate tutor meets about twice a year to discuss a particular course. All the tutors concerned are given advance notice of the meeting, and asked which of a number of dates and which of two places would be more convenient for them. From the replies, a date and place is selected. This is a good system for ensuring that as many people as possible come at the time and to the place which is best for them. It's particularly important in this instance as the participants are nearly all freelance consultants who have very varying demands on their time, and live in a wide variety of places. Asking people for their preferences beforehand not only ensures that as many people as possible will be able to attend, but means that people come to the meeting feeling that efforts have been made to take their wishes and circumstances into account.

2. *On-site or off-site?* There are advantages and disadvantages to both. On-site meetings are cheaper, quicker to convene, often more convenient. But sometimes (see above) central locations

can be better. Sometimes an off-site meeting in a conference centre or another building belonging to your company can mean that there are fewer distractions. Also, as everyone has had to make a special journey to get there, it can concentrate their minds on the importance of the meeting as they travel to it.

3. *What about security?* Are you going to be talking about a secret or sensitive issue? If so, make sure you are in a room which does not leak sound to rooms nearby and will not suffer too many interruptions or people coming in by mistake.

Lighting

For most meetings all that matters is that there is adequate light for working without being dazzled, and most rooms within organisations offer this. It is worth remembering, though, that sunlight streaming in through a window behind some participants can make it difficult for those sitting opposite to see well. Blinds and curtains, while shutting out the natural light prized in many modern buildings, can make it more comfortable to work.

Of course, putting 'the opposition' in the uncomfortable position may be a ploy that meeting organisers want to consider. The disadvantage is that while it might work in your favour at your meeting, you can be fairly sure that the 'opposition' will find a way of inviting you back for a return match when you can expect some equally hostile treatment.

If the meeting involves the use of visual aids, you will need to consider the suitability of the lighting. Do the lights need to be on or off during the presentation? Will this affect people's ability to make notes? Do they *need* to make notes? Are blackout facilities needed for the windows?

Heating and ventilation

Most office buildings these days are kept at a comfortable temperature for working. However, when you put eight people in a room which normally holds one or two, it can quickly become not only uncomfortably hot, but also stuffy and airless. When the ventilation in a room is inadequate for the number of people in it – and this can happen even in air-conditioned buildings – the oxygen levels go down and people become sleepy. If you have no control over the ventilation of the room, it may be necessary to have fairly frequent breaks so that people can move around and the door can be left open for a while.

Researchers have found that heating, ventilation and air-conditioning are among the most important features for comfort in the workplace, and that high and low ambient temperatures have been associated with discomfort, impaired task performance, irritability and antisocial behaviour. Put these ingredients into an important meeting and you have a recipe for, if not disaster, then something well below achievable performance.

The problem with a few people meeting in a very large room is that the room can often be cold – after all it is designed to hold a large number of people in comfort. Meetings have been known to be held in overcoats and gloves – not the best way to create a positive feel to the discussion. Grandjean (1986) quotes studies which show that overcool rooms can lead to restlessness and reduced concentration and alertness in the people who work in them.

To smoke or not to smoke?
This is a perennial problem. If smokers smoke, non-smokers choke. Many non-smokers are very uncomfortable working with someone who is smoking. This can distract them and detract from their performance. Also, even if only a few people smoke, the room can rapidly become smoky and airless. This is partly due to the fact that even light smokers seem to feel the need to smoke more when they are in meetings. This could be a mechanism to deal with stress, or it could be because many people smoke more in social situations, and a meeting is among other things, a social occasion. Some smokers find that they cannot concentrate, or that they become irritable without cigarettes, which, in turn, detracts from their performance. It looks like a no-win situation.

Many organisations now have a no smoking policy at meetings. In fact many organisations have a no smoking policy throughout the building except in a few designated areas. If you have a smoker or smokers at your meeting, the best way to deal with the problem is for everyone to declare their needs beforehand and then sort out a solution which meets these needs as far as possible. This might involve opening windows, regular breaks, air-conditioning, ionisers etc.

Tables and chairs

Chairs need to strike the balance between being so uncomfortable that people will be shifting from buttock to buttock before half an hour is out, and being so comfortable that people relax to the extent that they are in danger of dozing off. Chairs with arms are more comfortable to sit in for any length of time.

The question of whether or not there should be a table at meetings exercises some people quite a lot. The arguments in favour are that tables provide a useful working surface for notes. They also offer a handy place for a glass of water, leaning the elbows, putting down the spectacles, etc., and they give a businesslike atmosphere to the meeting. But a number of studies have shown that tables in front of members of a group act as a barrier to complete openness. For some meetings, the more informal atmosphere engendered by a lack of tables might be appropriate.

However, a lot of people feel more comfortable with a table in front of them, and the vast majority of business meetings where people sit around to discuss things, rather than listen to a presentation, do make use of a table.

Layout

If you are going to use a table, it's worthwhile considering who sits where.

Figure 4.3 overleaf is a fairly common meetings layout with person A in the chair. Some research has found that the person to the right of the chairperson is more likely to get his or her attention than the person to the left. So in this case, person J would get more attention than person B.

It is a well established fact that the position in which people sit, relative to other people, has an effect on the relationship between them. In the diagram persons B and C are sitting as if they are

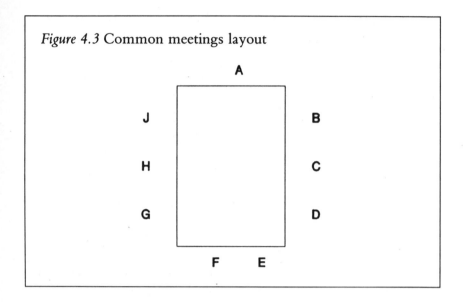

Figure 4.3 Common meetings layout

working together, whereas persons B and J are sitting as if they are in opposition to each other. In the House of Commons, the Government sits on one side of the House, the Opposition on the other.

Now if Mr J and Miss H were coming to the meeting hoping to convince Mrs B and Mr C of something, or if Ms G knew she was going to have a different opinion from Mr D then by sitting in these positions they are setting themselves up for a prolonged argument.

They would be much better off to sit next to the person they might want to influence, or if that is not possible, at least sit round the corner from them.

The arrangement in Figure 4.4 is much more likely to achieve a unified outcome. Now, no two people with opposing views are sitting opposite each other. B and C as the difficult-to-convince people have been split up so that they cannot confer and back each other up so effectively. No-one is sitting opposite anyone with whom he or she is likely to disagree strongly.

Consider too where the people with the most power and status sit. This is especially true if the table is longer, with a larger number of people at the meeting. There is a tendency for them to cluster at the end nearest the chairperson.

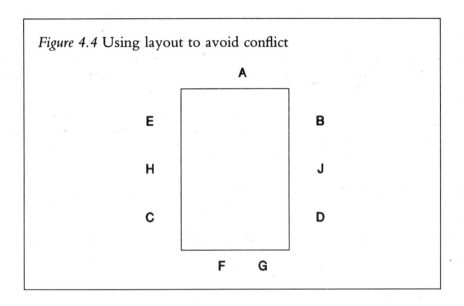

Figure 4.4 Using layout to avoid conflict

King Arthur is said to have favoured a round table so that none of his knights were more honoured than others. In many ways he had the right idea, because a round table does do away with some of the 'above and below the salt' placings which can creep into meetings at rectangular tables where people who want to get noticed try to sit next to the chairperson who is usually the individual with the most status.

This can still happen, though, even with a round table. The Cabinet table at Number 10 is described as 'coffin shaped'. We understand that in Cabinet meetings, only the people sitting next to, and opposite, the Prime Minister are allowed to speak at any time, the others have to wait to be asked.

When more than around 12 people attend a meeting, a single table is likely to be too small. For meetings of between 10 and, say, 30 people you might want to consider an arrangement of tables in a U shape. This is a favourite layout for training courses and has a number of advantages.

- it is easier for all participants to see each other
- it gives an open feel to the meeting, while retaining the use of tables

- if a presentation is involved everyone can see the presenter and his/her visual aids
- the presenter can walk about and distribute papers etc. from the middle of the U

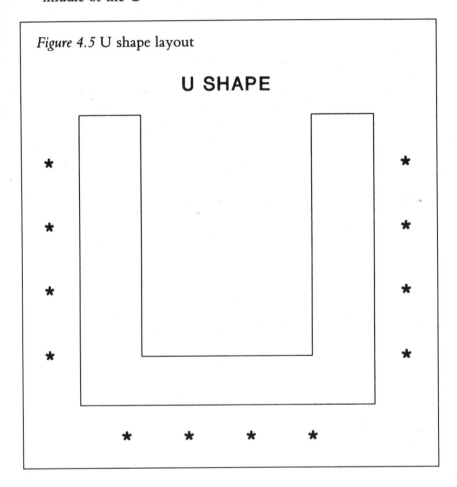

Figure 4.5 U shape layout

U SHAPE

Meetings where the main objective is the presentation of materials which might entail the use of visual aids are best arranged with all the chairs facing the front of the room.

A number of different layouts can be used, depending on the number of people attending, and whether or not they will need to make notes. A selection of layouts is shown in figures 4.6, 4.7 and 4.8.

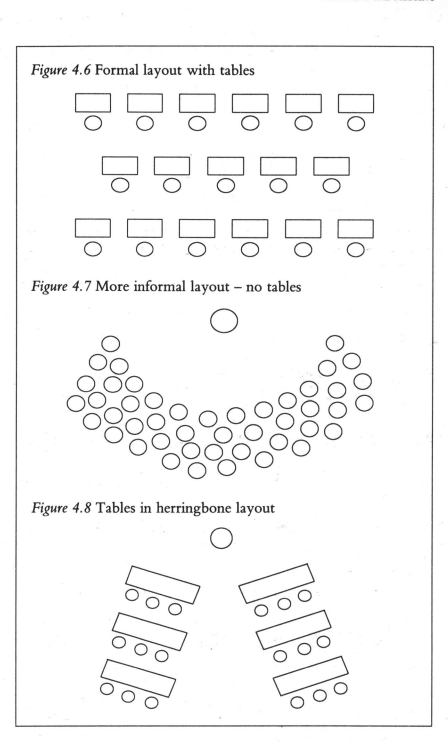

Figure 4.6 Formal layout with tables

Figure 4.7 More informal layout – no tables

Figure 4.8 Tables in herringbone layout

Distractions

The potential for distractions during a meeting is enormous, ranging from the internal musings of the participants to physical distractions. Let's look here at the physical distractions and leave internal musings until Chapter 7.

There may be distractions that you can do little or nothing about. For example, if your building is situated under the flight path from Heathrow, you may well be innured to most of the noise, but Concorde taking off could well stop a meeting in its tracks. All you can do in that case is wait a few moments before trying to hear or be heard again – unless of course you move to another building.

Try to deal beforehand with those distractions you can do something about. Telephone calls and people coming into the room are perhaps the most common ones if a meeting is held in someone's office, but these are easily eliminated with a little forethought.

Meeting rooms built specifically for the purpose ought, of course, to be ideal, but often, for the sake of flexibility and economy, meeting rooms are designed so that they can be either one large room or several smaller ones divided by screens. If you have ever tried to have a serious discussion whilst the next door meeting is being entertained by a John Cleese training video, you will appreciate the distraction problems inherent in this arrangement.

Perhaps even worse are meeting rooms with large windows at one side. A meeting of regional personnel managers for a large retail group was held off-site to hear some proposals and discuss how these would affect their staff. The room was at one side of an hotel, quiet, and overlooking open fields. The meeting started well but part way through, the presenter became aware that he did not have the full attention of his audience. As it was a subject close to their hearts he was somewhat puzzled until he noticed that in the field outside the window two horses were mating. His audience was completely absorbed – but not in what he was saying. The obvious, though perhaps unkind, answer to meeting rooms like this is to arrange them so that most people have their backs to the window, and/or the curtains are drawn.

Summary

The person who convenes a meeting has the responsibility for that meeting. He or she is responsible for the whole tone and climate of the meeting and can have an effect, even before it begins, on how well it achieves its outcome. Creating a positive climate for the meeting is achieved by:

- calling the meeting for the right reasons
- inviting the right people
- preparing an agenda
- providing the right physical surroundings

Use the following checklist to ensure that you have taken all the necessary steps to ensure your meeting is well planned.

CHECKLIST – PLANNING THE MEETING

PURPOSE
1. What is the purpose of the meeting?
   a) What do you need to achieve?
   b) What would happen if the meeting was not held?
   c) Is the purpose of the meeting to disseminate information, make decisions or a mixture of both?
   d) What outcome do you want from the meeting?
2. Does everyone who is to attend know the purpose of the meeting?

WHO SHOULD BE THERE
3. Why are you inviting people to the meeting?
   a) Do they have information to communicate?
   b) Do they need to be given information?
   c) Are they experts in particular fields?
   d) Do they have executive responsibility for an area under discussion?
   e) Will they be annoyed if they are not invited? If so, can you afford to annoy them?
4. Are the people you are inviting the right level to be able to make the necessary decisions and ensure their implementation?
5. Have you ensured a diversity of viewpoints?
6. Are your participants likely to be open-minded about the subject matter?
7. How diverse are the status levels of the people you have invited? If they are very different, how will you ensure that everyone who needs to, has a chance to be heard?
8. How big does your meeting have to be?
   a) Have you included everyone who needs to be there?
   b) Is it small enough to ensure participation?

PRE-MEETING PAPERS
9. Will you send out a notice of the meeting? This should include:
   a) purpose of the meeting
   b) topics to be covered

    c) date, time and place

    d) probable duration

    e) list of participants

10. Do you have an agenda?

11. Have you sent the agenda to the participants in good time before the meeting?

12. Are there any documents relating to agenda items which need to be sent out beforehand?

13. Does anyone need to present information? If so, do they know well in advance?

ARRANGE TIME AND PLACE

14. Have you arranged the date? Is it soon enough to deal with the purpose promptly and far enough away to be convenient?

15. Have you considered whether the time is convenient for people to get there easily? Is it early enough in the day for people to give their best performance?

16. Is the room the right size for the number of people to be invited?

17. Is the venue convenient for as many of the participants as possible?

18. Would an on-site or an off-site meeting be preferable?

19. Are there security considerations to be taken into account?

20. Do you need to consider the lighting?

21. Will the ventilation and heating be adequate?

22. Will you agree a smoking policy?

23. Are the chairs comfortable for long periods of time?

24. Will you use tables? If so, what layout will be most appropriate for your purpose?

25. Do you need to think about who should sit where?

26. Have you thought about, and eliminated, distractions as far as is possible?

5. *The Nuts and Bolts of Meetings*

'The MD invited us all to go for an "Ideas Weekend". It was very disorganised and involved long rambling speeches from a few of the full time staff. Almost no brain-storming took place. Several of us found excuses to slip away for part of the time and we didn't notice any difference when we returned. Worst of all, we reached no obvious conclusions and the policy document we were promised "soon after the meeting" didn't arrive for nearly three months.'

That quotation comes from a freelance member of a creative design and development agency. She is describing a meeting that aimed to be free thinking by not having an agenda, or any overt rules or procedures. In fact, all it achieved was being free with everyone's time, to obvious ill effect.

Most meetings have various rules and procedures which may be formally expressed or unspoken. While sticking too firmly to the rules and procedures can sometimes cause boring, unproductive meetings, used productively they are of great value. In this chapter, we consider agendas, the way formal rules can be applied to less formal meetings and the method by which the meeting is recorded.

THE AGENDA

The agenda is the backbone of a meeting. It gives the meeting structure and strength. Without an agenda, a meeting is far less likely to achieve its required outcome. The agenda acts as a control device which establishes the parameters of the meeting, assigns tasks, establishes order and sequence, and provides guidelines for timing.

The amount of information included in an agenda should be guided by the needs of the people invited to the meeting. Their need to know should be the paramount consideration of the person preparing the agenda.

Functions of an agenda

An agenda is an essential part of the preparation for the meeting. It has a number of critical functions not only for the person convening the meeting but also for those who are to attend.

1. Setting clear objectives

The person convening the meeting needs an agenda to focus his or her mind on what the exact content of the meeting should be. Writing down a list of agenda items can help to prioritise issues and clarify exactly what is needed.

2. Pre-meeting information

An agenda gives a lot of information to the people attending the meeting. It should tell them exactly what the purpose of the meeting is and what contribution will be expected from them. This means they will be able to consider the items that concern them before the meeting so that they come to it with any information they need to provide, or knowing what they need to ask or clarify. The agenda should also give them an indication of how long they can expect to spend on each item and how long the meeting is likely to take.

3. Inclusion of all relevant items

An agenda ensures that items are not accidently omitted from a meeting. If it is circulated before the meeting, participants have the opportunity to see that a particular subject isn't included and ask for its inclusion. Even if an agenda is prepared on the back of an envelope for an on-the-spot meeting, it gives those attending an opportunity to ensure that everything they wish to discuss is there. If items are not on the agenda, but kept in a person's head to be brought up when the time seems right, there are always dangers: the time is never appropriate, or is running out, or the person temporarily forgets about the idea because they are distracted by other things.

4. Structure
The structure of a meeting is very important and an agenda provides that structure. It gives the opportunity for items to be ordered by priority or by subject. They can be put into the best sequence to break the discussion into logical and manageable stages.

5. Timing
An agenda provides an opportunity to control the timing of the meeting by attaching time guidelines to agenda items.

Writing an agenda
The first thing to consider when writing the agenda is the question you presumably asked yourself when you decided to call the meeting: *what is the purpose of this meeting?* Everything else follows from that.

Consulting others
Who, if anyone, do you need to consult about what should go on the agenda? This may be especially true if you have regular meetings with the same team when members of the group may have specific items they wish to discuss.

When you ask people for information, you need to make the purpose of the meeting clear so that people know roughly what items are going to be relevant. Be sure to stress the deadline for receiving the agenda items,.

Requesting this information by letter or memo has a number of advantages: when you write you can be pretty certain the letter/ memo will arrive on the person's desk; it gives them a little time to think about what they want, and should also give them a deadline by which to reply. If they exceed the deadline their item shouldn't make the agenda.

Telephone calls can either be a very quick and less formal way of getting your agenda written, or extremely time-consuming and frustrating. You may have difficulty catching someone, or have to make a number of calls to remind them that they still haven't come up with the goods.

In many organisations, the use of electronic mail is becoming widespread. This can combine the best of both the telephone and the written word. Most systems give you an acknowledgement when the receiver has read the message which can be invaluable in identifying those who have *not* received it.

How many items?

Be realistic about the number of items that can be covered in the time available. If you know that you have a two-hour slot, estimate what can be covered properly in that time. Trying to squash too much in means that one or more of the following is likely to happen:

- items at the end of the agenda will be left out
- all the items will be covered, but not in enough detail
- items which are not covered in enough detail, or arbitrarily decided to be less important than others, will be held over for the next meeting

Limit the number of subjects to be dealt with at the meeting. If you have a long list of topics to be covered, it might be better to deal with them at short separate meetings. In any case, limit the length and scope of the meeting to avoid the fatigue factor.

If at all possible try to ensure that all the items on the agenda concern all the participants at the meeting. It is a great waste of someone's time to keep them at a meeting where the subject under discussion does not concern them. It is also a common reason why people feel resentful about attending meetings. If it is really impossible to avoid discussing items which involve some people and not others, order the agenda so that participants can leave after they have made their contribution.

Who should do what?

Consider whether you want to ask certain individuals to take the lead for various agenda items or part of them. If you do, give them some advance warning.

What information needs to be sent

At this stage think also about any information which needs to go out to clarify items on the agenda. A meeting can be shortened and made far more efficient if the people attending have had the opportunity to familiarise themselves with relevant information beforehand.

HOW TO WRITE AN AGENDA

What should be on the agenda?

For many meetings, there are certain standard items which need to be included on the agenda. These are:

1. title, date and place of meeting
2. apologies for absence
3. minutes of the previous meeting
4. matters arising from the previous meeting
5. other items to be discussed/decided
6. any other business
7. date, time and place of the next meeting

Items two, three and four will only be appropriate for meetings which occur at regular intervals (varying from once a week to once a year). Also, if you are holding a very informal meeting, you may not need to have these items or to set them out in this way, but if we deal with them one by one, you can omit those which have no relevance to your meetings.

1. Title, date and place of meeting

The reasons for including this information are self-evident. It's not much good having an agenda if you don't know which meeting it refers to.

2. Apologies for absence

These should be included because the information is useful to have in the meeting minutes. When you go back to look at the discussion and decisions made, it is often important to know who was, and was not, present.

3. Minutes of the previous meeting

Those present at a meeting are usually required to agree that the minutes of the previous meeting are correct, and they are then signed by the chairperson. This may seem pedantic and time-wasting but it does ensure that you have a signed and witnessed agreement which could be vital if there is an argument in the future.

4. Matters arising from the minutes

You should be careful about this item. It can turn into a monster which swallows up the rest of the meeting. In fact, it can sometimes be a virtual re-run of the previous meeting. So use it for its intended purpose which is to mop up information from the last meeting. Make sure that any large items which need to be discussed again, have their own place on the new agenda.

5. Other items

This should be the main bulk of the meeting. It is dealt with at greater length further on in this chapter.

6. Any Other Business

This is where anything not on the agenda, but needing discussion, is raised. Watch out for it, like Matters Arising it can also be a monster. Many well-run, well-timed meetings have gone on for another two hours because of AOB. It seems to be a particular problem for committees of voluntary organisations.

Any Other Business should not and need not be a monster. If the person convening the meeting has prepared properly and asked those attending for items they wish to put on the agenda, then AOB can usually be dealt with quickly and briefly, and can serve its purpose of catching anything which may have been omitted accidently, or cropped up since the agenda was written.

7. Date, time and place of next meeting
For regular meetings it is sensible and saves time to set the date, time and place of the next meeting when most of the people who will be attending it are present. It avoids countless phonecalls or letters to check whether people are available.

Order of agenda items
Take into account the following considerations when planning the order of items on the agenda:

*Logic. Items on the agenda may need to be in some sort of logical order – point of sale material, for instance, can't be designed until the kind of marketing strategy to be adopted has been decided.

*Routine. It may be sensible to deal with routine items first and get them out of the way quickly.

*Convenience. If some of the people attending the meeting are involved in only one or two of the agenda items, you may wish to put these items at the beginning so that the people concerned can leave once they have been discussed. It is better not to put them at the end as this can mean people have to hang about, or you have to send someone to round people up. Both are a waste of time.

*Difficulty. If you need to discuss difficult or complex items it is often a good idea to tackle them at the beginning of the meeting once everyone has settled down, but while participants are still fresh. It can be counterproductive to tackle important and difficult items near the end, when time, energy and patience are running out.

*Importance versus urgency. Sometimes items on the agenda are urgent, but not necessarily as important as others. It is often a good idea to deal with the most urgent items first, but to do it quickly so that due time can be given to the most important items.

Apportioning time
Consider allocating an estimated time for each agenda item. The advantages of this are that:

* it gives everyone a clear idea of how long you expect to spend on each item – which also indicates how complex, important or urgent you think it is

- it gives a firm structure to the meeting so that discussions have less of a chance of becoming long-winded and unproductive

However, since allocating time to agenda items is only a useful way of structuring the meeting, it shouldn't become an unbending rule, stifling useful and productive discussion. So, be flexible if it becomes obvious that the time you have allocated is insufficient. If other participants think that an agenda item will take longer than allowed, they should be encouraged to say so, giving their reasons, before the item is discussed.

When considering time and timings, bear in mind that concentration starts to fall off after 40–60 minutes. Build in short breaks to allow everyone to regain their powers of concentration. Grandjean (1986) quotes a study of World War II radar lookouts which found that 50% of sightings came within the first 30 minutes on duty. They then fell to 23 per cent in the next 30 minutes, eventually plummeting to 10 per cent in the final 30 minutes of a two-hour watch.

Begin on time
If you say you are going to start your meeting at 10.00, then start it at 10.00, not at 10.05. Green and Lazarus found that the most effective meetings started on time, while the least effective did so only about 50 per cent of the time.

Starting on time immediately introduces a business-like feel to the proceedings and makes it more likely that timings will be adhered to throughout the meeting.

It is particularly important to start on time in regular meetings. If you get into the habit of waiting five minutes for latecomers, you will irritate those who were there on time and they will start arriving five minutes later themselves and the situation deteriorates.

Clarify the content
When preparing your agenda it can be very helpful to be specific about the content of each item. Let us look at a typical agenda and see how it could be improved by the addition of more detail.

Figure 5.1 Office move agenda

NEW OFFICE MOVE SUB-COMMITTEE
Meeting to be held on 10th May 1993 at 10.00 in
Committee Room 1R

AGENDA

1. Apologies for absence
2. Minutes of previous meeting
3. Matters arising
4. Layout
5. Health and Safety
6. Washroom contract
7. Removals
8. Any other business
9. Date of next meeting.

The agenda shown in Figure 5.1 is actually more of a list than an agenda. It shows the areas which are to be discussed, but it does not give participants much clue about what will go on. It gives people carte blanche to have their own ideas of what should be covered for all non-standard items. For example:

Item 4. Layout
How offices are arranged is a subject dear to everyone's heart. Most people will have an opinion if not a firm demand. Are you there to discuss what everyone wants or to hear what the premises' department has to say? This could end up as a free-for-all, or a long and tedious item if you don't specify.

Item 5. Health and Safety
This is usually regarded as a boring subject by everyone except the Health and Safety Officer, so no-one will have thought about it much. Let us hope that the Health and Safety Officer has done some thinking and has something to say.

Item 7. Removals
This could mean anything from when the move will take place to who will do it, to what sort of boxes people require. Again, it offers almost unlimited scope for participants to bring their own concerns, rather than concrete information, to the meeting.

Specifying content of agenda items clarifies the purpose of the meeting. The agenda in Figure 5.2 overleaf gives a clear indication of what is to be discussed under each item with a time allocation. It means that everyone who comes to the meeting will have a good idea of what they need to prepare, what information they need to bring with them and which thoughts and opinions they might need to rehearse.

Name contributors

Putting a person's name against an agenda item tells them they need to do some preparation and bring information with them and also indicates to other participants that the item is not a free-for-all discussion but a response to some particular information about which they may or may not have something to say.

When people are named to speak on agenda items, remember that because they have been given official approval and speak first, their views and opinions may have a lot of influence on the group. Be sure to allow time for other people to respond to what the named contributor has said and offer their own opinions.

RULES

The procedures and rules that are used to govern conduct at a formal meeting have as their basis the same aims as any meeting. ie:

- allowing each person the opportunity to speak
- preventing unscrupulous domination of the meeting by people trying to gain something for themselves
- ensuring that the business of the meeting is carried on irrespective of individual personality and availability

Many organisations have a set of rules of conduct for their most formal meetings such as AGM's, shareholders' meetings. These

Figure 5.2 Office move agenda

OFFICE MOVE SUB-COMMITTEE
Meeting to be held on 10th May 1993 at 10.00 in
Committee Room 1R

AGENDA

1.	Apologies for absence	2 mins
2.	Agreeing minutes of previous meeting	2 mins
3.	Matters arising	10 mins
4.	Layout:	
	a. Feedback from survey on space requirements by Premises Department. (Jim Fisher)	10 mins
	b. Discuss implications of survey on layout and decide on future actions	20 mins
5.	Health and Safety	
	a. Proposal for multi-gym to be situated in basement (Anne Morris)	5 mins
	b. Discussions and recommendations for action	20 mins
6.	Washroom Contract	
	a. Discussion of tenders (AO to provide information)	10 mins
	b. Decision on contractor to be made	10 mins
7.	Removals:	
	a. Presentation of estimates from removal firms (John Sampson)	5 mins
	b. Discussion of removal estimates and decision	15 mins
	b. Departmental estimates of quantity of furniture and paper to be moved	15 mins
8.	Any other business	10 mins
9.	Date of next meeting	5 mins

rules are set out in articles of association, the constitution and in company law.

One of the reasons for such rules is the need for stability so it is often very difficult to change the rules of conduct for a meeting, for instance it might need a 66 per cent majority vote to make the change.

If you are involved with formal meetings, make sure that you are aware of the rules and work within them. Whole books have been written on formal procedures and it is not our purpose to repeat them here. However, there are four aspects of formal meetings which frequently apply to a wider range of meetings.

Notice of the meeting

Many meetings require a minimum number of days (or working days) notice to be given to attendees. This is intended to give everyone concerned sufficient time to prepare themselves and to make travelling arrangements, if relevant. As mentioned in Chapter 4, it is a good idea to discipline yourself to give everyone adequate notice of the meeting, otherwise you cannot expect participants to have been able to do the necessary preparation.

Quorums

Many formal meetings cannot proceed unless a minimum number of participants is present. Technically, this can mean that if someone has to leave the meeting to take a telephone call, for instance, and the meeting becomes inquorate, then business has to be suspended until the numbers are made up.

The concept of being quorate can be usefully applied to less formal meetings. If there are six of you normally at the project meeting, do the four of you who are caught in a traffic jam on the M6 really want the other two to go ahead and make major decisions without you? It may be helpful to agree at the start of a series of meetings who can deputise for whom, and which departments must be represented at all times.

Motions, proposals and amendments

When specific action is required from a formal meeting, it is normal for a motion to be put to the meeting before it is discussed. It may be the rule that motions have to be sent to participants with the agenda. After discussion, the proposal is often read to the meeting which may then vote on it. Proposers and seconders are asked to identify themselves for the original motion as well as for any amendments that have emerged during the discussion.

Most day-to-day meetings do not put forward ideas as formal motions nor do they have proposers and seconders. It is important though, that a subject is introduced so that everyone knows what they are talking about, and it may be useful to know whose idea it is. It is even more important to read out to the meeting exactly what action or decision you believe has been agreed so that everyone is clear before moving onto the next agenda item. The decision is recorded in the minutes (discussed later in this chapter).

Rules of debate

In formal meetings, it is normal for all contributions to be addressed through the chair. The chairperson is presumed to have great authority, and to be obeyed unquestioningly. In order to speak it is necessary to catch the eye of the chairperson and be given permission. It is also normal for participants to declare any personal or business interests they may have in the matter being discussed.

Much of the chairperson's role in an informal meeting is covered by the rules of debate. It does not help to have several people speaking at once, and it is important to ensure that the quieter aren't drowned by the louder and that the chairperson chooses who should speak next. Unfortunately, in many informal meetings, the chairperson has to fight to be heard, and cannot count on the other participants complying unfailingly with the rule of obeying the chair.

KEEPING A WRITTEN RECORD

Some of us have better memories than others. Some people can remember 30 or 40 telephone numbers while not being able to remember where they put their keys. Others can remember appointments weeks ahead, without needing to look in their diaries, and yet forget to collect their drycleaning on the way home. Old people have very clear memories of their childhood while being unable to remember what happened yesterday. The only constant in all this is that we cannot trust memory – neither our own nor other peoples.

So even the most informal meetings should have some sort of written notes. This may sound obvious for a formal meeting, but a bit excessive for an informal meeting between two people. However, if the meeting was worth having, the decisions were worth implementing – but this will be much harder without an agreed written record. Relying on yourself or someone else to remember accurately what went on is highly dangerous.

Some meetings such as company Annual General Meetings and Board Meetings are required by law to keep written records of their proceedings. Even meetings which do not keep formal minutes should have a written record of who was there and what was suggested and decided. These are the reasons for doing so:

1. When a decision is made, the action agreed needs to be recorded to ensure that there can be no argument about what happened at the meeting. Many staff disciplinary cases have dragged on for years because a manager warned a member of staff about their behaviour but did not record the conversation or the warning.

2. There needs to be a record of who was responsible for taking any action agreed if you are to avoid further meetings turning into recrimination sessions because Alf thought Bill was getting estimates for replacing the workshop roof, while Bill thought Alf had agreed to ask Annie which firm repaired the roof of the warehouse.

3. People who were not at the meeting but need to know what went on will require a record of what happened. They will need to know what was discussed, what was decided and who took responsibility for what.

4. Some time in the future it may be necessary to refer back to decisions taken at the meeting. It would be impossible to do this without a written record.

The record of the meeting should be strictly factual, describing what happened without distortion or comment. It should not reflect the opinions or comments of the person who took the notes, although it is hard to be completely unbiased (it has been said that the person who writes the minutes controls the outcome of the meeting).

The type of meeting often determines the sort of record taken. Usually, notes are taken and prepared afterwards into the record of the meeting. This record is known as the minutes by most meetings but more informal meetings may refer to it as 'notes'. Meetings at which major presentations are made sometimes have a written report which is a record of the presentation. For the rest of this chapter we shall refer to the record of the meeting as 'minutes'.

Minutes need to be:

- *accurate*, giving a true record of what occurred
- *clear and unambiguous*, so that they are not open to interpretation
- *structured consistently*, so that they are easy to read
- *brief*, summarising discussions and decisions rather than giving verbatim accounts

Who takes the minutes

Sometimes the person who takes the minutes of the meeting is the appointed secretary. This is often the case with formal committee meetings. In some cases, the secretary is a member of the committee in his own right with opinions to give and commitments to make. Other meetings may appoint a member of the meeting 'minutes secretary' or a junior person may be called in with the specific job of taking the minutes.

Sometimes the chairperson takes the minutes of the meeting. This is best avoided if possible, though, as it is difficult to concentrate on controlling the meeting if you are also trying to write down what is happening at the same time.

Whoever keeps the record of the meeting, and whether that record is formal or informal, the notetaker needs certain skills, abilities and knowledge.

1. The ability to listen carefully and understand what is being said. This may sound obvious, but if the notetaker is baffled by the subject matter, the resulting minutes may well be as baffling to those who knew what they were talking about at the time. It is thus

more sensible to have a minute-taker who understands what the meeting is about and can isolate the important from the unimportant.

2. The skill of jotting down a brief, coherent and accurate summary of what has been said or agreed.

3. Knowledge of the procedures and rules of the organisation concerned, so that the record is set out in the appropriate way and sent to the right people.

All of this argues against using a person who knows nothing about the subject but is dragged in because of their ability to do shorthand. Shorthand is not necessary unless a verbatim account of the proceedings is required – and in that case, a tape recorder will probably provide a better record.

What to include
Minutes should contain the following information:

- heading, including title, date and time of meeting
- names of the people present
- those in attendance (usually only at very formal meetings)
- apologies for absence
- numbered agenda items stating:
  - suggestions and proposals
  - the names of people who made major suggestions or proposals
  - decisions taken
  - actions agreed
  - the name of the person responsible for each agreed action
  - the date by which actions will be taken
- date of next meeting

Using the example of the New Office Move sub-committee, let us have a look at what goes in the minutes of a meeting. (The circled numbers refer to notes below the example.)

① **NEW OFFICE MOVE SUBCOMMITTEE**
Minutes of meeting held on 10th May 1993 at 10.00 in
Committee Room 1R

② PRESENT: Malcolm Sinclair (chairperson) Anne Morris
               Moira Clarke   Andrew Oppenheim
               Jim Fisher   John Sampson
               Sally Freeman   Sunil Srinivan

③

1. APOLOGIES: Apologies were received from Mark Hunter.

④ 2. MINUTES OF THE PREVIOUS MEETING
It was pointed out that item 4a should read 'the cost would be £3,500 not £35,000'. The minutes were agreed with this one amendment and signed.

3. MATTERS ARISING FROM THE MINUTES
(i) JF reported that screens had been ordered and the delivery date would be mid-July. They would be delivered to the new premises.
⑤ (ii) MC had met the architects to discuss the amendments agreed at the last meeting. These are now being put into effect.

4. LAYOUT
(i) JF presented the results of the survey on space requirements carried out by Premises Department. All departments had sent in their space requirements, including number of
⑥ desk spaces and room for equipment. JF suggested that in some cases the amount of space required had been exaggerated.
⑦ (ii) The implications of the survey on layout were discussed. It was agreed that the amount of space allocated to each department may have to be adjusted slightly to fit with the floor plans. The importance of having a clear path to fire exits was pointed out by the Health and Safety Officer

(AM). JF and SF agreed to draw up some draft plans for departmental layouts for the next meeting.

⑧ *ACTION:* JF and SF to draw up draft plans and circulate by 18/5.

5. HEALTH AND SAFETY

(i) Proposal for multi-gym: AM (Health and Safety) outlined a proposal for putting a multi-gym in the basement of the new building. Staff reactions to the idea were favourable and other organisation's experience was positive. The contractors would be able to carry out the work if informed within the next three weeks. The multi-gym would replace the planned table tennis and billiards room. The cost of the
⑨ equipment would be in the region of £10,000.

(ii) The question of supervision for the multi-gym was raised. AM said that for certain equipment expert supervision was not necessary as instructions were clearly visible on each piece of equipment. Most people present were in favour of the idea of having a multi-gym, but there was some concern about staff using the equipment unsupervised. Two suggestions were considered: 1. having a qualified trainer present for one day per week; 2. having a rota of qualified staff present at lunchtimes. AM was asked to look in to both these possibilities and find out what was the normal practice.

ACTION: AM to investigate ways of supervising staff using multi-gym and report back to the next meeting.

6. WASHROOM CONTRACTORS

(i) AO reported that a number of tenders had been received for the washroom contract. A summary of the services offered by each company, together with prices and costs, was circulated. AO pointed out that the cheapest tenders did not include as many staff.

(ii) The range of services offered was discussed. Stayclean

Systems, the contractor currently used, was more expensive than Washwell which offered the same range of services. The chairperson asked if Stayclean was providing a satisfactory service at the moment. AO said that there had been no problems with Stayclean over the last two years and they were very anxious to keep the contract. A concern was expressed that Washwell was an unknown quantity. After some discussion it was decided to offer Stayclean the contract if they would reduce their price to match Washwell's, otherwise the contract would go to Washwell.

ACTION: AO to negotiate with Stayclean and to agree contract with Stayclean or Washwell, depending on the outcome of the negotiation. Decision to be reported at next meeting.

7. REMOVALS
(i) JS gave a summary of the removals estimates provided by Pickerings, Dodwells and Offmove. These were all very similar but Dodwells would be unable to provide cartons until one week before the move.
(ii) The various estimates were discussed and it was agreed that Offmove would be used. They would be asked to provide cartons three weeks before the removal date.
(iii) The estimated number of desks, filing cabinets, other furniture and number of cartons to be moved had been received from all departments except Information Services. This was felt to be a problem as they were likely to have a lot of equipment which might need special treatment. SS offered to chase them up again.

ACTION: 1. JS to draw up contract with Offmove
2. SS to chase Information Services for estimated quantities to be removed

8. ANY OTHER BUSINESS
(i) SF reported that there had been a problem with the

carpet supplier who had had a breakdown on the production line. This was now sorted out and the supplier was working overtime to try to make up for lost time. It was likely that the carpet would not be ready by the date agreed, but that the delay should not be more than a week. SF was asked to keep a close eye on the matter.

ACTION: SF to monitor progress and report to next meeting.

(ii) The architect's design consultant will be coming to the next meeting to advise on colour schemes.

10. DATE OF NEXT MEETING
The next meeting will be held on 21 May 1993 at 10.30 in the Board Room.

① Heading
The heading of the minutes should include the title of the meeting, where it was held and the date. The title and date are particularly important for record purposes.

② Those present
This is important as it shows who may not have been present for important decisions. It also tells people who were not at the meeting whether or not their department was represented. The chairperson is usually listed first, followed by other participants in alphabetical order. Sometimes is is helpful to indicate which departments are represented. At other times this is unnecessary. It depends really on who is to read the minutes and for what purpose they are to be used.

In attendance
This is usually only used in formal meetings. It is done, for example, in council meetings where the elected members of the council would be listed as 'present', but the council officers or an official

secretary would be 'in attendance'. This means that they do not take part in the meeting as such, but are there to provide some sort of service to the people actually having the meeting.

③ Apologies
Sometimes this space is used to indicate who is not there – i.e. anyone who has not turned up, irrespective of whether or not they did in fact offer their apologies. With other meetings, only the names of those who did tender apologies are listed.

④ Number items
It is helpful to number the items recorded as this makes it easier to refer to them again. As far as possible follow the numbering of the agenda.
⑤ Usually, the initials of participants or their title – 'the chairperson' or 'the MD' – is used in minutes, rather than their full names.
⑥ Decisions and suggestions should be recorded using reported speech, i.e. 'It was decided that . . .' 'JN suggested that . . .' 'The chairperson asked BG to . . .'
⑦ Each paragraph should outline a subject, summarising discussions and decisions. There is no need to record all the details, just the main points. Specify proposals or reports made by specific presenters.
⑧ Names should be put against actions to be taken, which should be summarised at the end of each section. You need to say who is to do it, what is to be done, when it is to be done by and any other criteria agreed by the meeting, such as a budget.
⑨ If statistics and figures are crucial to an argument, they should be included in the minutes.

Written follow-up
It's not enough to simply take the notes or minutes, something has to be done with them afterwards. The following section deals with: whose responsibility it is to distribute written follow up; who should receive it; when it should be done.

Whose responsibility

It is one of the many responsibilities of the person who convened the meeting (often also the chairperson) to ensure that the meeting is recorded and that a copy of that record is distributed afterwards to the participants and other interested parties. Let us assume that Alistair convened and chaired a meeting of departmental heads to discuss the implications of the budget cut which was to be imposed next year. After the meeting Alistair would need to:

- check the accuracy of the minutes with the person who took them
- allocate responsibility for typing up and distributing the minutes
- agree with that person when and to whom the minutes should be sent

Who gets a copy?

Everyone who attended, or was invited to, the meeting should receive a copy of the minutes. There may also be other people who need to receive a copy for information. The circulation list for the minutes of regular meetings can often build up over a period of years, with the minutes disposed of in filing cabinets or waste bins and seldom read.

So it's worth asking yourself who really needs to see the minutes. You may find that many people on the distribution list don't need to be there at all, so save time, ink and trees by omitting them. Conversely, when you question who really needs the information, there may be people to add to the list. Sometimes minutes are sent to people for political reasons, their status, position or reputation requiring they are kept informed of everything that is going on.

A simple way to check how many people genuinely read the minutes is to insert a question in the next set of minutes asking people to reply to you if they wish to remain on the circulation list. This invariably cuts it down and also gives you some idea of who is really interested in your meetings.

If people have queries about the content of the minutes, these can usually be raised at the next meeting, or dealt with by a simple telephone call.

Public record

When the minutes represent a public record of the meeting, then it is usual to circulate a draft for comments which is returned and amalgamated into a final version. In these circumstances the minute-writer may need to exercise some control to ensure that the meeting does not get rewritten to favour each of the participants. If feelings have run high, then considerable diplomacy may be needed to get a finished and agreed set of minutes.

Timing

The written record of a meeting, whether it consists of typed-up notes or a formal set of minutes, should be distributed as quickly as possible after the meeting. This shows an efficient businesslike approach and gives the impression that you, the sender, regard the meeting and its outcome as important.

Minutes as a list of decisions

One of the most efficient ways of writing up the minutes is simply to record the decision taken for each agenda item and the people responsible for implementation. This format can look a little stark but is a good way of demonstrating, for instance, that only two implementable decisions came out of a three-hour meeting.

SUMMARY

Agendas, rules and minutes give structure to meetings and act as control devices for ensuring both that the meeting arrives at its intended outcome and that that outcome is recorded and implemented. They can be used to ensure that ideas are encouraged, considered, assessed and that the meeting achieves its full potential. They need to be set up to help rather than hinder. The way the agenda is used can help a meeting achieve its objectives faster. Rules, together with someone to implement them, can prevent the outbreak of open warfare – although those of us who listen to 'Yesterday in Parliament' may have our doubts! Minutes can aid the implementation of actions by providing an accurate record of the outcome of the meeting.

CHECKLIST – THE NUTS AND BOLTS OF MEETINGS

PREPARING AN AGENDA
1. Decide the purpose of the meeting
2. Consult the people you need to
3. Be realistic about how much you include on the agenda
4. Put the items in a logical order
5. Be specific about what is to be covered by agenda items
6. Estimate time guidelines for each item
7. Allocate named people to speak on items where appropriate

RULES
8. Give adequate notice of the meeting
9. Check whether or not you need a quorum
10. Ensure that proposals and amendments are clearly understood
11. Use the chairperson to keep the meeting on course.

MINUTES AND RECORDS
12. Keep a written record of the meeting, which should be:
    a) accurate
    b) clear and unambiguous
    c) consistently structured
    d) brief
13. Choose an appropriate person to take the minutes, ie. someone:
    a) with some knowledge of the subject
    b) with the skill to summarise
    c) who knows the rules and procedures of the organisation
    d) who is not the chairperson
14. Include in the minutes:
    a) title, date and time of meeting
    b) names of people present (and in attendance if appropriate)
    c) apologies for absence
    d) numbered agenda items
    e) date of next meeting
15. When writing the summaries, include:
    a) suggestions and proposals
    b) the names of people making major suggestions or proposals

c) decisions
d) actions agreed
e) the name of the person responsible for each action
f) date by which action will be taken

16. It is the responsibility of the chairperson to ensure that a written record is made, checked and distributed
17. Check that your circulation list includes everyone who needs to be on it, but is not unnecessarily long
18. Distribute minutes as quickly as possible after the meeting.

6. Chairing the Meeting

John and Mary are having lunch and comparing the afternoon meetings they have to attend. John will be in a meeting called by his boss Megan – known as Megan the mugger since she takes no prisoners. Mary will be with William the regional manager – known as William the wimp because, well its obvious really, isn't it?

John: *'The problem is that Megan is so competent, so experienced and so confident, that she overwhelms us all. She sets the agenda and is often the main speaker. If you have to talk about an item she questions you so closely that it might as well be a two-person discussion in her office, nobody else gets a look in. Ideas are fine as long as they are hers, or are known to comply with her views. God help anyone who steps out of line.*

    'But the worst thing is that none of us learn anything during her meetings, she does it all herself, and we gain no experience at all. I hear she says she's overworked, it would be nice if she trusted us to do a bit more than fetch and carry for her, then we could share some of her workload.'

Mary: *'William is just the opposite. He does not bring any control to the meeting at all. Some of the other regional managers are very tough and they will talk and talk until they get their way. I've seen them be very unfair to Paul in accounts who has done some good work, but is never recognised for it. I expect he will be looking for a better job soon.*

> *'Despite our suggestions, William still hasn't grasped the value of an agenda that tells you what is going to be talked about and by whom. Everything just ends up as a free-for-all. Because of this lack of control the meeting goes on too long and ends too late. If there is anything serious that really has to be decided, then we all go to the pizza place across the road afterwards to talk about what we need to do.'*

Somewhere between these two sad, but not untypical, examples is effective chairing. In this chapter we try to show how you can adopt appropriate skills, techniques, styles and approaches to ensure that no-one can make complaints similar to those above about your chairing ability. Fortunately there are many ways to be a good chairperson. Part of the trick is to recognise your own strengths and weaknesses, and build on the strengths while finding ways to compensate for the weaknesses. We look at the various aspects of chairing a meeting that combine to make the difference between a meeting which achieves its objective speedily, with good humour, or becomes increasingly bad tempered without reaching any satisfactory conclusion. These are:

- the purpose of the chairperson
- crucial tasks
- leadership skills
- facilitating skills
- dealing with problems

KNOW YOUR PURPOSE

Let us return to our favourite catechism: *What is the purpose?* You need to ask this question in two ways:

- What is the purpose of the meeting?
- What is your purpose as the chairperson?

Purpose of the meeting
Do you, the chairperson, really know why the meeting was called and what outcome is expected from it? We would suggest that

unless you can answer both the above questions in a simple sentence you are not suitably prepared to conduct the meeting – however good your chairing skills. Chapters 3 and 4 explore the question of purpose extensively, so please refer to them for more detail.

Purpose of the chairperson

Your overall objective should be to get the best outcome possible from the meeting. In order to do this you need to have a clear idea of what success criteria can, or will, be applied to the meeting.

Some meetings are easy in that everyone knows what will be a 'good' result. But there are more difficult meetings when different people or power groups want different outcomes, which will require you to weigh up priorities. Even more difficult are meetings where different groups want opposing or contradictory outcomes. Here, you may need to spend some time negotiating success criteria before you can begin the meeting proper (see Chapter 12: Politics and Power).

TASKS

The major tasks of the chairperson are:

- opening the meeting and setting it on course
- structuring the meeting, with reference to agenda, time and to achieving the overall purpose
- summarising at intervals and at the end
- ensuring that a written record of decisions and actions is agreed and followed through

Opening the meeting

From the very beginning you can set the tone of a meeting by the way in which you introduce it. You can ensure a positive, brisk, purposeful meeting, or a dull, tedious, frustrating one. The things you say and the way you say them can have a profound effect on the outcome. You are leading the meeting at this stage and the other participants will take their cue from you about the sort of meeting it is going to be.

- Be positive in both your tone of voice and your body language. Look and sound as if you expect the meeting to achieve its objective easily and without pain.
- State the purpose of the meeting and set out its structure. Give an overview of what will be covered and name the people who are to give specific information or make other pre-planned contributions.

    'We are meeting this morning to discuss a number of issues about the move to the new office in City Street. We need to discuss and decide space requirements for each department – Andrew has some information for us about this. Anne has a proposal about a gym to encourage staff fitness. We need to discuss the tenders for the washroom contract and to hear from John about removal firm estimates and make a decision about which firm to use. Lastly we need to set a tentative date for the move'.

- Give a clear indication of how long the meeting is likely to take. You may also wish to indicate roughly how long you think you need to spend on specific items on the agenda.

    'I'm hoping we can finish this meeting by 11.30. Is everyone happy with that?'

- Tell people about anything that is going to affect the meeting, such as certain people needing to leave, or others arriving later.

    'Anne has to leave at 10.30 because she has to investigate an accident at Hounslow branch, so we'll deal with the item about the staff gym first if that's OK with everyone. Oh yes, and there's a fire alarm test at 11.00, so don't all run away when it goes off.'

Recap

If the meeting is a regular one, you may need to recap on the previous meeting. *Keep it short.* Don't waste time giving the assembly a complete summary of the previous meeting – after all most of them will probably have been there and they should have read the minutes. Just recap on any business which is still outstanding, or actions agreed that will be reported in this meeting.

    'In our last meeting we agreed that we could not allocate space to individual departments until we had a clearer idea of how much space they thought they needed – although this may not match how much space they are given, of course. Andrew has been doing some research into this.'

Structuring the meeting

The chairperson has to control the structure of the meeting. This means making sure the meeting moves through the agenda efficiently and effectively, making the best use of the available time and ensuring that the required outcome is achieved. The appropriate *style* of control will differ depending on the purpose of the meeting, but the tasks which enable you to control the structure remain the same. These are:

- deal with each item in turn
- facilitate discussion
- stay on course
- keep to time limits

Deal with each item in turn

Deal with each item in the order in which it appears on the agenda. When you wrote the agenda you took care to put items in a logical order taking into account the convenience, difficulty and importance of items. Occasionally, there may be special reasons for rejigging the order, as in the example above where one member has to leave unexpectedly, but this should be the exception rather than the rule.

Each item needs to be introduced by the chairperson, perhaps recapitulating previous discussions, giving some background information or bringing people up-to-date on the current situation.

'Anne has a proposal to make about a gym for staff use in the basement of the new building. As the Health and Safety Officer, Anne's remit covers the physical well-being as well as the actual safety of staff. She has some information for us about what other organisations our size are doing in this area and some feedback from our own staff.'

Facilitate discussion

Having introduced Anne and let her have her say, you must ensure that other people who have suggestions or opinions have the opportunity to voice them and that they are discussed. The whole point of meetings is that they deal with issues that cannot be decided or dealt with by one person on their own, so a number of views on a subject are likely to be expressed. (The skills of facilitating discussion are discussed more fully later in this chapter.)

Stay on course

It is your job to keep the discussion under control, ensuring that it neither wanders off the point nor degenerates into pointless argument. You need to strike a balance between allowing participants enough time to examine proposals and suggest ideas, and allowing too much time so that the subject becomes tedious from over-repetition or clouded by side issues. We will explore the necessary skills later in this chapter.

Keep to time limits

It is your job as chairperson to ensure that the meeting stays within the time contraints. If you have put rough timings for each item on the agenda, try to ensure that they are adhered to as far as possible. Having said that, you do, of course, need to be flexible. Sometimes a discussion is worthwhile and useful, perhaps dealing with aspects of the subject which have not been considered previously but are relevant. Moving the discussion on while issues are left unresolved in order to keep to time is not the most effective way of running a meeting.

> *Paul:* 'Before we leave the multi-gym, what about supervising the people using it? Who would do that?'
>
> Wrong: *Chairperson:* 'We're out of time on this item, Paul – deal with it at the next meeting'.
>
> Right: *Chairperson:* 'We are running a bit behind time here, but that is an important point, Paul – are there any regulations about this Anne?'

Summarise

Summarising is an important skill and a useful control mechanism. When you are chairing a meeting you can use summaries to:

- control the discussion
- recap
- clarify decisions and actions
- check commitment
- provide material for the minutes

Control the discussion

Summaries can be used to signal to a contributor that he or she has had their say and it's time to give someone else a turn.

'Can I summarise where we seem to have got to so far? Jack, you think that the maintenance of the building would be best served by employing contractors because we could get specific jobs done quickly, when we needed them. We would pay the price for the job and save the cost of National Insurance and salaries. Does anyone else have a view?'

You can also use a summary to close one area of discussion and move the meeting on – to making a decision, allocating responsibility for action or moving to the next subject.

'We have decided to keep two permanent maintenance people for day-to-day convenience and routine jobs, but contract out special or large jobs. We now need to allocate responsibility for the management of the outside contracting and decide who will work with personnel to deal with the redundancies.'

Recap

Sometimes the discussion has been long and far-reaching and before any further progress can be made, a summary is needed to put into a nutshell what has happened.

'So, Anne has given us the reasons why she thinks it would be a good idea to have a multi-gym in the basement and told us of some staff's enthusiasm for the project. She has also given us a rough estimate of the costs involved. We've discussed the pros and cons and Andrew has suggested we do a bit more research as to the exact cost involved.'

Clarify decisions and agreed action

When a decision is made, or some action agreed, it is your job as chairperson to reiterate and clarify that decision to ensure that everyone is clear about what has been decided or agreed.

'So, to research the cost of the multi-gym, Anne is going to find out exactly what equipment is available and how much it costs and Andrew has agreed to get some estimates for installing a suitable floor from the builders. They will bring those figures to the next meeting and we will hope to make a decision then about whether or not to proceed.'

Check commitment

Groups do not always reach agreement easily. When you summarise a discussion, or, especially, a decision or agreed action, you have the opportunity to check whether the members of the group have reached some sort of consensus. Unless people are committed to the decisions made in the meeting, they are unlikely to be committed to implementing them. We deal in more detail with the way groups work in Chapter 7.

Provide material for the minutes

The summaries of discussions, decisions and actions made by the chairperson often provide the minutes-taker with his or her material as the minutes of the meeting are essentially a summarising activity. If you are doing your job properly as chairperson and summarising at intervals you are making the task of the minute-taker a lot easier.

Following through decisions and actions

This involves:

- closing the meeting
- recording the meeting
- follow-up

Closing the meeting

At the end of the meeting the chairperson needs to give a clear, succinct summary of the major issues discussed and decided, with a recap of the action to be taken.

Often, this is the most appropriate time to set the date of the next meeting as the participants can be consulted about convenient dates. It avoids a lot of telephoning to check on availability – or even having to cancel a planned meeting if a key contributor cannot be there.

Recording the meeting

It is your job as chairperson to make sure that a record of the meeting, such as minutes, is kept. It is particularly important to ensure that decisions, actions and the people to take the action are recorded accurately. Many people when acting as chairperson like to make their own note of decisions and actions agreed so that they have their own record in case of any doubt or mistake. However do not make the mistake of trying to take the minutes and also act as Chairperson – if you do, you will do neither job well.

Follow-up

When you finish chairing a meeting, you cannot breathe a sigh of relief and say 'Thank goodness that's over' as the last participant leaves. Your job is by no means completed. It is the responsibility of the chairperson to ensure that the minutes are prepared and distributed to the appropriate people, that any relevant information is sent out, that agreed actions are taken, and that the decisions made at a meeting are implemented. We deal with the how, what and why of this in Chapter 13.

LEADERSHIP SKILLS

As chairperson you are seen to be the leader of the meeting and people look to you to fulfil this role. Leadership used to be regarded as no more than planning, organising and controlling, but modern thinking suggests it is more to do with vision and the communication of that vision.

Leadership is needed to prevent people getting lost; people in meetings can get lost remarkably easily. The effective leader helps to prevent this by bringing three skills to bear on the meeting. They are:

- *vision* – to capture attention, and indicate direction
- *communication* – to give the vision meaning, and to harness energy
- *appropriate control* – applied through flexible choice of style

Vision

Leaders have vision: they can see where they are going when others cannot. In the case of a meeting, vision will usually be translated into clarity of purpose which as we said earlier in the chapter, is essential to the effectiveness of the meeting. However, it sometimes happens that once a meeting is underway, it becomes clear that the original purpose is no longer appropriate. If a team is meeting to discuss the next steps to be taken on a particular project, but it becomes apparent immediately that there are fundamental differences between the team members, sorting out their differences might be a more appropriate purpose for the meeting before embarking on any new project plans.

Leadership can be shown in a meeting by anyone, it is not just the prerogative of the chairperson, but it is to the chair that participants will turn when they need guidance. And it is part of the job of the chairperson to ensure that the participants receive guidance when they need it.

The meeting has been discussing the possibility of installing a new telephone switchboard. Charlie has become very emotional about the 'vast amount of money spent on electronics and computing when I can't even get a new forklift for the warehouse'. The meeting is beginning to break up into recriminations and justifications of budgets past, present and future. The chairperson intervenes with a similarly emotional statement, only his concerns the future of the organisation. He reminds everyone round the table how they have worked together since the management buyout 12 months ago, and accepts that times are still tough for every department. But he also recalls the 'vision' that united them at the buyout, and asks if they all still subscribe to the same aims. If so, he suggests, it must be possible to make a decision keeping that vision in mind.

Except at meetings concerned with future planning, it is unusual for vision to appear on the agenda. But the chairperson must never lose sight of the vision of the organisation, and must be prepared to remind the meeting whenever it seems to be getting off-track.

Communication

Leadership is about turning vision into action. The first stage of this process is to communicate the vision in such a way that it has meaning for the people who are going to implement it. In a meeting, that may involve the chairperson helping one or more participants translate the overall vision into a reality they understand. IBM successfully translated its vision of service and support to the customer into the phrase, 'no-one ever got fired for buying IBM'. It's a catchy phrase if you are a worried computer purchaser and its meaning is attractively clear.

Appropriate control

The most obvious leadership skill to the other people at the meeting is the way the chairperson controls the meeting.

> A colleague sits on an international committee of specialists. The committee is made up of representatives from several European countries, plus a chairperson. The chairperson is from one of the countries represented at the meeting and his job is to chair the meeting impartially.
>
> The chairperson of this meeting controls the meeting firmly, moving the discussion on when he feels that enough has been said. Some of the people who attend the meeting feel that he uses his power to manipulate the subjects which are discussed at the meeting. If he feels that a subject is not important or of no interest to his country, he spends little time on it and does not allow those who feel strongly about it to give it the attention they feel it deserves. On matters which do concern his country, he gives more space and time to those who support the point of view which is held by his countrywoman on the committee.

The resentment felt by some of the people who attend this committee is two-fold. They are resentful of the fact that the chairman controls the meeting so firmly that some subjects are not discussed fully. They are doubly resentful as they perceive that he is not playing his impartial role, but is stifling discussion about subjects of little interest to his country and allowing plenty of time for those which are of interest to him, but perhaps not to others.

Writers on leadership have identified three basic styles of control: *autocratic*, *democratic* and *laissez-faire*.

Autocratic

People with a natural tendency to use an autocratic style of control have a concern for getting things done their way. They assume a high degree of control. Their style is authoritarian, they tell people what they want them to do and expect them to do it. Their main concern is to get the task performed and they show less concern for the people involved than for the task itself. In meetings, an autocratic chairperson will probably state her own view at the beginning of a discussion, keep very firm control over the discussion, and ensure that the structure of the meeting is firmly adhered to.

Democratic

People with a natural tendency to use a democratic style of control are concerned to ensure participation. They involve the people working for them as much as possible in the decision-making process. While the best of them do have a concern for the task to be performed, their main concern is for the people who are to perform the task. In meetings, a democratic chairperson will ask for information and opinions from many participants, and do her best to ensure consensus is reached.

Laissez-faire

Laissez-faire means literally 'let someone else do it'. People who adopt this style assume little or no control of the meeting. They allow the group to go its own way without interfering. They show little concern for the task or for the people involved. A laissez-faire chairperson will sit back and let the meeting happen, without controlling the agenda or the discussion.

Appropriate use of control styles
Each of these styles may be appropriate at certain times and when chairing a meeting you may wish to use different styles for different meetings. The really skilled chairperson will be able to move from one to the other at different stages of the same meeting, depending on which is most appropriate.

Using the different styles inappropriately can cause frustration among participants and the task will not be completed with optimum effectiveness. Megan, at the beginning of this chapter, adopted an autocratic style, while William's style was laissez-faire. John felt that Megan was controlling the meeting too firmly, she was not allowing discussion or debate and had her hands firmly on the reins at all times. Mary felt that William didn't take enough control; he allowed things to drift along so that the real work had to be done outside the meeting.

For most meetings within organisations, a strong flavour of democratic control is most likely to achieve a positive result in terms of committing the participants, plus achieving the required outcome. However, if a democratic style is used exclusively this brings problems of its own: it can make it difficult to control the structure of a meeting effectively:

Chairperson:	'Well, do you all think we have come to an adequate decision about that?'
Group:	'Yes', 'Yes', 'I think so', 'I'm not sure', 'No'
Chairperson:	'What do you think we ought to do now?'

The style in which you control the meeting will have a profound effect on the way it is conducted and on its outcome, so vary your style: a formal, structured meeting to present the annual accounts to the Board for their approval, will, for example, need a different method of control from an unstructured, informal meeting which has the purpose of generating creative ideas.

The effective chairperson needs to keep the balance between controlling the structure of the meeting firmly enough to keep it on track, and having the confidence to allow the participants to contribute as much and as well as they can. The aspects to be balanced are shown in figure 6.1.

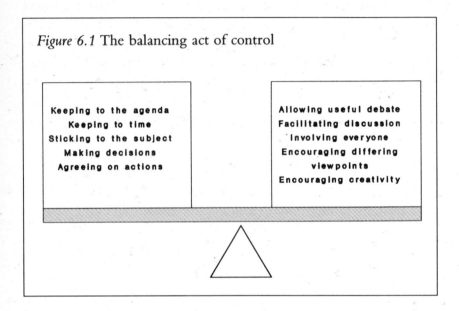

Figure 6.1 The balancing act of control

Keeping to the agenda
Keeping to time
Sticking to the subject
Making decisions
Agreeing on actions

Allowing useful debate
Facilitating discussion
Involving everyone
Encouraging differing viewpoints
Encouraging creativity

How to combine the elements of control

1. Tell people what to expect during the meeting. Outline the structure and define the purpose.
2. Ask the views of other participants before giving your own. Telling people what you think before they have a chance to speak gives the impression that the outcome is already decided.
3. Facilitate discussion between participants, but control the meeting with summaries and ensure that the discussion stays within relevant parameters. Tell people it is time to move on if necessary.
4. Take less control of creative sessions. Be prepared to sit back and listen rather than tell them what to do.
5. Ensure that decisions and actions are clear-cut and that responsibility for implementation is assigned.

FACILITATING DISCUSSION

The vast majority of meetings involve some sort of exchange of views or discussion between the participants. One of your tasks as chairperson is to ensure that this exchange of views is as productive as it can be. This may involve drawing people in to the conversation, shutting others out, asking for clarification etc. This involves a degree of skill at facilitating discussion. If you are skilful enough, you can get the tasks and structure wrong but still hold a successful meeting.

The skills you need to apply to facilitate discussion are:

- listening
- questioning
- encouraging
- harmonising and conciliating
- praising and complimenting
- building and integrating

Listening

At first glance this might seem an unlikely candidate for top of the list, but it's crucial: if you do not listen to what is going on in the meeting, you will not know when to use other skills such as conciliating, praising and so on. It is one of the hardest skills to learn, as it is so easy to be distracted. The skills of active listening are covered in Chapter 9.

People who chair meetings need to listen more carefully than anyone else in the group because they need to:

- juggle the contributions of all group members
- be aware of undercurrents of bad feeling and hidden agendas
- pick the right time to move on
- know when to insist on continuing the discussion until the point has been thrashed out
- clarify points when people are getting in a muddle
- summarise the medley of viewpoints and opinions so far
- identify when the time has arrived to push for a decision

- completely understand the points which contributors are making

Questioning

Questioning is a very versatile skill, you can use it for many different purposes. Using questions, you can structure and control the meeting, open up a discussion or close it down, draw somebody out or shut them up. These are some of the ways a skilful chairperson can use questions to control and structure a meeting.

Questions to open up discussion

Open-ended questions encourage people to talk. These are questions that begin with words such as how, what, when, why, tell me about. They are almost impossible to answer with yes or no so an open-ended question will open up a subject for discussion. Contrast the answers you might get to the following two questions:

'Do we all agree that the revised estimates now fall within our budget?'

'What are the implications of those estimates for our budget?'

Asking the first question would mean that you would then need to ask a lot of extra supplementary questions if you wished to start a discussion; the second question opens up the subject straight away.

Questions to close down a subject

Closed questions are useful for ending a discussion. Questions which begin with do, did, can, are, is, encourage people to answer yes or no. The question: 'Do we all agree that the revised estimates now fall within our budget?' can be the signal for terminating that particular discussion and moving on to make a decision or take some action.

Closed questions are also extremely useful for bringing the talkative to a halt. If Paula is pontificating about the pros and cons of installing a mobile phone in each sales rep's car, a simple closed question can bring her contribution to an end and gives you the opportunity to ask someone else for their opinion. For example:

'Do you recommend that we give everyone a phone?'

'Is that the course of action you would prefer?'
'Did you ask the sales people themselves?'

Other uses of questions

A skilled chairperson will use questions for many other purposes during a meeting. As we look at the other skills needed, the value of questioning will reappear frequently. They can't be any old questions, though, they must be appropriate at the time. However, fortunately, questioning is a skill which can be learned.

Encouraging

It is part of the chairperson's job to encourage participants. This takes two forms:

1. Encouraging people to give their best performance during the meeting (giving them enough time to prepare and showing them that you expect them to have done so is crucial here).

2. Encouraging people to speak on subjects about which they have some information, expertise or opinion.

The skill involved in encouraging people is partly showing your own enthusiasm, partly being aware of who has not spoken and using open questions to encourage them to speak. You need to develop a 'helicoptering' technique so that you are aware of what is being said and your own reactions to it, while at the same time, mentally hovering above the meeting, watching everything that is going on, being aware of who is keeping their head down, who is trying to get a word in and failing, and noting that Harriet is irritating Nancy.

Encouraging the silent

Some people do not speak at meetings. This may be due to shyness, natural taciturnity, lack of interest or for various other reasons. On the basis that most people should not be at the meeting unless they have something to contribute, it is an important part of the chair-person's job to encourage everyone at the meeting to speak, prefera-bly without drawing attention to the fact that they never speak unless spoken to. So the simple: 'What do you think, Martin?' is what is needed here, not: 'We haven't heard from you for a long time Martin, what do you think?'

Harmonising and conciliating

When participants at a meeting start throwing verbal grenades at each other, damage limitation is the chairperson's job. Conflict can be healthy in that it encourages new ideas and ways of solving problems. While participants are disagreeing, it is the chairperson's job to ensure that everyone has a fair say and a fair hearing so that the full range of ideas and suggestions can be considered. This may be difficult if one person has very strong views and is extremely vocal, while another with equally strong views is not as loud or persistent. You as chairperson may need to say something like:

'I think it would help us make a decision if we heard equally from all sides of the discussion, so George will you hold back for a moment so that Robin can give us his views.'

Harmonising and conciliating become more difficult when participants at a meeting start attacking each other or each other's departments on a more personal level. When, for instance, put-downs and sarcastic remarks start being bandied about:

'Well, that's personnel for you, isn't it?'

'Typical sales insensitivity'

'Of course if anyone in finance could actually count'

'I regard that remark as typical of your usual attitude, John.'

A way of tackling this situation before it escalates into open warfare is to confront the people involved directly. Saying something like: 'I think it would be better if we stuck to discussing the facts rather than attacking each other' may be a bit startling to the protagonists and their audience, but has the effect of exposing the personal attack for what it is and usually has the required effect.

If a meeting becomes very intense, the chairperson can try to lighten the atmosphere with humour – when people are laughing it is difficult for them to be angry with each other. Some people have a natural gift for using humour in this way and can do so very effectively. But, beware, if you are not really a humourist, it is easy for your attempt to come over as heavy-handed sarcasm and this can make the situation worse, not better.

Praising and complimenting

People are encouraged by praise, when you tell them they are doing well they are motivated to keep on doing well. So, when someone produces a useful report for a meeting, tell them how useful it was. Similarly, if someone comes up with a good idea, or provides valuable information towards making a decision. Result: they will be motivated to produce more good ideas and valuable information.

Some people do not find it easy to praise others, or compliment them on the work they do. Perhaps they are afraid of sounding condescending or patronising, or find it embarrassing. If this applies to you, the best way of paying a compliment or giving praise is to be specific about what you are praising and own the praise yourself.

'I like some of your ideas about saving money, Jeremy. I particularly like the one about moving out of the Andover warehouse, which seems to be eminently sensible. You've obviously been very thorough in your research and you presented it well.'

This chairperson has been specific about exactly what he liked: the actual idea, and the fact it was well presented and researched. It gives Jeremy positive feedback about exactly what he did well.

As the chairperson is saying 'I like some of your ideas' he is owning the praise himself. He is not saying 'those are good ideas' – a value judgment which might annoy others who don't agree with the ideas.

Building and integrating

A major part of the chairperson's job is to help participants at the meeting build on each other's ideas and integrate them into the final solution. The chairperson can achieve this by clarifying and summarising what each person has said to ensure that others have a clear understanding, then asking for other ideas to enlarge it or take it forward. Since the chairperson should have an overview of what is going on he or she should be able to suggest various ways of integrating ideas or information to help achieve a coherent decision.

HANDLING PROBLEMS

When chairing a meeting you need to be able to identify and deal with problems. Problems can be caused by the other people at the meeting or by yourself.

Problem people

In any group of people there are bound to be some you perceive as more of a problem than others. Problem people come in many shapes and forms. We have called them the 'W's'. They are: *Whisperers*; *Wizards*; *Wanderers*; *Whingers*; *Why me's?*; *Worriers*.

Whisperers

You have all met the Whisperer. The Whisperer is not content with having one meeting, he likes to have an extra meeting with one or two other people, at the end of the table, sotto voce. Often their meeting seems to be a lot more amusing than the one everyone else is having.

Your body language probably offers you the most effective way of dealing with the Whisperer. Stop listening in an obvious way to the person speaking to the 'main' meeting, signalling to them with your hand to stop if necessary, and look directly at the Whisperer and cronies, waiting in silence for them to stop speaking. Often this will be enough.

Sometimes you may need to ask the Whisperer to stop talking and pay attention. It will probably be very tempting to speak sharply to him as if you were the teacher and he a wayward child (Eric Berne has described this as being in a Critical Parent frame of mind), but this can be dangerous, as it can engender resentment (who does she think she is?), or it can create rebellion – the rebellious child reacting to the critical parent.

The best approach is to use non-verbal skills – it's not what you say, but the way that you say it. If you say: 'Would you like to share your ideas with us, John?' in a sarcastic voice, you risk the rebellious child response. If, however, you say the same sentence in a tone of voice which sounds as if you sincerely mean it, John will either do just that, if it is relevant, or subside into embarrassed silence if it is not.

Another useful phrase is: 'John, could we just listen to Alex for a moment please and then we'll come on to you' implying that you think they are jumping the gun, although you may secretly believe they are only talking about the show they saw on Saturday.

Whingers

Whingers can always find something to complain about. However brilliant the plan, however cunning the execution of it, there will always be something about it which will have an adverse effect on them personally, or on their department. Their hunting cry is 'Yes, but' and they can be relied upon to find a point about which to nit-pick on every occasion.

If the Whinger is shouted down by the rest of the group, if her objections are overruled, she will revel in being the voice of doom for the whole project, ready to cry 'I told you so' as soon as anything deviates even slightly from plan.

The best way to deal with the Whinger is to thank her for bringing up the problem. Hail her as devil's advocate, then suggest that she is the person who is clever enough to think of a way of resolving the problem she has just raised. For example:

'Thank you for raising the point about the fact that not everyone eats fruit, Mary. Do you think this should make us reconsider altogether our plan of giving all the children a packed lunch? What do you think would be the best way of overcoming this problem?'

Why Me's?

The Why Me is often quite vocal and helpful while a discussion is going on but likes to keep his head down when action is called for. He has never been known to volunteer to find out information or carry out a particular course of action. If he is asked to do something, he usually has a very good reason for being unable to do so.

One of the authors once served on the committee of a voluntary organisation of which all but three members were Why Me's. The Why Me's were full of praise for the hard work which the three active members carried out, but never volunteered to do any of it themselves. If asked to do something they had so many other commitments that they knew they would not be able to do a good job, so gracefully withdrew, leaving the field clear for the few.

The best way of dealing with the Why Me, when he gives good and fulsome reasons for being unable to help with finding a builder to repair the roof, or to canvass reactions in his department about replacing real plants with plastic ones, is to acknowledge his

105

problems. Having acknowledged how very busy he is and how grateful you are that he has been able to spare the time to attend this meeting, move in with an open question.

'As we've just said, Martin, we do realise how busy you are. How do you think you may be able to use your time to the best advantage in helping us to achieve . . . ?'

Wanderers

Wanderers wander off the subject. A discussion about resurfacing the car park may lead the Wanderer into reminiscences of how terrible the parking arrangements were in her previous firm. This sort of reminiscence is very catching. Everybody has a story to tell about parking and before you know it, half an hour has gone – and so has the subject of resurfacing the car park.

The Wanderer needs a firm hand. Unless reminiscences are cut off almost before they begin, once someone has told their story other people begin to feel hard done by if they don't get their chance. So it is best to be ruthless and jump in straight away.

Wizards

Wizards can do everything and know about everything. They come in various forms and guises, but usually have in common the belief that they can speak with authority on most subjects. If they are not able to fix something themselves, they know someone who can. Often, they will offer to implement many of the actions needed, leaving little for others to do 'Just leave it to me, I'll fix it in no time' is their cry.

Sometimes, on first meeting the Wizard, a chairperson is lulled into thinking what a good and useful member of the team he will be. Disillusionment often follows at the next meeting, when the Wizard hasn't had time to work his spells on half the actions he undertook to do.

Worriers

People who play the part of devil's advocate can be extremely useful to a group which is trying to come to a conclusion or make a decision. The problem with the Worrier is that she takes the search for possible difficulties too far. She always has a concern about whether the right decision has been made. Have you really taken everything into account? Have all stones been well and truly turned over? Worriers can also be known as What Ifs. What if the transport system breaks down? What if there is a flood or a fire?

One way to cope with a Worrier without letting them worry you, is to use their predilection in a positive way and actively give them the role of identifying potential problems so making use of their natural talent. The very fact that they have been given a specific role seems to have the effect of concentrating their minds on raising major, rather than minor, issues.

Problems with yourself

Unlikely though it is, there is just the possibility that the problem is you! The symptoms may emerge through your use of leadership skills and particularly in the way you tend to control a meeting.

Often, if a person is not confident about their chairing ability, they tend to adopt either the laissez-faire approach, or, in complete contrast, the autocratic approach. Sometimes, the person who is chairing the meeting is the most senior person present, and feels for reasons of prestige or status that he has to have the final word on all decisions which also leads to autocratic control.

Identifying the way you use control at a meeting can be a very useful piece of management development work. If you can improve the usefulness of your meetings by improving the way you chair them, you are indirectly increasing the efficiency and productivity of your organisation.

SUMMARY

The way in which a meeting is chaired is of crucial importance to how well a meeting functions as a management tool. Many people are asked to chair meetings because of their status or their position. A few may be asked either because people like them, or because they weren't quick enough to duck. It is questionable how many are asked to chair meetings simply because they are known to be skilful at doing so.

The chairperson has to be extremely clear about her own purpose and the purpose of the meeting. She has to undertake certain crucial tasks in order to make that meeting work. The leadership style with which those tasks are performed can have a huge effect on the outcome of the meeting – not only what is achieved, but the way in which it is achieved. The level of skill which a chairperson brings to handling the tasks and the people involved in the meeting, will produce positive involvement and commitment, or boredom and frustration. Developing the skills of leading a meeting are discussed further in Chapter 15.

CHECKLIST – CHAIRING THE MEETING

PURPOSE
1. Be aware of:
   a) the purpose of the meeting
   b) your purpose as chairperson

TASKS
2. Open the meeting and set it on course:
   a) give a clear and positive introduction
   b) recap on previous meetings if necessary
3. Structure the meeting:
   a) deal with each item in turn
   b) facilitate discussion
   c) stay on course
   d) keep to time limits
4. Use summaries to:
   a) control the discussion
   b) recap
   c) clarify decisions and actions
   d) check commitment
   e) provide material for the minutes.
5. Follow through decisions and actions.

LEADERSHIP
6. Leadership skills involve vision, communication and control:
   a) use vision to provide guidance
   b) use communication to turn vision into action
   c) use control to get the most out of participants at the meeting.
7. Use an appropriate style of control for your meeting, balancing the need to structure with the need for participation.

FACILITATING
8. Facilitate discussion by:
   a) listening
   b) using questions appropriately

c) encouraging participation
d) harmonising and conciliating
e) praising and complimenting
f) building and integrating.

DEALING WITH PROBLEMS
9. Be aware of some of the problems which you may need to deal with; those posed by other people and by yourself.

7. How Groups Work

Your plane has crashed on the edge of a lake 150 miles south of the Canadian Arctic Circle. The pilot was killed in the crash but the six or seven passengers have managed to escape unharmed and have waded ashore. It is cold and you are wet. But miraculously you have saved 15 items from the plane's luggage hold. How will you survive? How will you make best use of those items? And which will be the most important for your survival?

Exercises like Sub-Arctic Survival, Desert Survival and Lost at Sea, are often the first introduction managers have to understanding the behaviours they show in groups and meetings. Most people go to meetings to get something done or to hear something they didn't know. Power, position in the hierarchy, expertise, and suspicion of politics will all have an effect on how much a person speaks and how much they contribute to each of the meetings they attend. Exercises like the one outlined above are one way of getting behind those imposed constraints in order to see what skills individuals bring to meetings.

In this chapter we will put aside the content and the purpose of the meeting. Instead, we will concentrate on the behaviours that are shown during the meeting. People sometimes talk about the words and the music of a meeting. The words being the content and the music being everything else that was going on at the same time, but which never gets mentioned in the minutes.

A greater appreciation of the behaviour that happens in meetings – ie. the music – helps the chairperson and the contributor, in three ways:

1. It helps understand what is actually going on in the meeting – often what people say is not what they mean.

2. It helps to anticipate many of the sources of fruitless conflict, and do something about them before the conflict becomes destructive.
3. It also helps to appreciate that the skills of working effectively with one other person are very different from those required when working with a group of other people in a meeting.

Since R.F. Bales and later Neil Rackham, Peter Honey and Michael Colbert produced innovative work on observing, classifying, and finally understanding how small groups work, there has been a considerable explosion of interest in the dynamics of groups and the skills individuals can bring to them. There are probably hundreds of ways of observing how the individuals in a meeting make the thing work or fail. However, it is possible to say that the kinds of behaviours that are visible during any meeting tend to fall into a small number of categories. We have identified four:

1. task
2. maintenance
3. task and maintenance
4. non-functional

Task behaviours
The group is meeting for a purpose, and the task is directly concerned with that purpose. We have dealt in Chapters 3, 4 and 5 with meetings which have no declared purpose or an inadequately defined purpose. However let us assume that the group of people in the meeting understand why they are there and what their task is. In the Sub Arctic Survival group exercise, for example, the task would be to rank order the 15 items which the survivors of the crash had to use in order to survive.

In a business meeting the task might be to come up with new suggestions to defend a product from a competitor, or to take 10 per cent out of the group budget, or to investigate why the scrap and rework rate on line number three was 15 per cent higher last week than the other two lines.

Typical task behaviours include:

1. *Initiating activity:* this involves suggesting ideas, proposing solutions to the problem, putting forward new definitions of the problem or new ways to deal with it, or perhaps some new view or reorganisation of the data that is available.

   'If we were to divide the regions into areas by post code, then we could correlate the market awareness data with income groupings.'

2. *Seeking information:* asking for clarification, asking for information or additional information, asking who has the facts.

   'How many sale staff do we have who can speak German?'

3. *Giving information:* offering facts or ideas, clarifying a point whether asked to or not, giving opinions or stating beliefs, particularly concerning the value of suggestions rather than the factual basis of them.

   'In my view, the Japanese product, although more expensive, does not have the same robust construction as the Korean machine.'

4. *Building and elaborating:* developing or extending a proposal which has been made by another person at the meeting. Giving examples and developing the idea or meaning of a suggestion that you or someone else has made. Trying to envisage how a proposal might work if it is adopted by building scenarios.

   'So if we took your idea for an internal customer help line, could we link its use to our drive for quality by making each new problem a case for our quality improvement project team?'

5. *Co-ordinating:* showing the relationships between various ideas or suggestions, trying to pull ideas and suggestions together also activities of various sub groups or members.

   'If finance can provide the data using the same spreadsheet as purchasing, then they will not need to exchange long print-outs, a single disk will do until the computing people can get the network running again.'

6. *Summarising and testing understanding:* bringing together related ideas or suggestions, and not just those made by the individual concerned. Restating suggestions after the group has discussed them. Establishing whether an earlier contribution has been understood.

'We have agreed that within four working days of the end of every calender month you will all fax your sales figures and stock variances for that month to Mary's department, she will produce outline figures for our market review meeting.'

Maintenance behaviours

The previous section dealt with behaviours which were concerned specifically with achieving the task of the group. Maintenance behaviour is the equivalent of the lubricating oil in an engine. If you take the lubrication away, the engine overheats and soon is unable to move and achieve its task. Maintenance behaviour is therefore not directly concerned with the task as described, but it is concerned with helping the individuals in the group achieve that task. Typical maintenance behaviours are:

1. *Encouraging:* being friendly, warm, responsive to others, offering praise to others and their ideas, agreeing with and accepting the value of the contributions of others. You can encourage without having to agree with everything that someone says.

   'I like that suggestion, Jean–Claude, but I don't think it would work with this particular gauge of nylon, could you expand on your idea?'

2. *Gate-keeping:* trying to make sure that every member of the meeting is able to contribute. Directly asking the quieter members of the group what their views are, or what data they may have that is pertinent to the task. Holding back the louder members of the group to ensure that others can take part.

   'Hold on a moment Geoff, let us hear from Frank, I know he has experience with Unix.'

3. *Standard-setting:* expressing standards for the group to use in choosing content or procedures, or ways of evaluating the decision of the meeting. Reminding the group when it is likely to break or challenge the standards it has previously set.

   'We did agree at the previous meeting that we would set a time limit of no more than 30 minutes for the discussion on point of sale material.'

4. *Following:* accepting other people's ideas, listening to other

members of the meeting as they offer their views, not just remaining silent or reading papers, but actively signalling through body language that you are prepared to listen.

5. *Expressing group feeling:* summarising the feelings of the group and the reactions individuals have to the way the group is working together. Summarising behaviour of individuals within the group without making judgements about it.

'We seem to have our biggest disagreement on item three, where John is strongly opposed to the use of a mail shot, but apart from that, we are reasonably happy with the way the project is going.'

Task and maintenance behaviours

There will be times when behaviours fall into both the task and the maintenance categories.

1. *Evaluating:* submitting group decisions or achievements for comparison with group standards and measuring those achievements against the task goals of the group.

'As a piece of new business, the turnover, contribution and ROI figures seem to be within the boundaries that we set ourselves, what about the projected growth?'

2. *Diagnosing:* determining sources of difficulties, taking appropriate steps, analysing the main blocks to progress.

'Our main difficulty seems to be that our staff still see themselves as working in a bank, whereas we want them to think of our organisation as a centre for financial services.'

3. *Testing for consensus:* checking for group opinions in order to assess how close the group is to reaching consensus on a decision, testing out sub-sections of group opinion if factions are beginning to form.

'So we have agreed on the need to produce longer prestige documentaries for international distribution, but how close are we to agreeing what we give up in order to find resources for these more demanding projects?'

4. *Mediating:* harmonising between individuals or sub groups,

bringing together different points of view, looking for the common thread between opposing arguments.

'If we were put the ten pence-off sign on the shrink wrap, rather than on each individual bar, then production wouldn't have to wait for the new paper wrappers. Would that meet both your needs?'

5. *Relieving tension:* helping to ease tension with humour, putting the conflict into perspective, reconciling and acknowledging the importance of people's views.

'If the competition could see George getting so excited about the plastic casing they'd probably give up and go home at the thought of what he will be like when we get onto the motor and gear train!'

Non-functional behaviours

If we only went to meetings where task and maintenance behaviour was all that was practised, the authors suspect meetings would be a lot simpler, a lot shorter but probably a lot less memorable. Non-functional behaviour, like a piece of grit in the engine, is often the reason why meetings take too long, stray off the subject, and generally fail to achieve their purpose in the most efficient manner. It is also through non-functional behaviour, that most people show they are human!

There are many categories of non-functional behaviour, but we are listing eight here. If the reader wishes to have a check-list of how to disrupt a meeting simply by using inappropriate behaviour (you need know nothing of the content of the meeting or why it was called) then the following eight behaviours are as good as any. They usually derive from unfinished business that has occurred, or failed to be resolved, outside the meeting. The attempt to resolve that unfinished business becomes, in effect, a meeting within a meeting. This can often be very disruptive and an effective chairperson and the meeting participants will soon spot what is going on and find an appropriate way to deal with it. See Chapter 12 for a complete wrecker's guide.

We have not given examples of these kinds of behaviour since we have found that they are usually very obvious to most meeting participants, and if for some scurrilous reason you wanted to copy any of these behaviours then we certainly don't wish to encourage that!

1. *Being aggressive:* improving your own status at the expense of others. Blaming, criticising, showing hostility against an individual or a sub-section of the meeting, deflating the ego or status of others.
2. *Blocking:* rejecting the ideas of others without listening to their content. Often, if there is an unresolved conflict between two members of a meeting, it may be that one person will consistently contradict every suggestion or statement of the other. This behaviour has nothing to do with achieving the task of the meeting, although it may be necessary for those two to go and resolve their differences before they can make any effective contribution to the present meeting.
3. *Self-confessing and sympathy-seeking:* telling long complex and usually unrelated stories concerned with the individual's feelings or point of view, and generally getting away from the subject or task. Trying to get other group members to be sympathetic to your problems or misfortunes, either personal or organisational. Making a great play of the awfulness of your own situation, or offering self-defeating arguments in an attempt to gain sympathy.
4. *Competing:* challenging and competing with others to produce ideas, say the most, talk the loudest and be seen to 'win'.
5. *Special pleading:* arguing for yourself or your department as a special case, generally suggesting that the rules and systems being used satisfactorily by everyone else in the meeting should not apply in your case. Often in conjunction with:
6. *Seeking recognition:* attempting to draw attention to oneself by loud, dramatic, or other unusual or extreme behaviour.
7. *Negative humour:* clowning, negative jokes that are purely disguised aggression or blocking, behaviour that is designed to irritate and call attention to oneself rather than the kind of humour that relieves tension.
8. *Withdrawing:* acting indifferently or impassively, day dreaming, doodling, whispering to others about subjects unrelated to the task and generally wandering from the subject.

Lights on, nobody home

The authors have conducted a small and rather lighthearted study on the last of the non-functional behaviours. We wondered how people could withdraw from a meeting with the least noticeable physical evidence. After all, it is easy to withdraw from a meeting by going to sleep, or by starting to write memos or whatever, but to have mentally left the meeting and not have anyone notice would require more skill. We asked a number of managers we met as part of our consulting and training work what methods they had seen in action, and which was the most effective. The most popular was to write notes on the pad in front of you about whatever it was that most concerned you at the time. The really skilled would combine this with occasional lifts of the head to make it seem as if they were paying rapt attention.

The second most popular, and in our view the more subtle, was to lift the eyes about ten degrees above the horizon. This appears to enable most members of the meeting to perceive that you are day-dreaming, without making the body language so obvious that people feel offended. We have found that people who lift their eyes only about five degrees from the horizon still find members of the meeting talk to them, since they misread the body language.

The serious point about all this is that whichever way people mentally leave meetings, it is up to the other participants and the chairperson to offer them the choice of whether they stay and contribute, or leave and do something else. Why have a meeting of six bodies when only five minds are present?

The importance of perception

In looking at all these classifications, personal perception is of tremendous importance. This is especially true if the meeting is composed of people who have grown up in different cultures. What to one person is non-functional seeking recognition, or blocking behaviour, to another culture may be hard bargaining and totally appropriate behaviour.

These detailed behaviours are most easily seen when reviewing video tapes of meetings. If you are going to a meeting with some clear targets to achieve, you will be very hard pressed to observe and react to all the various behaviours listed above. You will almost certainly be doing this at an unconscious level, but consciously to process different types of behaviour and then consciously decide on an appropriate response, is too much of a load for most people.

However, it is perfectly feasible to be aware of the kinds of behaviour that people are using at the meeting, and to point it out if it seems that some behaviour is being particularly non-functional and is distracting the meeting from its purpose.

Another simple assessment of how a meeting is developing is to count the numbr of 'I's' and 'we's' used. It is usually healthy if people are expressing their own beliefs and expectations: 'I think we should paint it green,' and 'In my opinion, the response time is too long'. But if they are still owning, rather than sharing, their wants: 'I must decide who is allocated to each sales department, it is no-one else's business,' then it is only a short step to the taking of sides.

LEADERLESS GROUPS

The survival exercises mentioned at the beginning of this chapter are also used to demonstrate several other components of meetings and group discussions.

One outcome of an effective meeting is that the contributions and discussions have created a better and more usable set of data than any of the individuals previously had access to. This is particularly useful when a meeting is called to discuss a subject about which there is no real expertise in the group. In the western world, it is traditional to find experts to aid us with solving our hardest problems. But sometimes a meeting has to face the fact that it doesn't have expertise, and it doesn't have access to expertise. The group of people trying to survive the plane crash have to make do with what they know at that time, and the equipment they have available in that place. So it is essential that they maximise the use of their ideas and the materials that are available to them. This is not such a different position from that which many managers find themselves in when running their businesses. In times of continuing and increasing change, many organisations are facing markets or environments in which there is little known expertise.

Many meetings face the need to haul themselves up by their 'boot straps' for the tasks they are setting themselves. Working in an effective leaderless group can produce tremendous synergy which can lead to creative and useful outcomes which pull the meeting up to a higher level of operation and effectiveness.

The survival exercises always have a recommended ideal solution. This is normally produced by military or other experts who have practical experience in the region or environment being described. Participants in these exercises compare the difference between their own ranking of items with that of the experts. If you take the average of the individual rankings, and compare it with the group decision for a ranking, on most occasions the group result is closer to the experts' result than the average of the individual results, thus demonstrating that an effective leaderless group will get closer to a good solution than a group of individuals. There are several constraints however.

Speed

First, it takes much longer. For a leaderless group to meander around the problem, discuss it, challenge each other etc. takes a lot longer than one individual to review the problem in their own mind and make the same set of decisions. Typically in these exercises, an individual can produce a ranking of the 15 items in about five minutes. Usually groups need at least 30 minutes and sometimes longer before they reach anything like consensus.

Listening to the wrong expert

Secondly, if there is one strong individual in the group who claims (whether accurately or otherwise) to have some expertise in the problem being tackled, then there is a good chance that this individual will lead the others to produce a group ranking close to his or her own. If it turns out that the individual is quite wrong and has been leading the group away from the correct answers, then the group score will be worse than the average of the individuals.

Ignoring the true expert

Thirdly, one of the people in the group may have an individual score which is better than the final group score. It is often the case that, by contrast with the self proclaimed expert, there is a real expert in the group. Sadly, it is not always the case that the group is able to identify that expertise or able to listen to it, as this sobering story from the history of the development of the Sub-Arctic Survival exercise demonstrates.

> *The designers of the exercise had the opportunity to see how a group of Eskimos from a relatively remote area would handle the survival exercise. These were people who had considerable understanding of what you might describe as the technology of survival in this remote region. They themselves when completing the exercise felt they would try to escape from the situation (not the preferred solution of the Transport and Rescue Squadron of the Canadian Airforce which had acted as experts) but estimated their chances of survival to be only 50:50. Yet they felt they should try to get out of the situation because of reasons to do with self esteem. They certainly recognised there was no way of walking out, so they were going to construct a canoe and escape by water.*
>
> *The depressing part of the story is that soon afterwards the designers of the exercise asked a group of businessmen on a fishing holiday if they would also do the exercise. They were asked to include one of the Eskimos, who was acting as their translator and guide, as part of their group. Although this group of (North American) fishermen had an Eskimo – a real expert – in their midst they ignored most of his contributions, and rejected his choice of priorities. These men did not listen, they didn't question and they didn't check on their own assumptions. As one of the designers ruefully put it 'to be sitting in the middle of the Canadian sub-arctic with an experienced Eskimo trying to solve this problem and not to listen, is symptomatic of the difficulty we have in so many interpersonal relationships'.*

How often in meetings do we have an expert in our midst, but fail to make effective use of his or her expertise?

Speed versus quality

The leaderless group provides useful guidance to consider when making a choice of who should be in the meeting, and indeed whether to call a meeting at all. The guidance concerns the trade off between speed and likely quality (see figure 7.1). It does depend on whether the problem being tackled has any known solution, or if it involves the invention of a solution that is new to all the participants. At one end of the scale, if speed is required and there is expertise, then asking the person who has greatest expertise is likely to produce a fast and good quality result. If the expert is confident that he or she has met a problem like this before and knows the answer, then there is scarcely any point in calling a meeting, just let the expert advise on what the answer should be. Unfortunately, there are very few business and organisational problems where the right answer is confidently known. After all, dealing with this kind of problem is what managers are generally needed for.

At the other end of the scale, where speed is not required but there is the danger that a poor decision will turn out to be catastrophic for the rest of the organisation, then a group should spend a considerable amount of time brain-storming and building so that the best possible solution can be produced. Remember, it is the leaderless meeting that is most likely to come up with original and innovative solutions.

Somewhere in the middle is what many organisations use most frequently, which is the chaired meeting where the agenda, and sometimes the chairperson or some other strong contributor will influence the direction of the group. This will probably occur at the cost of some contributions from quieter members of the meeting and of innovation generally. The dangers are that good ideas are lost because the chairperson or other strong participants will railroad the group into a solution which is appropriate for some and not for others.

GROUP NORMS

In all areas of human activity people observe and try to live up to group norms. It is comparatively easy for a group of people who meet regularly, who get on well together, and are in some way insulated from external views and opinions, to form norms which over a period of time become the overriding determinate of that group's output. Those readers who have teenage children will know

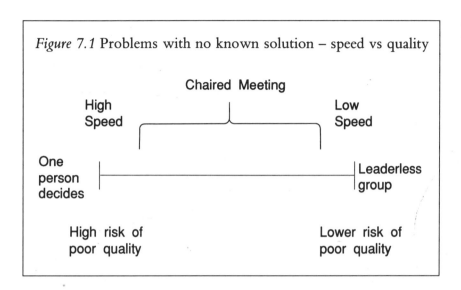

Figure 7.1 Problems with no known solution – speed vs quality

the effort and concern that goes into their offsprings' avoidance of breaking a group norm which is seen to be important by their peers. The same is true, although less dramatically, for groups of people that meet and work together frequently.

Even a group that has never met before will set norms for itself quite quickly. When a group of people meet for the first time the first few minutes of that meeting are often very significant and will set the tone and style for the rest of the meeting. It is well known that at an interview or a sales call or some other first time event, initial behaviours and transactions leave a long lasting impression. The same is also true for a formally convened meeting. If one person is very assertive and others are rather quiet, if the tone of the meeting is sombre, or irreverent, these norms will have an overall effect on the subsequent style of the meeting.

One observer described the development of a meeting as going through four stages:

1. *Forming:* that is the initial manoeuvring and testing out of position and influence.
2. *Storming:* whereby any major disagreements on values, process methodologies or what the task is, are brought to the surface and hopefully resolved.

3. *Norming:* having had argument and debate the members of the group now establish some workable rules to which they all subscribe.
4. *Performing:* operating to the best of their ability and in a high performance manner they have now set their rules and agreed their methods of working so can move on to achieve the goal they have set themselves.

Of course the norming phase can also be quite negative.

Stanley Milgram conducted some horrific experiments many years ago by placing an advertisement in the local paper in New Haven asking for volunteers in a learning experience. The volunteers were told that a subject was going to do some tasks in an experiment on adult learning, and would be punished with an electric shock if he failed to do the task accurately. In fact the subject was actually an actor and was not visible to the volunteers. They had a dial which was calibrated from mild shock up to dangerous, and yet with the encouragement of the proverbial man in the white coat, the expert who encouraged them to continue the experiment, 70 per cent of the members of the public who took part in this experiment were prepared to give dangerous or lethal shocks to an unknown victim on the other side of a wall.

The only encouragement was the man in the white coat with the clipboard who instructed them to continue with the experiment. We can assume that the ordinary people who took part would not normally have caused suffering if they felt directly in control of all components of their behaviour. Simply by detaching the victim to the other side of the wall (although his simulated screams could easily be heard) and by creating the authority figure of the man in the white coat, most of these ordinary male and female volunteers were prepared to take drastic and terrible action without apparently appreciating its true consequences.

Milgram's experiment is a horrific reminder of how easy it is to set unlikely, unreasonable or damaging norms and still have people try to live up to them. How often do we allow this to happen in our own meetings?

Conflict

The storming part of a group's development is a reminder that conflict may be a useful and essential stage a meeting has to work through. Many people find that conflict in meetings is unpleasant and therefore conclude that it is undesirable. But it is the way that the conflict is resolved that may be undesirable. In the days of the Wild West when 'there wasn't enough room in this town for the both of us', conflict was resolved by a shoot-out producing, at best, the short-term satisfaction of only one party in the dispute, and the long-term satisfaction of the undertakers. If that is a widely held model of how conflict gets resolved, then no wonder many people are not keen to get involved in some sort of shoot-out at the next meeting.

However it is possible to deal with conflict without spilling blood, real or metaphorical, and a good negotiator will use many of the techniques that are necessary. The important thing to recognise is that the meeting may be the best place, and sometimes the only place, in which the conflict can be resolved. Therefore effective meetings should not necessarily avoid conflict, but should take it as part of the task they are called to achieve.

So far in this chapter we have looked at the kinds of behaviours that are normally involuntary. For the most part, participants at meetings do not intend to use one piece of behaviour or another, the behaviour emerges as part of an attempt to put a point forward, argue a case, prove someone wrong etc. In the next section we look at what preferences affect the behaviour people use in teams and meetings. While we all have preferences about the kinds of behaviour that we use in meetings, once we understand our preferences and those of others, it is then possible to adjust behaviour to suit the needs of the task, or the other members of the meeting.

BELBIN CATEGORIES OF BEHAVIOUR

The work of Meredith Belbin on teams has been well known in the UK for some time. After observing teams in organisations and running business games, Belbin came up with eight kinds of behaviour that need to be available for any team to work effectively.

Subsequent work has added an extra behaviour which is also sometimes necessary in a team. Although this book is not about teams, it is true that many of the behaviours shown by effective teams are also necessary in effective meetings. For more information on effective team operation see the companion volume to this one called *Quality: Change Through Teamwork.*

The nine behaviours which are now identified in the Belbin approach to teams do not require that all meetings should have nine separate participants. The expectation is that each member of a meeting should be able to bring to that meeting more than one kind of behaviour. In addition, as the meeting develops, different kinds of behaviour will be required for the different stages the meeting passes through. This is particularly true for the management of a long-term project which may go through several stages.

Plant

A Plant is one of the two sources of new ideas in a meeting. Plants have new ideas, are creative, and as a consequence are sometimes difficult to manage. Just when the rest of the meeting thought it had sorted out a problem, the Plant will leap in with a completely new version of how it could be tackled and suggest that everything they have done so far should be discarded. If this happens too frequently Plants can get themselves quite disliked. The problem with Plants is that they will spend too much time and energy on ideas which catch their attention, without devoting themselves necessarily to the task of the group. If their own ideas are not being accepted or listened to sufficiently, they may feel rejected and may withdraw from the group.

Resource Investigator

Resource Investigators are the other source of new ideas, not because they invent them themselves, but because 'they know a man who can'. Resource Investigators are always on the phone, or out at meetings. They are usually sociable, extrovert, and great listeners. They make contact easily and are good at seeing the possibilities of someone else's idea. They tend to get bored if asked to work on their own, and may not follow up all the tasks they are given by the meeting, since they prefer to follow their own nose. Also they can be distracted by what the rest of the meeting regards as irrelevances.

Co-ordinator

This role, which was previously called chairman, is the one that keeps the group together and acts the part nearest to that which, in formal meetings, is frequently called chairing (see Chapter 6). Effective Co-ordinators are good at gate-keeping and all the other maintenance behaviours described in the previous section. Often it is difficult for a person with a very strong personal view to act as a good Co-ordinator since their own views keep bursting through to affect their judgement. Co-ordinators keep the meeting focused on the objectives and goals they have set themselves. Sadly, in many meetings the chairperson is the most senior manager present, not the person with the greatest Co-ordinator skills. The authors have recently found encouraging evidence, in a number of client companies, that the most senior manager will influence the choice of the most effective Co-ordinator to become chairperson, and will not hog the job for him or herself.

Shaper

Shapers like to have an impact. They like and understand power. They want to push and challenge and move everything forward. If there is to be someone who owns the vision of the group then it is likely to be the Shaper. They will most frequently show self confidence and drive and a strong need for results. Meetings can waste huge amounts of time when several Shapers gather round the same table. Shapers, who are competitive by nature, can have a wonderful time in non-functional behaviour by competing with other Shapers. It's great fun, but it does not achieve anyone's objectives. The effective Co-ordinator and indeed the rest of the meeting may need to exert their combined influence to ensure that the Shapers make useful contributions. However, two or three Shapers who are agreed on their purpose and are not in competition are a formidable power source for any meeting.

Monitor Evaluator

This is a role which is not widely valued in a meeting since it tends to be seen as the person bringing bad news. When the Plants and Resource Investigators, egged on by the Shapers, have come up with brilliant and creative new plans, it is the Monitor Evaluator who will ask quietly 'but can we make money from it?'

Monitor Evaluators are good at assimilating and interpreting large volumes of data. The Monitor Evaluator will then go on to use that data in order to criticise or comment on the proposals of the meeting. Sometimes huge amounts of money have been wasted when members of a meeting have become over enthusiastic and blinkered by the brilliance of their ideas or the persuasiveness of their rhetoric. It is the Monitor Evaluator who brings them down to earth and prevents them from wasting too much time or money or other resources. There are moments in the life of a project when this role is absolutely essential.

Team Worker

Team Workers are, along with the Co-ordinators, the other major source of maintenance behaviour in a group. In extreme cases the Team Worker really isn't interested in the objectives of the group, merely that the group works well together. They are good and willing listeners, able communicators and are prepared to listen to the emotional component of communications as well as the data. Team Workers are especially valuable when a meeting is under pressure and competitiveness between Plants or Shapers is beginning to reduce overall effectiveness. Team Workers sometimes dislike direct confrontation, and may occasionally find themselves put down by the less interpersonally skilled members of a meeting.

Implementor

The Implementors are the engine room of a meeting. After ideas have flowed and been debated, visions traded, evaluations made, someone actually needs to do the work. This is the Implementor. Implementors are stable and loyal, but do need to be clear about their objectives. Give them an objective and they will go out and achieve it, but they must first be clear about what the objective is and how it fits in with their other work. Ideally they are methodical and well organised. These are the people who come into their own towards the middle or end of a project. When, as they would put it, the real work needs doing.

Finisher

The Finisher is the person who actually gets the job completed. Finishers worry about what might go wrong and whether the entire project can be brought to a successful conclusion. They have a sense of urgency, particularly after all the ideas have been traded, which often communicates itself to the meeting. Finishers like deadlines and get worried when other people disregard them. In most organisations, senior managers can delegate much of the Implementor and Finisher tasks to other more junior staff.

In recent years there has been an increase in the number of top manager and director level projects. At this level where a project team is composed entirely of senior managers, there is a tendency for the early stages of the project to go very well as ideas are generated and concepts are argued, but in the latter phase where Implementor and Finisher behaviour is required sometimes the project can hit the rocks. If a meeting is primarily concerned with progressing a task at senior level, the members of the meeting may need to take special care to ensure that the work gets done and gets finished on time and on budget. It is not unknown for the chairman's secretary to assume the role of temporary director to ensure that the other participants in the meeting actually complete the work.

Specialist

The new behaviourial role which has been added in recent times is that of the Specialist. Specialists are mainly concerned with their area of expertise. If they are unassertive, then they can easily be ignored by the rest of the meeting. As with the Eskimo in the Sub-Arctic Survival exercise – a man who was not assertive by nature – life-preserving data was ignored and unused by the other members of the meeting. Tragic examples of failure to make use of life-preserving data – the NASA Challenger disaster was a very public example – demonstrate that although we have known about experts since before the time of the Romans, we sometimes fail to make effective use of them.

The value of understanding these roles is that members of the meeting can make public the particular behaviour needs they have in order to tackle the problems they are facing. For instance at the beginning of a project it may be necessary to have a lot of creative behaviour, and very little Monitor Evaluator behaviour. However as a project progresses Monitor Evaluator behaviour will become more significant, followed by Implementor and Finisher behaviour.

SUMMARY

There are four major kinds of behaviour seen at meetings. Three of them – *task*, *maintenance*, and *task and maintenance* – contribute in some way to the achievement of the task or the maintenance of group cohesion around the task. Non-functional behaviour is of no value as far as the declared task of the meeting is concerned, but often takes up a lot of the meeting's time.

Speed of decision against quality of decision is a trade-off that can be made depending on the availability of expertise, and the originality of the solutions needed. A high quality original solution is more likely to come from a leaderless group than one which is heavily controlled by a person who wants to put their own views across.

A group of people meeting for the first time will usually go through four stages: *Forming*, *Storming*, *Norming* and *Performing*. Norming is a process with potential pitfalls as well as advantages for a meeting.

We all have preferences for the kinds of behaviours used in meetings. The nine categories of Belbin team behaviours are a useful guide to the changing behavioural needs of a team, particularly when managing a project over a series of meetings.

CHECKLIST – HOW GROUPS WORK

1. How much attention do you pay to the behaviours – the music – in your meetings?
2. What task behaviour do you and others use?
3. How much do you and others use building and summarising behaviour to develop and clarify ideas at the meeting?
4. How much maintenance goes on at your meetings?
5. Check if all the members of the meeting feel that they are getting sufficient encouragement.
6. Who acts as gate-keeper? Are the quieter participants being allowed to speak?
7. Is group feeling being expressed or suppressed?
8. How often do you or others test for consensus?
9. How much non-functional behaviour gets in the way of the task?
10. Who identifies non-functional behaviour, and how does the meeting deal with it?
11. How many people are physically at the meeting, but mentally elsewhere? What do you do about it?
12. How have you made the trade-off between speed and quality of decision when no expertise is available?
13. How do you use experts and specialists? Do they get a word in edgeways?
14. Are you listening to the right expert?
15. What norms is your meeting setting for itself? Are they all consciously agreed?
16. At what stage of development is your meeting? Are you still storming, or have you started performing yet?
17. Do you welcome conflict in order to resolve it, or do you try to hide from it?
18. Which of the Belbin categories are most strongly and least strongly represented in your meeting?
19. What are you doing to manage your Belbin strengths and compensate for the meeting's weaknesses?

8. Non-Verbal Behaviour and Listening

NON-VERBAL COMMUNICATION

We have a dog. His ambition in life is to eat as much and as often as possible. He is able to communicate this ambition to us quite clearly. He does a most spectacular breakfast dance which it is impossible to ignore; he fusses and pushes at us when he thinks it is teatime; and in between he sits next to the cupboard in which his food is kept and looks at it meaningfully. Although we ignore most of his demands for extra food, we are left in no doubt about what he wants.

Animals conduct all of their social life non-verbally. Although humans have the advantage of words we do, in fact, convey far more non-verbally than we do verbally. Non-verbal communications have a far greater impact than verbal communications when you want to convey whether you are friendly or hostile, important or inferior, comfortable or uncomfortable.

Michael Argyle and colleagues (1970) carried out an experiment where they gave groups of people two different messages. The verbal content of one message conveyed that the group was clever and able. The verbal content of the other conveyed that the group was stupid and inept. The messages were delivered in non-verbal styles which sometimes matched and sometimes did not match the verbal message. Argyle found that the non-verbal style of delivering a message had about five times as much effect as the verbal content of the message. People took more notice of the non-verbal signals than the words.

In this chapter we will look at non-verbal communication and the effect it can have in meetings. It's not just what you say at the meeting, the way that you say it sometimes has even more effect. We will look at the ways you can learn to use non-verbal behaviour to improve your communication skills. We will also examine the frequently underused skill of listening and look at how better listening can lead to better meetings.

HOW HUMANS COMMUNICATE NON-VERBALLY

Proximity and distance

One of the ways we communicate non-verbally is by the amount of distance we place between ourselves and the person with whom we are communicating. As we mentioned when talking about room size in Chapter 4, we each have an invisible bubble or comfort zone of proximity around us, which varies in size depending on the people or the situation. If you know someone well and feel friendly towards them, you are more likely to stand or sit close to them than if you don't know them well or don't like them. If you are a lowly junior manager, meeting the managing director for the first time, you will probably stand further away from him or her than you would from a colleague whom you know and like.

Stand in front of the mirror and move to where you would feel comfortable standing if the mirror were the following people:

- your wife/husband/partner/lover
- the Queen
- your boss
- someone you met for the first time at a cocktail party
- the Chief Executive of your company (if you are the Chief Executive, think of the most senior person you want to impress)

Positioning

We have already mentioned positioning in the chapter on Planning a Meeting. The place where you position yourself is a way of communicating non-verbally. For example, when people chair a meeting, they normally sit at the end of a rectangular table, rather than at one side or the other, thus demonstrating their status. Those people who want to have a lot of influence on the chairperson try to sit close to him or her – those at the bottom of the table are also usually at the bottom of the pecking order.

The following diagrams show the various positions which indicate co-operation, discussion and antagonism. Position X and Y also indicate superiority/inferiority.

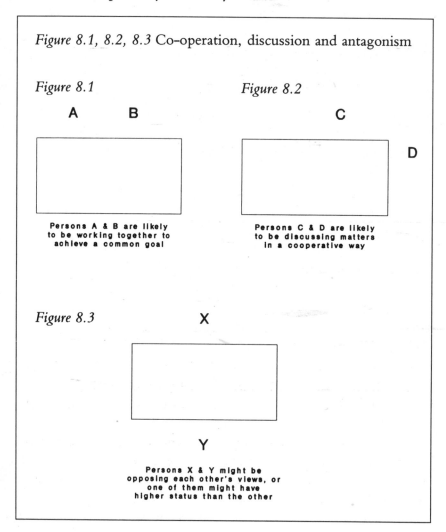

Figure 8.1, 8.2, 8.3 Co-operation, discussion and antagonism

Figure 8.1

A   B

Persons A & B are likely
to be working together to
achieve a common goal

Figure 8.2

C

D

Persons C & D are likely
to be discussing matters
in a cooperative way

Figure 8.3

X

Y

Persons X & Y might be
opposing each other's views, or
one of them might have
higher status than the other

Posture

A lot of nonsense is talked about posture. Some writers attribute specific attitudes and feelings to specific postures. This is unwise because your posture is only part of the message you are conveying. The complete message also uses all the other aspects of body language – proximity, tone of voice, facial expression etc.

However, posture is an important part of the message. The way you sit or stand can, with other elements of non-verbal behaviour, communicate a great deal about the way you are feeling. Here are some of the common interpretations of frequently seen postures.

Sitting back	**Sitting forward**	**Arms folded**
relaxed *or*	tense *or*	angry *or*
don't care *or*	interested *or*	anxious *or*
not interested *or*	going to ask a question *or*	tense *or*
at home here *or*	anxious	stern *or*
not listening *or*		cold
I've got this one sewn up		

As you can see, posture alone will not tell you all you need to know to properly interpret whether someone is feeling anxious / angry / tense or stern etc.

Gestures

Some people use a lot of gestures: they 'talk with their hands'. We use gestures to clarify and amplify our spoken words – sometimes even when we cannot be seen. How many of you, we wonder, have stood giving directions to a friend on the telephone, pointing hands left and right and drawing little circles in the air when instructing friends to go round the roundabout?

Gestures can also be used in a threatening or submissive way. Pointing at someone could indicate that you want them to speak next, or it could indicate that they have displeased you in some way and you have the power to make them tremble in their shoes. Some teachers make a lot of use of the threatening point. Again, it's not just the gesture that sends the signal, it's the combination of the gesture with the posture, tone of voice, proximity, etc.

Head movements

Head movements are a particular form of gesture. In Western countries, we nod our heads in agreement and shake them from side to side in disagreement. This is not universally true throughout the world and has occasionally been the cause of confusion between people of different nationalities and conventions.

We use head-nodding a lot to show that we are listening to someone. We also use it to indicate that we have listened for long enough and that it's our turn now. When we use head nods during listening, they tend to be fairly slow. When we think that it is our turn to speak, we nod very fast to indicate to the other person that we have something to say.

Head-shaking can indicate disagreement, puzzlement or incredulity. Again, the head shake itself is not the full message. It has to be read in conjunction with the speed of shake and with facial expression and posture.

Another head movement commonly recognised in the West is the jerking back of the head, usually accompanied by the casting up of the eyes, to indicate incredulity, usually of a negative nature. Because this is so universally recognised, it is a very obvious and usually deliberate piece of non-verbal feedback, one to be used with caution.

Facial expression

The face is the most expressive part of the human body. Much of our facial expression is under our control. We smile at people we like or at people to whom we want to signal our approval. We frown at those to whom we want to signal our disapproval.

Sometimes, though, our facial expressions are not as controlled as we would like them to be. We may smile involuntarily at a child or something which touches us. We may smile automatically at someone who smiles at us in the street – and then think 'Now who was that?'.

We can use smiles in particular to send non-verbal messages

which can enhance our communications. If you smile at someone, you are sending them a message of approval. This makes it more difficult for them to disapprove of you. In fact, because smiling at someone who smiles at you is almost a reflex reaction, smiling at your enemy can be the quickest way to a peaceful settlement – so long as it is a genuine smile. People instantly recognise if you are smiling with clenched teeth.

Other facial expressions are even less under our control. Studies have found that the pupils of the eyes enlarge when you look at someone you like or find attractive. Also, that if people are shown two pictures of the same person and asked which they prefer, they are attracted to the one with the larger pupils. We may not know that this is happening, but it shows quite clearly that we are sending and receiving non-verbal signals without being aware of it.

Eye movements

Eye movements are probably our most powerful signalling device. Think of all the phrases in the English language which refer to eye movements 'eyeing someone up', 'the sidelong glance', 'a frosty look', 'seeing eye-to-eye', and many more. We signal not only with the direction and intensity of our gaze, but also by the length of time we look.

'Eye contact' is a well known phrase to anyone who has been on a management skills course. But when we talk about 'eye contact' what we actually mean is looking at the top half of someone's face, not an eyeball to eyeball gaze.

Eye contact is a two way process and with it we signal our interest and intentions. A friend of ours brought his new girlfriend to visit us. She was pleasant and chatty in a quiet way, but after they left, we agreed that she had not gained our seal of approval. When we analysed the reason we realised that she had never once looked at us while speaking. As we could not consider her shifty, we had interpreted her behaviour as dislike, disapproval or lack of interest in us.

Fiona and William are having a conversation.
When Fiona is listening to William, she will look at William at lot

more than William looks at her. William will look at Fiona, making contact with her eyes and the top half of her face, subconsciously checking that she is looking at and listening to him. He will also, however, look briefly out of the window for inspiration, glance at his hands, the floor, his papers. These glances away from Fiona's face are to avoid the long stare, which no-one except young lovers is comfortable with.

Fiona will be quite happy about this as long as William keeps the level of looking at her high in comparison with all the other places he looks. If he never looks at her she will interpret this as shifty, nervous, lacking in confidence, or she will assume that he is not interested in her.

When William is coming to the end of his turn in the conversation, he will look at Fiona, to signal that it is her turn to speak. As Fiona is about to speak, she will look away from William, then she will fall into a pattern of looking at him and glancing away occasionally. If William looks away from Fiona, she knows that he is no longer attending to her.

Think about the following examples. You may well have had similar experiences.

You go into your boss's office at his request. He glances up to see who it is, then goes back to shuffling his papers while he talks to you about the customer he wants you to see this afternoon. He doesn't look at you while he is talking – he keeps his head down.

You are in a meeting at which someone is asked to speak. She presents quite a lot of information, all the time looking down at the paper or table in front of her.

You ask your son or daughter to go and tidy their bedroom. They say 'Yes, OK' without glancing up from the television programme they are watching or the guitar they are strumming.

Our reactions to these actions will be frustration in one form or another – fury, impatience, a feeling of rejection. They clearly demonstrate that we expect eye contact with the person to whom we are speaking, or who is speaking to us.

Using eye contact in meetings

When you are speaking at a meeting, whether you are presenting information or making a point arising from the discussion, the more people you can make eye contact with the better. They will feel that you are speaking to them, not just to the chairperson or to the person with whom you happen to disagree at the time.

Make eye contact with the chairperson when you want to make a point. You can signal very clearly with your eyes that you would like a turn to speak.

Always look around the group when you are speaking. Make eye contact with each one in turn. Because you are talking to more than one person you do not need to worry about staring at them, you don't need to break eye contact by glancing away. Do not look down at your notes except for quick glances to make sure you are on the right track. Notes can be a comfort blanket – we look at them because they are familiar and reassuring – but remember that you may be creating a negative impression if you do so.

Grunts and groans

Prehistoric man probably communicated with grunts and groans, different sounds having different meanings. Although we have the benefit of speech and language, we still use grunts and other audible non-verbal communication. A heavy sigh can sometimes be far more effective than words in expressing our feelings.

Pitch, pause and emphasis

'I didn't like her tone of voice'
'Don't you take that tone with me'
'She sounded really fed up'

It's not what you say, it's the way that you say it. The tone, pitch, emphasis and use of pauses in speech convey far more than the actual words themselves. It's also the only form of non-verbal communication we can use on the telephone.

Try the following exercise with a colleague or friend.

Exercise

Say each of following phrases in such a way that it reflects the meanings on the right.

1. That was really difficult
   a) It wasn't difficult for me
   b) I'm amazed that you found it difficult
   c) It really was difficult

2. I'm really pleased to be here
   a) I really am happy to be here
   b) I'm extremely fed up that I'm here
   c) There's a bit of a problem about my being here

3. This is a brilliant report
   a) What a mess of a report!
   b) You mean that you think this is brilliant?
   c) This is an extremely good report.

CONSCIOUS USE OF NON-VERBAL COMMUNICATION

We use non-verbal behaviour unconsciously more than we use it consciously. Sometimes our unconscious use of it conveys things we are feeling, but don't really want to convey. You can learn to use non-verbal behaviour consciously to:

Communicate attitudes
Communicate or hide your feelings
Support your verbal communication
Signal when you want to speak
Synchronise verbal communication
Give feedback to other people
Build rapport quickly and easily
Pace other people's attitudes
Lead people in the direction you want them to go.

Communicate attitudes

Tone of voice
Given that we are all so aware of the tone of voice people use, it's surprising how little it is deliberately made use of when trying to

influence others. If you have an idea which you are not sure other people will like, the easiest way to ensure that they too will be unsure is to sound tentative and apologetic when you talk about it. If you sound enthusiastic and positive about something, your listeners are likely to become enthusiastic and positive themselves.

When chairing a meeting, you can use your voice to attract attention. A strong positive voice gives the impression of a strong positive chairperson, even if you are mentally shaking in your shoes.

Listen carefully to the evenness of sounds a person's voice creates. A wavering tone can be caused by the muscles of the chest and throat not contracting smoothly and therefore not producing a regular flow of air. This often indicates nervousness or other strong emotion. This wavering is audible irrespective of the particular tone. Hesitations and breaks of speech also indicate nervousness – they also encourage the less nervous to jump in before you have finished.

Posture

Deliberately use your posture to show that you are interested. If your natural way of concentrating hard is to draw complicated doodles on your pad, be aware that other people may put a different interpretation on your doodling.

If you want to look as if you are paying attention, lean forward slightly with your head erect. When your head is down, people may think you are not interested, not paying attention, bored, rude etc.

Facial expression

Remember, smiling at someone sends a positive message. They can interpret it as liking, approval, sympathy, or agreement. You can also use facial expressions to signal your doubt about a proposal, which saves you putting that doubt into words.

Communicate or hide your feelings

You will probably find it easy to use body language to communicate your feelings non-verbally. After all, you've been doing it all your life and it comes naturally. It is a little more difficult to use body language to hide your feelings, but not impossible.

A colleague of ours told us this story:

'I was recently at a meeting where I had very little patience with the views and opinions of some of the other people. I thought they were being boring and tedious. However, I knew two things:
1. That they felt very strongly about the subject
2. That for various reasons I did not want to alienate them, I needed them on my side.

After the meeting, I came away feeling pleased with myself. I had not shown that I found the subject boring and I knew the people involved thought I had been positive and helpful. I achieved this by smiling a lot at the person who was getting het up about the subject, whilst making non-committal grunting noises. When I spoke I used a warm and friendly tone and I made sure that my posture indicated interest and commitment. The contributions I made were all to do with the process of the meeting, suggesting things that would move the discussion on, and I managed to come away with everyone except myself involved in carrying out some action.'

To some extent this was manipulation and our colleague was not being open about her own views and feelings. However, she knew that the only alternative was a major row and she did not want to precipitate a rift which would have taken many months to smooth over.

Support your verbal communication

Use tone of voice to support the actual words you say. As we have already mentioned, tone of voice is a way of expressing your feelings if you feel enthusiastic about something and you can also express doubt, worry and many other feelings with your voice.

Suport your verbal communication with gestures. Use gestures to emphasise your points. It may sound rather old hat, but supporting your points by counting off your fingers one by one, does draw attention to the fact that you are making, for example, three points.

Lean forward to emphasise that you are saying something

important. Lean back to indicate that you have finished and you are willing for others to speak.

But when you are supporting verbal points non-verbally, do make sure that the way you choose to do it will be regarded as appropriate. The famous occasion when Nikita Khrushchev took off his shoe and banged it on the lectern when making a speech to the United Nations was actually due to a misinterpretation of cultures. William Ury in *Getting Past No* revealed 30 years later that Khrushchev had been advised that Westerners loved passionate political debate. He thought this was the thing to do but his gesture was actually interpreted as an attempt to intimidate!

Signal when you want to speak
There are a number of ways you can do this. You may need to use only one of them, or all of them together. Lean forward, with head up and back straight. If you open your mouth slightly at the same time you are making an unmistakeable signal. 'Catch the eye' of the chairperson by looking directly at him. If you also raise your hand from the table slightly, with fingers pointing upwards, it will be an insensitive chairperson who doesn't give you a chance to speak.

Synchronise verbal communication
You do this with your eye movements, signalling to others that it is their turn to speak, or that you want to speak. When you want to speak you will look at someone more closely and for longer periods without looking away. When you are giving them their opportunity to speak you finish your turn by glancing at them.

Give people feedback
We do this all the time. We communicate whether or not we like or approve of what people are saying. You can do it deliberately, sometimes positively, sometimes negatively.

The Chief of one Social Services Department had the unpleasant habit of sitting with his head in his hands, covering his eyes whenever one of his new deputies spoke at a meeting. As a confidence builder for a new deputy, this behaviour was at best inept and at worst malicious. No wonder deputies did not stay long in that department.

Build rapport

In order to get on with other people, work well with them and influence them, you need to have a rapport with them. It can often take a time to build rapport with people you don't know very well – and in meetings you often don't have time to spend on rapport building before you get down to the business in hand. Non-verbal communication can help you build rapport more quickly.

Mirror posture and gesture

When you see two people who obviously have a rapport, how can you tell? Often the answer is that they are sitting or standing in similar positions. When you meet a couple who have been happily married for a long time, don't you sometimes notice that they have similar postures, gestures and turns of speech?

You can increase and build rapport with people by consciously mirroring or matching their body language. Not in an obvious way by copying every change of position and mannerism – a game which children play to annoy one another – but by subtly echoing someone's postures, gestures and language. Lean forward when they are leaning forward, hold your hands in similar positions, match the way they hold their heads.

This is a powerful way of rapidly increasing rapport with someone, but it is a skill which requires practise. Practice in situations which are not crucial – on your colleagues in the office, friends in the pub, strangers you get chatting to when the train is late. When you feel confident of being able to mirror other people's body language in an unobtrusive way, start using it at meetings.

Match tone and pace

Imagine you are feeling really down and someone asks how things are going. You reply in a grumpy tone of voice that you just need another 10 hours in a day and all will be well. The content of the enquirer's reaction doesn't matter too much, but the tone of voice in which they make it will have a huge impact on whether you regard them as insensitive or sympathetic with a real regard for your wellbeing.

Matching the tone and pace of someone's delivery can increase the speed with which you gain rapport with them. When you feel there is some rapport, you can move on to the next step which is:

Lead people in the direction you want them to go
If you start off by talking to people in a matching tone of voice, you can gradually lead them, with your own voice, towards a more positive frame of mind.

You are in a meeting. You put forward a suggestion in a positive and enthusiastic manner. Your opposite number in the finance department leans back in her chair and shakes her head. She puts forward her doubts and objections in a slow and deliberate tone. If you then ask her questions or answer her questions, still using an enthusiastic tone, you are underlining the differences between you. If, instead, you answer her points slowly and deliberately to start with, and then build up to the positive and enthusiastic, this will indicate to her that you have some understanding of the way she feels and she is more likely to come round eventually to your proposal.

SUMMARY

The non-verbal messages we send and receive are a much more powerful way of communicating than the words we use. This is why if we want to make absolutely sure we get our message across in the right way, we often take the trouble to go and see the person we want to communicate it to, rather than write or telephone them.

We are all very good at reading and understanding non-verbal messages, even when we are unaware we are doing so. We do it without thinking about it, indeed we do it well *because* we don't think about it. We can tell when someone is unhappy, excited, nervous etc. This means that we have to be very careful about the sorts of messages our non-verbal signals are sending if we are to give the sort of impression we want. Being aware of your own body language and that of other people and making appropriate use of it can help you communicate better at meetings and elsewhere.

LISTENING

Communication involves two parties, the broadcaster and the receiver. BBC radio may be broadcasting the fact that the M1 Southbound has a tailback from Staples Corner to junction 5, but unless you have turned on the radio, you may still get stuck in the jam.

Does the following conversation ring a bell?

Partner 1. 'Come on, don't sit there, we have to get ready to go to the dinner party/football match/parent's evening/lecture on frogspawn'

Partner 2. 'WHAT? You didn't tell me we had to go out this evening, I wanted to watch the next episode of Coronation Street/play with my stamps/write this report'

Partner 1. 'Of course I told you . . .'

There is more to listening than just hearing. Although it is not possible to listen without being able to hear, it is certainly possible to hear without listening. Just think of all the things you do without listening to background sound. Working in an office we learn to shut out the sounds of those around us. When we are shopping or eating in restaurants we are frequently unaware of the piped music or other people's conversations. When we are not listening it is only the sharp or intrusive sound we hear – a nearby telephone or a screaming child.

There are some occasions when we actually want, or ought, to be listening, but our learned ability to shut out sound overpowers our want or need to listen. In this section we will review the barriers to listening and the techniques which help people become high performance listeners.

There are two ways in which we can increase our powers of listening.

1. Overcome the distractions.
2. Active Listening Techniques.

Overcome the distractions

There are enormous numbers of internal and external physical and mental distractions to listening. Becoming aware of them can help you realise that you are distracted and not listening actively enough to the conversation.

Internal

Internal distractions can be *physical* or *mental*:

a) Physical

Physical distractions are usually related to bodily comfort. If you are hungry or thirsty, if you are sitting on an uncomfortable chair, or if you are aware that you really shouldn't have had that extra piece of apple pie for dessert, then your awareness of your body's needs or discomfort is a distraction from listening.

b) Mental

Your body may be sitting in the meeting, but your mind can be somewhere else altogether. Some people cultivate and perfect the ability to sit and look as if they are paying attention whilst their minds are processing completely different information, related to what they will be doing next weekend, or how they will handle the difficult interview with the Health and Safety Executive.

However, sometimes we are distracted mentally without realising it. The sort of things that can distract us in this way are:

- a train of thought triggered off by something someone has just said
- thinking about what you are going to say next
- concentrating on your chance to get a word in edgeways
- worrying what the other people on the committee will think of your contribution
- being appalled by the rubbish some people speak

External

External distractions (covered more fully in Chapter 4) are nearly all physical to begin with, although they are often compounded by the fact that they may set off a distracting train of thought. You will also be distracted from listening by physical discomfort in the shape of extremes of heat or cold, by interruptions such as phones ringing or people coming in, by excessive aeroplane or traffic noise. The talking of colleagues in the meeting can also become just background sound and only a sudden or loud noise will refocus our attention.

ACTIVE LISTENING TECHNIQUES

Active listening means listening in such a way that you communicate to the person who is speaking that you are hearing and understanding them; that you appreciate and accept not only what they are speaking about, but the feelings which underlie the words. It is a very demanding skill, because:

- you have to concentrate hard and give a high degree of attention to the person speaking
- you need to be able to respond with patience and empathy even when someone is expressing ideas which you feel to be misguided, illogical and generally or totally wrong. It does not mean you have to agree with them, merely show that you understand their point of view

Wide Band listening

Active listening means listening on the wide band – picking up not just the verbal content of the message, but the underlying meaning of it.

There are a number of techniques which you can use to improve and enhance your listening skills. They are:

- testing your understanding by clarifying content
- reflecting back feelings and emotions
- asking probing questions
- summarising
- sending non-verbal signals

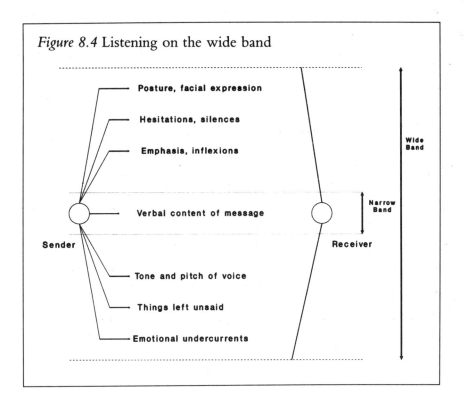

Figure 8.4 Listening on the wide band

Testing understanding

Testing understanding has two benefits:

1. you ensure that you do actually have the facts correctly
2. you demonstrate that you have understood what the speaker is saying

Getting the facts correct is one of the fundamentals of active listening. It is essential to ensure that you are receiving the message you think you are. You can do this quite simply by rephrasing what the speaker has said and repeating it back to test whether or not you have heard accurately.

'So can I just check, you're saying that . . .'
'As I understand it, what you're saying is . . .'
'Do you mean that . . .'
'So your point is that . . .'
It is important not to repeat what the speaker has said parrot-

fashion, which can be a real irritant, but to rephrase it to demonstrate your understanding of the content.

Reflecting

Reflecting back feelings and emotions also has two benefits:

a) it gives you the opportunity to check that you have accurately understood the feelings of the person speaking

b) it allows you to show empathy by demonstrating that you have understood how the person feels about the subject.

Listen to the way the message is spoken as well as the words being said. The emphases, the inflections, the hesitations of speech, the pauses, the tone and pitch of the voice show how people feel about what they are saying. Sometimes these reinforce the message, at other times they contradict it.

As we noted in the exercise earlier in the chapter, it's possible to deliver words such as 'I'm really happy to be here' in such a way that the listener knows that they are intended to convey the exact opposite. The words 'Guess what, I've been chosen to play in a lacrosse match!' would indicate excitement and pleasure for most people. When uttered by our daughter they indicate the highest degree of tragedy imaginable!

Sometimes these spoken but non-verbal clues are so obvious that they are almost impossible to miss by anyone who is having a conversation in their own language. At other times you have to be a more skilled listener to pick up the inflexions and other spoken non-verbal clues which indicate feelings and the inconsistencies between what people say and what they mean.

Understanding feelings

Reflecting back in order to check that you have understood the feelings behind the words people are saying means picking up and rephrasing what people say and then giving your interpretation of the way they said it. For example:

'You say you'd like to come and stay with us at Christmas, but you don't sound very sure about it'.

'You seem to be very keen on doing that'.

'You say that you're willing to be involved, but you seem a bit doubtful about it'.

Showing empathy

Reflecting back in order to show empathy, that you understand the feelings of the person to whom you are listening, means picking up the emotions involved and expressing them in your own words. For example:

'So your boss really gets under your skin when he behaves like that'.

'It sounds as if you've been having a really hard time recently'.

'That must be really exciting'.

It may be a fairly obvious point to make, but ensure that when you reflect back people's feelings, *your* voice and non-verbal signals are congruent with what *you* say.

Asking probing questions

Asking questions may seem a funny way of listening to people, but asking appropriate and probing questions which follow on from what people have said, and encourage them to say more, are one of the ways you can demonstrate your listening ability.

Any interviewer will tell you that asking appropriate questions, pertinent to the answer the candidate has just given, is one of the hardest skills of interviewing. The reason being that the interviewer's mind is often filled with what needs to be asked next and what else needs to be discovered about the candidate.

Similarly, when listening in meetings, you may be concerned with what you want to say about the subject, or you may be wondering how long Harry can go on talking about landfill sites. If you are not actively listening, you will not be able to ask the questions that could increase your knowledge by probing more deeply into the subject. If you are able to ask pertinent questions, you are establishing yourself as one of that rare breed – 'good listeners'.

Summarising

Summarising is one of the key skills of an effective chairperson. Of course, an effective chairperson needs to be a listening chairperson. Even if you are not the chairperson, summarising is a critical skill for active listening and can be used effectively by anyone at the meeting. Summarising has three benefits:

1. it clarifies and reinforces the message for both listener and speaker
2. it finishes off one subject, creating the opportunity to move on to the next
3. it gives the speaker the opportunity to correct the listener if they summarise inaccurately

For example:

'So the main problem seems to be that the bread slicing machine is not available 24 hours a day.'

'So we have agreed to restrict our trial market to the City of Swansea and agreed that we need to prioritise the main actions we need to take before September. Let's move on to look at what the priorities are.'

'As I understand your proposal, the cost of servicing would be borne by your company for the first twelve months. After that it would be the subject of a separate agreement.'

Sending non-verbal signals

We have already identified the fact that non-verbal messages are more powerful than verbal ones. When you are listening you can send powerful non-verbal signals to show that you are. If you don't bother to do this, you have to rely on the assumption that the speaker will know that you always concentrate most fiercely when staring out of the window, or doodling on your pad. But this is unwise since the speaker is more likely to assume you are not listening.

Your facial expression and posture should be attentive and turned towards the speaker. Nods and sounds indicate that you are following the content of the message. The direction of your gaze and eye contact show the other person whether or not you are paying attention.

SUMMARY

Listening is more than just hearing. This is perhaps why the phrase 'I hear what you say' is so irritating to many people – one of those phrases which people interpret as meaning the opposite to the words used. Active listening means understanding the content of the message and the feelings behind it. It means disentangling the confusing messages you may get when words and meanings seem to conflict. It involves a certain degree of rapport and empathy between speaker and listener. It is a skill which can be developed with practice and is essential for anyone who wants to be effective at meetings or at any other means of interpersonal communication. It is a skill particularly necessary for those who want to chair meetings effectively.

Use the checklist on the following page to monitor your non-verbal and listening behaviour.

CHECKLIST – NON-VERBAL BEHAVIOUR AND LISTENING

When you communicate with someone in a meeting, make the best use of non-verbal communication by doing the following:

1. Sit or stand at what you feel is a 'comfortable' distance from the person.
2. Position yourself so that you indicate non-verbally that you anticipate a discussion or collaboration, rather than a confrontation.
3. Keep your posture and gestures congruent with the sort of message you want to get across.
4. Use head movements and facial expression to support, rather than contradict, the statements you make.
5. Make eye contact with the person with whom you are communicating.
6. Use the tone and pitch of your voice to add emphasis and meaning to your statements.
7. Deliberately make use of non-verbal signals to:
   a) communicate attitudes using voice, posture, facial expression
   b) communicate or hide your feelings
   c) support your verbal communication and signal when you want to speak
   d) synchronise verbal communication using eye movements
   e) give feedback to other people
   f) build rapport quickly and easily by matching or mirroring body language
   g) pace other people's attitudes and feelings, then
   h) lead people in the direction you want them to go.

Whether you are chairperson or a participant, to be effective in meetings you need to listen actively:

8. Be aware of distractions, internal and external, and ignore them as best you can.
9. Test your understanding of what people have said.

10. Reflect back feelings and emotions.
11. Ask probing questions.
12. Summarise.
13. Send appropriate non-verbal signals.

9. Making Effective Contributions

'Why are you at the meeting, Eccles?'
'Everybody has to be somewhere.'
(with apologies to the Goon Show)

'What did you do in your meeting today, Dad?'
'I sat there and nodded when the boss spoke.'
'Is that what you have to do at meetings, Dad?'
'No, son, I don't usually have to work that hard. Usually it's enough to turn up 80 per cent of the time.'
(with apologies to Woody Allen)

In a meeting, the chairperson has an acknowledged role and tasks to perform. What are the roles and tasks of the other people there? Is it sufficient just to 'turn up 80 per cent of the time'? In this chapter we want to distinguish between those who feel they have done their bit just by turning up, and those who are there to add real value to the outcome of the meeting.

Some contributions made to meetings are more useful than others. In this chapter we suggest a number of techniques you can use to make your own contributions more effective.

We look at:

- useful behaviours
- behaviours to be avoided
- using questioning effectively
- getting the timing right

- saying what you want to say
- what to do when you don't agree
- helping the meeting to flow smoothly
- interruptions
- behaving confidently in meetings
- changing your attitude to meetings

Research carried out by Rackham and his colleagues at the Huthwaite Research Group on the behaviour of skilled negotiators can also be applied to making your contributions to meetings more effective. The research group compared the behaviour of negotiators who had a significant track record of success, with average negotiators. Much of the behaviour used by the skilled negotiators can also be used by those who wish to increase their effectivness at meetings. For instance:

- signal your intention
- ask questions
- test understanding
- summarise
- say how you feel

The types of behaviour which should be avoided are:

- using irritators
- diluting arguments
- making counter proposals
- getting into defence/attack spirals

USEFUL BEHAVIOURS

Signal your intentions

Give the meeting a warning about what you want to do. If you want to make a point, say so. Say 'I'd like to make a point', 'I'd like to make a suggestion', 'I'd like to ask a question'. This serves a threefold function:

1. you get the attention of the meeting

2. everyone hears the whole of what you have to say rather than losing the first half of the sentence

3. it gives you time to formulate your thoughts and your words. So rather than saying 'Er – actually the feedback loop from that information system has been obsolete for a long time', you will be saying 'I'd like to make a point here. The feedback loop from that system has been obsolete for some time'

Ask questions

Asking questions can be one of the most useful and crucial behaviours used in a meeting. Questions help clarify what is going on for you (and possibly for a lot of others as well). Questions can stop someone who is well launched into a detailed and highly technical discourse and force him or her to explain what they mean in lay language. They act as controls for a meeting. They also offer you a way to be seen as a contributor to the meeting. Once you are established as a contributor, you will be expected to contribute, so it might make it easier to get your voice heard first when you want it to be.

Test understanding

Testing understanding is one particular form of questioning. When you test understanding you say something like 'So what you are saying is that if we adopt course C, we will have to allow for outcome D'. By doing this you are clarifying your understanding and allowing space for further explanation or making sure that someone confirms what they have said. You are also of course, establishing yourself as a valuable contributor and demonstrating your grasp of the subject.

Summarising

In most meetings this is left to the chairperson. In fact, most people who chair meetings well see this as one of their main functions and become rather annoyed if they think other people are trying to usurp their role. If your chairperson is doing their job effectively, you shouldn't need to summarise. However, if you are in a meeting where the chairperson is totally ineffective, and there are one or two of those around, summarising is a useful skill to have.

Say how you feel

If you are finding a meeting confusing, or losing track of the argument, or if you think someone is lying through their teeth, then say so – but carefully. Don't make accusations to individuals or to the meeting.

wrong 'That's a downright lie, you devious toad.'
right 'I feel a bit doubtful about what you just said, Mark.'
wrong 'This is very confusing.'
right 'I feel a bit confused.'

Now while you may feel that avoiding the first statement is fairly self-evident if you want to preserve your job – and your teeth – you may think there is very little difference between the second pair of statements. The difference is that 2a is more likely to be perceived by the receiver as a criticism and he can argue with it. Maybe he or she doesn't think it's confusing at all. Whereas 2b is a statement about how *you* feel – much less threatening and impossible to argue with.

BEHAVIOURS TO BE AVOIDED

Avoid irritators

When the Huthwaite Research Group talk about 'irritators', they are referring to the way some negotiators come out with phrases of self-praise such as 'Our very reasonable offer' – implying of course that the other party is unreasonable in not accepting it immediately. This applies equally well to meetings. Similarly, there are other words, phrases and bits of body language that can be used deliberately or accidently to irritate the other people in the meeting. Here are a few: 'With respect' (or even worse, 'With great respect'); 'I hear what you say'; 'At this point in time', etc.

There are also non-verbal irritators – the heavy sigh, the casting up of the eyes, etc. If you are thinking to yourself 'Why doesn't the boring old whatsit get on with it and make his point so that someone with sense can get a word in edgeways,' be careful that your body language isn't telling him exactly what you are thinking. As we said in Chapter 7, we are all extremely good at reading other people's body language without even being aware that we are doing it. We are not so good at hiding our real feelings – our non-verbal behaviour can have a nasty habit of giving us away.

Don't dilute your argument

The researchers found that skilled negotiators do not weaken their argument by bringing in a number of less important points to back up the major one, because their opponents can then knock the minor points off one by one. Instead, they start off with one or two good reasons for the course of action they wish to take and support them later (if necessary) with other minor points in favour.

A way of using this technique in a meeting is to say 'There are a number of good reasons for this; let me tell you about one or two of them'. Then hit them with your major reasons for wanting to take a particular action. As often as not you won't need to bring the minor arguments out of the woodwork at all.

Avoid making counter proposals

The Huthwaite Group's research found that skilled negotiators make fewer immediate counter proposals than average negotiators. This makes a lot of sense.

> *Imagine that you are having a discussion about how to build a bridge. You suggest that a good way of doing it would be to sink supports in the bed of the river and put planks across the top. You think this is a pretty clever idea. No one says what a clever idea it is. Instead, Joe, hardly waiting for you to finish speaking, says that he disagrees, and that he thinks you ought to build a suspension bridge by tying ropes from handy trees each side of the river and suspending the planks from the ropes.*

How likely are you to give Joe's idea the careful consideration it probably deserves? Not very likely is almost certainly the answer at this stage in the meeting. Joe has not given any recognition to your idea, but has made an immediate counter proposal of his own. You may regard this as a put-down of your idea, get offended because no one has taken any notice of your proposal, or see it as an attack which you need to defend. However you perceive it, Joe has not contributed to the general health and wellbeing of the meeting. We will look at ways that Joe could have been more adept in putting forward his ideas later on in the chapter.

Avoid defence/attack spirals

The Huthwaite Group found that when people are negotiating they often become heated and use emotional or value-loaded behaviour. When this behaviour is used to attack the other party, or to make an emotional defence of a particular standpoint, it is termed defending/attacking. It is not uncommon for people in meetings to become heated and emotional, especially if they feel strongly about the subject under discussion.

If someone makes an impassioned defence of, for example, his model of a bridge, it can be perceived as an attack by someone else in the meeting who has a different model of a bridge. He may well reply with an equally passionate defence of his model, which in turn could be seen as an attack . . . etc., etc.

USING QUESTIONING EFFECTIVELY IN MEETINGS

Questioning, as we've seen, is a useful technique for making effective contributions. We talked briefly about using questioning for controlling the meeting when acting as chairperson, but questioning has many other uses. It is such an important and worthwhile skill to have – one which can really move the meeting forward, help make a decision, calm down a storm etc. – that it is worth giving it more attention.

You can use questions to:

- gain information
- get the details
- clarify and test understanding
- show you are taking someone's idea seriously

- defuse anger
- introduce yourself as a contributor

Questions to gain information

The most obvious sort of question is one where you are seeking information.

'How big is the area for development?'

'What effect would that have on the number of people required?'

'Why is it important to do that sift first?'

'Who is likely to be involved in the move?'

When you ask this type of question you are extending your knowledge and the knowledge of all the other people in the meeting. It means that you want more information upon which to base any reaction.

Very often a person who knows a lot about a subject leaves out all the simple nuts and bolts explanations, because he or she is so familiar with the subject they feel everyone else must know it too. So you are doing yourself and others in the meeting a favour by asking for more information. (See Chapter 14 for a more detailed review of talking to experts.)

The questions you are asking here are called *open* questions. The words you use to start them off with, such as *what, how, explain, why* make them difficult to give a 'yes' or 'no' answer to, so they compel people to open up the subject, to explain more about it.

Questions to collect detail

When you understand the overall concept you may still need to ask questions to get the facts and details absolutely precise.

'Does that price include transport?'

'Is that the final draft?'

'Can we be sure that we have the commitment from purchasing?'

Questions to clarify and test understanding

Making an assumption that you understand what is going on can sometimes get you into very deep water. Far better to ask a question to clarify a point for yourself and ensure that you really *do* understand. In a similar style to active listening, described more fully in

Chapter 8, clarify and test understanding by using questions with phrases such as:

'So can I just check . . . you are saying that the balance of widgets is so low that we can expect to run out within three weeks?'

'Can I just get this clear in my own mind . . .'

'Let me make sure I've got this straight . . .'

You can also clarify and test understanding by repeating the essence of a statement someone has made, but by inflection turning it into a question.

'So the long term effects could be quite drastic?'

Questions to show that you are taking someone's ideas seriously

When someone puts forward an idea or a suggestion, asking him or her a question sends a signal that you are interested. This is where we go back to the example of the bridge. If, having heard your proposal, Joe had asked some questions first, instead of immediately coming in with his own pet idea, you probably would not have taken umbrage.

Let's look at an alternative scenario for the bridge suggestion. You suggest a bridge with piles in the river bed and planks across the top. Perhaps Joe asks you how you propose to dig the holes in the river bed, or exactly how you propose to support the planks. He appears to be giving your idea some thought and consideration. If he then goes on to say that he has another option the meeting might also like to look at, you may be happy to give his idea thought and consideration in return.

Questions to defuse anger

Sometimes people get angry at meetings. All too often one person becoming angry can lead to a number of others becoming angry – a defence/attack spiral is set up, as in the following example:

> Andrew is angry that his department hasn't been consulted about a new appointment. Because he is angry about this particular incident, he says some cutting things about Personnel. Susan gets annoyed at this, because Andrew's department never replies to memos – and in any case is very slow at sending in appraisal documents. The scene is set for a

*good old argy-bargy which could easily turn into a free for all, wasting
a lot of time and reaching no useful conclusion.*

Using questions to defuse someone's anger is a useful technique
that can be used at any time, as well as in meetings.

When someone is angry, the things he or she says are often fairly
generalised. Statements like:

'That bloody Personnel department has mucked it up again. Why
can they never get anything right?'

'Typical Marketing. Look what they've gone and done now!'

If you happen to represent the Personnel or Marketing departments you may well feel your hackles rise. Don't let them; try a few
questions instead. Even if you are not on the receiving end of the
criticism, the generalised nature of the complaint is not conducive to
sorting out the problem. What you need is information.

Asking for specific information has the effect of calming people
down. If they have to present you with concrete facts, they need to
marshall their brain into bringing out those facts in a straightfor-
ward way that you will understand, so their brain has less time for
producing adrenalin to fuel their anger. Concentrating on facts
means that they are diverted from the general to the particular.

Another way of using questions to defuse a situation is to challenge the generalised nature of the criticism. So for the first example
above you could ask:

'They *never* get it right? Never sounds a bit strong; what precisely
are you criticising?'

In the second example you might ask

'What exactly is it that is *typical*? What have they done in the past
that was similar?'

Questions to establish yourself as a contributor

If you are going to be seen as a contributor to a meeting, rather than
a passenger, asking questions can be a way of establishing your role
early on.

Sometimes you may not have any useful ideas or information to
contribute to a discussion, but you don't want to keep completely
quiet. So ask a question. It doesn't have to be very profound, but it

does need to be intelligent. All you have to do is to ask a clarifying question:

'So the band will play for as long as we want during the evening?'

Once you have established yourself as a contributor the other participants will expect you to contribute, which means they are more likely to notice that you are speaking, leave space for you when you want to speak and to listen to you.

GET YOUR TIMING RIGHT

Making an *effective* contribution to a meeting is often a question of getting your timing right. Sometimes useful and important points are ignored because they are not made at the relevant time.

If you are not sure of the relevant time to make your point, check with the chairperson.

'Is this a good time to mention . . . ?'

Better late than never?
Sometimes, if you leave making your contribution until after everyone else has moved on, you might as well not make it at all. Imagine the following scene.

> The discussion has been flowing hot, strong and long about the need for abolishing the tea lady and replacing her with drinks machines. The pros and cons of various machines have been presented and debated and a decision has been made about which company to use to service the machines. The terms of redundancy for the tea lady have been agreed. All that remains is to decide where on each floor the machines should be situated.
>
> All this time, Harold has been thinking about the tea lady. He is not happy that she should go. He has understood the time-saving and money-saving implications, but he thinks she serves a useful social purpose because everyone stops to have their tea together and enjoy a little break, rather than just carrying on with their work, tea on desk.
>
> So Harold says: 'Just a minute I'm not quite happy that Betty should go because . . .' and the rest of the sentence is either drowned out by his irritated colleagues, who cannot understand why he has left it

until **now** *to make his point, or totally ignored by other impatient colleagues. 'We dealt with that hours ago, Harold . . .'*

So your contributions need to be made at the appropriate time. Don't sit and mull it over in your head for too long – the discussion will have moved on and you may have lost your chance. Late might just as well be never.

Signal late contributions

If you do actually think of something that would genuinely put a new light on a subject and this only occurs to you when everyone else seems happy and about to make a decision, *signal*. Say something like:

'Oh dear, I've just thought of something that might change the way we approach that', or

'I'm afraid something has just occurred to me.'

When you say 'Oh dear' or words to that effect, you are demonstrating to your colleagues that you are aware of the effect your bombshell may have; that you know your timing isn't right, but that you have thought of something too important to be ignored.

Being ahead of the game

Sometimes you may feel that unless you say what you've thought of straight away you'll burst, or forget what you were going to say. So you say what you want to say even though it doesn't exactly fit into the discussion at that moment.

It's not quite so drastic to be too *early* with your contribution. With any luck, because you have made it once and been asked (or told) to hang on to that point, you or someone else will remember it when the appropriate time arrives. However, it is not so effective a contribution as if you had waited until the appropriate time.

If you do have something which is burning a hole in your mental pocket until you say it, do one of two things.

1. Make a note of it, then bring it up at the appropriate time or

2. Flag up the fact that you want to talk about it later. Say to the chairperson, between agenda items rather than interrupting one, if possible,

'When we get to the item about budgetary analysis, I've got a point I'd like to make', or

'I'd like to just flag up that I've got a suggestion I'd like to make when we get to the point about fundraising.'

SAYING WHAT YOU WANT TO SAY

Getting across the point you want to make is not always as easy as it should be. All sorts of things may stop you making your contribution when you want to and in the manner you want to. Ways of increasing your chances are to:

- prioritise
- make it short and snappy
- ask for reactions
- use examples
- use visual aids

Prioritise

Have you ever come across those people in meetings who have something to say about every single issue and want to say it at great length?

When you want to make a positive impact on a meeting, prioritise the issues on which you want to have a say. Decide which are the critical issues as far as you are concerned, and when, if necessary, you will make a stand. If you can involve yourself as well in the discussion on other items, as the more often you contribute, the more effect you are likely to have. However, restrict yourself to making a firm stand on a limited number of items because your contribution will have more impact than if you are seen as having strong and persistent opinions on everything.

Make it short and snappy

Keep your contributions short and to the point. Remember that the longer you speak, the smaller percentage of what you say will be assimilated by your audience. However riveting a speech you may make, the human brain will not take it all in.

Ask for reactions

Asking other participants at the meeting for their reactions to what you have said can be one of the most effective ways of ensuring that your contribution is heard, and that notice is taken of it. You can do this straight after making your point: 'I'd like to hear your reactions to that', but it's most effective when no one seems to have taken much notice of what you have said.

'Chris, what do you think of my suggestion about the total quality scheme?'

'I'd like some reactions to my point about the Christmas discount'

'I'd like to hear what everyone thinks about the wording amendment I suggested just now'

'How does my proposal about the air conditioning tie in with the overall plan?'

When you do this, you call people's attention back to your point, without having to sound peevish that nobody noticed it the first time. If the other participants didn't hear, they may well ask you to repeat your suggestion. If they've forgotten it, you recall the suggestion to the front of their minds. If they've ignored it, then the suggestion gets another chance to be considered.

Use examples

Illustrate your argument with examples. Examples make a statement come alive. Examples are stories, and stories enliven dull facts and make people remember them.

> *President Jimmy Carter told America that he was in control of a multi-billion dollar budget. Although this sounded impressive, it didn't mean anything to most people. President Ronald Reagan told America to think of a stack of $1000 dollar bills as high as the Empire State Building. The budget of one trillion dollars would be equal to 30 Empire State Buildings. Most people could picture that, so the budget had some meaning.*

Visual aids

If you need to present the sales figures for the year, remember that the human brain limits the amount it can take in through the ears, so use some form of visual aid. In very large presentations these can take the form of films, slides and overhead projector transparencies. In smaller meetings, sometimes the overhead projector is used, but more often a flip chart diagram or individual handouts are talked through. Don't forget that if you have a large amount of complicated information to get across, send some of it as papers to the other participants before the meeting.

WHEN YOU DON'T AGREE

Having to say that you disagree, or don't like someone's idea, is not always easy, especially when you are in the minority. There are some techniques you can use to make life easier for you if you do disagree.

1. *Give reasons*
   If you disagree with a suggestion or opinion, it is sensible to give your reasons for doing so before firmly stating your disagreement. Thus:
   'I think there are a number of flaws in this option, so I don't think we should consider it' is less likely to annoy the person who suggested it than:
   'I disagree. I think this option has so many flaws that it is a non-starter'.

2. *Prioritise*
   Decide how important the issue is to you and make a firm stand only on the most important. Try not to be the one voice crying in the wilderness on every item on the agenda.

3. *Ask questions*
   As mentioned before, asking questions and showing interest, rather than dismissing someone else's suggestion out of hand, will get you a better hearing.

4. *Give way gracefully*
   If you are obviously losing, it makes sense to give way gracefully. If you do it positively, you may well gain some support

for your stand on another subject. In any case, giving way with bad grace will only get you the reputation for being crabby, bad tempered and a bad loser. Compare the following statements:

Negative 'Well I suppose as you're all against me, I'll have to go along with it.'

Positive 'I'll fall in with the majority and go along with the idea.'

Negative 'OK, if that's really what you want, but no good will come of it, you mark my words.'

Positive 'As I'm obviously in a minority, I'll agree to the suggestion, but I would like my reservations to be noted.'

Changing your mind

Occasionally, other people may have a better idea than you. If so, gracefully accept their idea in place of your own. Some people find this difficult because they are afraid of being thought fickle or a soft touch and this makes them hide the fact that they have been persuaded.

If you are genuinely swayed by an argument and change your mind, do it openly. Make it clear that someone has persuaded you, made you see things in a different light. If you do this you will build yourself a reputation for being reasonable and open. If you are seen to be changing your mind grudgingly, because you are afraid of being thought fickle, you may gain yourself a reputation for being stubborn or bloody minded, e.g.:

Grudging 'Yes, all right, you win, I suppose that would work better.'

Open 'I think that's a much better idea, let's do it that way.'

HELPING THE MEETING TO FLOW SMOOTHLY *OR* BACK-SEAT CHAIRING

Making effective contributions does not necessarily mean coming up with brilliant ideas and profound expositions every time. Suggestions and proposals that help the progress of the meeting can be just as valuable. Make your suggestions to the chairperson, for politeness' sake, but often the chairperson will be grateful to you for making constructive suggestions about structuring the meeting.

If your chairperson is not very effective, then your suggestions will have even more importance – they may be the only way to get any structure at all into the meeting. Some of the ways that you can facilitate the structure and process of the meeting are:

- suggesting a finite finishing time
- proposing a limited time for specific items
- suggesting that Annie might like to illustrate her point on a flip chart
- asking if the meeting has heard all the available information on that item
- proposing a different, more logical order for the items on the agenda

There are obviously many more, and if you are unfortunate enough to have an unskilled chairperson you may need to become skilled yourself in the art of chairing the meeting from the back seat.

INTERRUPTIONS

Interrupting others

The rule with interruptions, by and large, is 'Do as you would be done by'. Try not to interrupt other people when they are in full flow as this shows little regard for what they are saying. If you are successful in talking them down they are quite likely to feel resentful. If you are not successful and they talk you down, you may be left looking foolish.

The exception to this is interrupting those people who just go on and on and on. Sometimes it is necessary, if not essential to interrupt someone who plainly could talk about the necessity of implementing BS 5750 until midnight.

The best way is to wait until they draw breath, then signal your intention: 'I'd like to make a point about that.'

Signalling your intention in this way means that you are saying something very short, but something which grabs the attention of the chairperson and the rest of the group. It gives the chairperson the opportunity to turn the spotlight in your direction.

Being interrupted

Don't let other people interrupt you if you have not finished what you want to say. If someone does interrupt, by starting to talk while you are still talking, *don't stop*. If you stop talking they have successfully interrupted you. You have two options:

1. To carry on talking louder – this can be a successful tactic because many people give up the attempt to interrupt and stop talking if you carry on. However it sometimes has a limited success, because a) you may not have a very loud voice, and b) it can lead to a general free for all.
2. To say something about the interruption. Use phrases like, 'I'd like to just finish the point I'm making' or 'I haven't quite finished yet, Tom.'

Of course, if a lot of people seem to be trying to interrupt you, it may be a signal that you are banging on too long yourself!

BEHAVING CONFIDENTLY AT MEETINGS

A lot of people hate going to meetings. They don't mind meeting with a few people they know, but having to go to a meeting full of relative strangers from other departments, many of them more senior, all with different wants, views and knowledge is a form of refined torture.

Sometimes people feel overawed and awkward in meetings because they are the most junior, or among the most junior attending. Sometimes it is because they are the only woman or the only man and as such are treated differently, or *feel* as if they are. At other times it can be because they know that they have something to say which the other participants are not going to want to hear. Sometimes it may be that they are just not used to meetings and need a bit more practice to gain confidence. Large meetings often engender far more feelings of being overawed than smaller ones. These are some of the horrors which haunt people before, during, and after meetings.

The right moment never comes

One of the problems in getting your point across at meetings is finding the right moment to make it. You wait for other people to have their say, but then the discussion moves in a slightly different direction and somehow the point you were going to make doesn't seem to fit in with what everyone else is now talking about.

Getting attention

Sometimes when you do pluck up the courage to speak and make your point, it seems not to get heard in the general discussion. You've made your point and no one has taken any notice. Of course, this is not a great encouragement for the next time you want to say something, and a lot of people become so disheartened that they sit back thinking 'No one pays any attention to me so I might as well not bother'.

Even more discouraging is when you make a point which no one seems to hear, but which is then repeated by someone else five minutes later and hailed as the idea to save the world.

Tying your tongue in knots

You've got the attention of the meeting, they are all listening to you and – horror of horrors – the sentences that were so clear in your head come out as a disjointed jumble. Perhaps the word that would clarify everything disappears from your brain, perhaps you forget everything and you are reduced to the ignominy of saying: 'It doesn't matter, I've forgotten what I was going to say'.

They are all far more important than me

This is a common problem in meetings where there is a large difference in the status of the people attending, or where one person is much younger or more inexperienced than other participants. The young, lower status or inexperienced person feels embarrassed to speak for fear of feeling foolish in the eyes of the other people.

I'm a token

Rosabeth Moss Kanter in her book, *Men and Women of the Corporation*, identifies the concept of 'tokens' – people taken into an organisation (or onto a committee, etc.) so that the organisation or committee is seen to be fully representative. The most common 'tokens' are token women, but you also find token men, black people, disabled people, etc. What all tokens have in common is that the committee where they are represented would deny that they *are* token. Now the problem with being, or feeling that you are a token, is that the other people on the committee may expect you to behave like a woman, black, man, disabled person, because they have a certain stereotype of you. Even if they don't, you probably think they do. Also, you are expected to reflect the views of all those people you are supposed to represent. This gives you the burden of making sure that you are specially good at whatever it is you should be doing. Of course, this is in addition to representing the views of your department, or whatever you were supposed to be there for in the first place.

WHY YOU LACK SELF CONFIDENCE

The internal critic – the nagging voice of doom
All of us have a little voice inside us that comments on the way we handle our lives, giving us praise and blame whether we want it or not. Unfortunately, for many people, it tends to be very quick off the mark to point out anything that wasn't quite perfect and to nag on about it in a very unfriendly way.

It also warns us of dangers. Sometimes this warning voice can be very helpful and necessary, but for some of us it tends to be over-cautious, and warns us off things that we are really quite capable of doing. 'Watch out in case you make a fool of yourself', says the voice, 'You'd better not do that in case you get it wrong'.

Your beliefs about yourself
If you want to behave more confidently at meetings, you may have to make certain changes to your beliefs about yourself. Perhaps you believe that you are not very articulate, that you never manage to say things at the right time, that your ideas are not as good as other peoples.

Some of the problems people encounter at meetings which make them lose confidence are self perpetuating. If they are unsuccessful at getting a point across, because they are shy and left it too late or said it too quietly, this means that the next time they go to a meeting they will be aware of their previous failure and their approach may be even more tentative. Success breeds success, failure breeds failure. If you think you are going to fail, you are more likely to. Failure becomes a self-fulfilling prophecy, a vicious circle of self put-down.

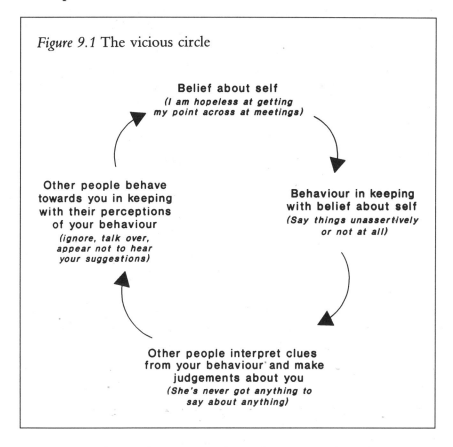

Figure 9.1 The vicious circle

Belief about self
(I am hopeless at getting my point across at meetings)

Behaviour in keeping with belief about self
(Say things unassertively or not at all)

Other people interpret clues from your behaviour and make judgements about you
(She's never got anything to say about anything)

Other people behave towards you in keeping with their perceptions of your behaviour
(ignore, talk over, appear not to hear your suggestions)

We can break into this circle and sever the chain of self doubt at a number of stages. We can break it at the stage of our beliefs about ourselves, and at the stage of the behaviour we use. It's easier to change behaviour if we have a change in belief first. Then the vicious circle can change into:

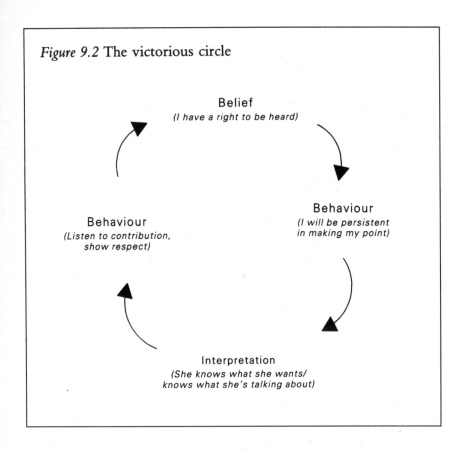

Figure 9.2 The victorious circle

Belief
(I have a right to be heard)

Behaviour
*(I will be persistent
in making my point)*

Behaviour
*(Listen to contribution,
show respect)*

Interpretation
*(She knows what she wants/
knows what she's talking about)*

Exercise

Think about the last meeting you attended. If there were times when you feel you could have behaved more confidently, chart your behaviour on the vicious circle. Now see how you could break into the circle to transform it into a victorious circle. What shifts in your behaviour would it be feasible for you to make next time? Now identify a future meeting where you could try out the victorious circle and go and do it.

CHANGING YOUR ATTITUDE TO MEETINGS

There are a number of things you can do to help you feel more confident at meetings – and feeling more confident will help you to behave more confidently.

Prepare

Make sure that you prepare thoroughly for the meeting. Go through the items on the agenda which concern you and ensure you have all the facts at your fingertips. Knowing that you can't be faulted will make you feel more confident. Knowledge is power. If you are an expert, make sure people know it.

Prepare visual aids for any complicated point you may wish to explain. These don't have to be elaborate, at most meetings you can hand around a paper if you don't have the nerve to stand up and use a flip chart.

Look at all the items on the agenda to identify areas where you might need to ask questions. Prepare a few questions to have up your sleeve. Asking intelligent questions can help in establishing yourself as one of the key contributors to the discussion.

Your general approach

When you go to a meeting to which you have been invited, it may help to think along the following lines:

> I HAVE BEEN INVITED TO THIS MEETING
> therefore
> I HAVE A CONTRIBUTION TO MAKE
> therefore
> I HAVE CERTAIN RIGHTS

Ken and Kate Back in their book *Assertiveness at Work* suggest that you have certain rights which are particularly appropriate at meetings. Some of these are:

- the right to make suggestions
- the right to disagree, to state opinions which may be different to those of others
- the right to have other people listen to you and take you seriously
- the right to understand what is going on

- the right to know the purpose and rough time-scale of the meeting beforehand
- the right to use your time in a productive way

Everyone in the meeting has those rights – even the most boring people. Remembering that *you* as well as the others have them can help you feel more confident in speaking up. Remembering this can also help you to be tolerant when listening to others.

Watch out for your internal critic
Here's how to handle the voice inside you that keeps on nagging away at your self-confidence, saying things like:
    'If you speak now they'll think you're cheeky'
    'Better wait and see what everyone else thinks first'
    'You can't say that, it's absolute rubbish'
    'You can't say that, it contradicts the Big Boss'
    'If you ask that they'll all think you're stupid'.
    Find a name for the voice so that you can tell it to 'Go away Fred. Don't bother me now'. Argue back – tell your voice that you know what you are doing and go ahead and do it.

Listen
If you are not very confident at meetings, you probably feel that you spend too much time listening and not enough talking anyway. This is different. Listen actively. Let everyone know that you are listening. Look at the speaker, not at your notes. Use eye contact to show that you are listening and nod at appropriate points. If you are actively listening and showing that you are listening, it is much easier to get the attention of the speaker to show that you want to speak next.

Use non-verbal behaviour assertively
Use eye contact when speaking as well as listening. When you do speak, *don't* look down at your notes, using them as a visual comfort blanket, but *do* look at the other people in the meeting. Turn your head when speaking so that you include everyone in your gaze, rather than speaking to the only other person you know, the

friendliest looking person there, or in extreme cases, the jug of water in the middle of the table.

Make sure your voice sounds assertive and confident. Use a strong, even tone. If you are normally quietly spoken, turn up the volume a bit. Try not to turn up the pitch, though. A high pitched voice sounds more nervous than a low pitched one. Imagine you are talking to someone with whom you are normally very much at ease – it doesn't matter whether it's your friend Jack, your child, your dog or the milkman. Remember that tone of voice and use it at the meeting.

Ask for reactions

As we've already mentioned, this is an extremely valuable technique for ensuring that your ideas and suggestions are noticed at a meeting and don't fall by the wayside because other people are so interested in what *they* are saying that they take no notice of you.

It is particularly important if you do not feel very confident. Unfortunately, if you feel self-conscious about saying something at a meeting, when you do pluck up the courage to say it, it often comes out in a small and timid voice. This, of course, makes it easy for other people to ignore you, or not to pay attention because someone else speaks immediately afterwards in a more assertive way.

If you lack the confidence to ask the whole meeting for a reaction to your idea, pick out someone who looks sympathetic and ask him or her for a reaction. Make sure you don't pick the meeting 'mouse'; pick someone who has already proved to be fairly vocal.

Agree actively

If you don't have anything new to say at the meeting yourself, or somebody else has just said what you were about to say, don't sit there passively agreeing, do it actively. Say something like: 'Yes, I agree with John because . . .'

By doing this, you are a) establishing yourself as a contributor, which may make it easier for you next time, and b) making a useful contribution to the meeting by building on John's suggestion.

Be persistent

If your suggestion is lost in the maelstrom of ideas being generated, don't give up. If you don't like the idea of asking for reactions to it then make the suggestion again – and again, until it is noticed. Often, the other people at the meeting do hear the suggestion you made and then instantly forget it because they are involved with something else. If you are persistent, then the second or third time around it will be welcomed and dealt with, 'Oh yes, what about the XYZ?' is a fairly typical reaction. While you are breathing a mental 'phew', the others are now discussing your idea.

Remember, nobody but yourself knows what an effort it takes to be persistent and keep on making a point. Other people will be very matter-of-fact about discussing suggestions and ideas – they will not think about, let alone take into account, the fact that you could have crawled under a stone when they ignored your idea the first time, and that although you would rather have jumped out of an aeroplane than say it again, you did it and are proud of it.

Be assertive

Remember that you have a right to be at the meeting and a right to be heard. Say what you think or feel in a clear and direct way. Make your body language positive and upright; hold up your head. There is a difference between being assertive and being agressive, so don't hammer home your point at the expense of other people. Acknowledge their right to contribute to the meeting as well. Tell yourself that your contribution is just as valid as everyone else's and make it confidently.

SUMMARY

Making effective contributions to meetings is not always easy. There are many reasons why people may feel unsure about what to say and the best way to say it. There are a number of skills and techniques which it is possible to learn to help you ensure that the contributions you make to meetings are both useful and noticed.

Certain types of behaviour are positively helpful in ensuring that your contributions are effective, whereas others are best avoided.

Questioning can often be used to help the meeting to move forward positively. It is important to get your timing right if your suggestion or information is to have the most impact. The way you go about saying what you want to say and disagreeing when you need to, is as important, if not more important, than what you actually say. You can help the chairperson of the meeting by making suggestions about the structure of the meeting.

You can learn to behave more confidently at meetings by identifying in advance the issues which cause you to feel unsure of yourself. There are a number of steps you can take to change your attitude to meetings and acquire a more positive approach.

Use the checklist on the next page to find out if the contributions you make at meetings are as effective as they could be, or if you could improve the quality and quantity of your input by using some of the skills and techniques identified in this chapter.

CHECKLIST – MAKING EFFECTIVE CONTRIBUTIONS

1. Signal your intentions, giving the meeting a warning about the kind of contribution you are about to make.
2. Ask for information.
3. Test your understanding of what has been said.
4. Summarise what others have said.
5. Say how you feel about the way things are progressing rather than making judgmental comments about the meeting.
6. Avoid using words, phrases and non-verbal behaviour that could irritate the other people at the meeting.
7. Stick to one or two really good reasons for doing things your way rather than diluting your argument with many minor reasons.
8. Avoid making immediate counter proposals when someone has made a suggestion.
9. Try not to get involved in a spiral of attack and defence.
10. Use questions in a positive and versatile way to:
    a) gain information
    b) amass the detail
    c) clarify and test understanding
    d) show you are taking ideas seriously
    e) defuse anger
    f) establish yourself as a contributor.
11. Get the timing of your contributions right, not too soon before the meeting has started thinking about the topic, nor after everyone has moved on.
12. Prioritise the issues you wish to make a stand about.
13. Keep your contributions short and snappy.
14. Ask for reactions to your suggestions, especially when they don't seem to have made an immediate impact.
15. Use examples to illustrate your points.
16. Use visual aids to help to put over complex information.
17. When you disagree, give reasons, and try to give way gracefully when you don't get your own way.
18. Change your mind positively rather than grudgingly.
19. Make suggestions about the process of the meeting (e.g. timing,

order, etc.) rather than its content, if this will help it to progress.

20. Avoid interrupting others except when absolutely necessary and try to prevent others successfully interrupting you.

21. Analyse why you are not as confident as you could be at meetings.

22. Boost your confidence by preparing thoroughly so that you know what you are talking about.

23. Be aware that you have a right to be at the meeting and a right to make your contribution.

24. Actively listen and agree with others even if you don't say anything new yourself.

25. Be persistent and assertive in getting your point across.

10. Influencing a Meeting

'I went to the meeting, I told them all the facts, but they still wouldn't accept my argument.'

'Even though they understood me, they didn't want to help, what's the use of trying to get anything done in this place?'

'The only way to get things done here is to have some power behind you. When the guy from production comes along he has his director's backing, there is nothing I can do in the face of that.'

These three quotations are from individuals who failed to get the most out of a meeting. From time to time everyone feels a sense of futility because an opportunity has not been seized or made the most of. Meetings offer great opportunities for influencing people, but if you fail and other people observe your failure, you will find it much harder to influence those people in future. This chapter looks at the techniques that can improve your chances of having an influence at the right moment.

Influencing means getting other people to take your ideas or needs into account in their own decision-making especially when you do not have direct power over them (see Chapter 12 for Politics and Power.) It does not mean always getting your own way, nor that you can always come out smiling when the odds are heavily loaded against you. However, even when they are, effective use of influencing skills can improve the situation. For instance, the British and American hostages held in Beirut prove that even when you are chained to a wall you can still exert some influence on your captors. One hostage always made a point of welcoming his captors into 'his' cell. This very slightly altered the imbalance of power, so that when that hostage was finally released his captors even apologised to him for detaining him for so long.

So how can you bring your own influence to bear at a meeting? You first need to know three things:

1. the person
2. yourself
3. the circumstances and need

KNOW THE PERSON

Here is a valuable way of looking at individuals, based upon work by Elias H. Porter. He produced a motivational model of how humans relate to each other called Relationship Awareness Theory. It argues that people use methods of behaviour to reach goals that are important to them. If you understand a person's goals then it is easier to understand and predict his or her behaviour. You can also appreciate which styles of behaviour they will find rewarding, and which they will find unrewarding or threatening. If influencing is about achieving a 'win-win' outcome, i.e. both parties achieve most of what they want, then knowing what the other person regards as a 'win' outcome will help you to influence them. You will be more likely to influence people if they think you are helping them to achieve *their* goals as well as your own.

People at meetings tend to fall into four motivation categories:

- helpers
- activists
- thinkers
- generalists

Helpers
These are people who enjoy looking after and giving protection to others, often with little interest in any personal reward. They care about other people's feelings. Helpers by definition are drawn to

opportunities where they can be of help. They are frequently good team-workers and will instinctively try to help a meeting flow smoothly. Comments like: 'Before we get too heated, let us first see where we agree' or, 'People's feelings need to be considered in this proposal; it's not good enough just to work out the logic' are typical. Helpers dislike competition and strong aggressive emotions, especially directed against themselves.

Activists
Activists like achieving, taking control, and using power. They like to win and are often perceived as aggressive. Action is the name of their game.

'Don't just stand there, *do* something,' is one of the activist's typical remarks. When influencing activists, remember they are attracted by drive, energy and the chance to win. They like competitors, and will sometimes find competition where it doesn't really exist. The style of influencing that works with a helper will be dismissed by an activist as weak and feeble. Activists also like time pressure, and are attracted to deadlines. They are also frequently seen as dynamic and energetic.

Thinkers
Thinkers are self-reliant, independent and good with data. They like to review the logic of a situation before they take action. Thinkers are influenced by data that is well prepared, clearly laid out, and above all logical. They find demonstrations of emotion, whether of the caring helper kind or the competitive activist kind, somewhat distasteful. Thinkers may be seen as cool and as loners, but they regard themselves as the only truly objective people at the meeting. They are often specialists, and because they may not be particularly forceful verbally, are easily overlooked by more vocal contributors to the meeting.

Generalists
Generalists share all three of the previous basic behaviour patterns. It is tempting to believe that they are the ideal managers but viewed through the eyes of a strong helper, activist or thinker, generalists

may seem to be sitting on the fence. They can side with anyone and appreciate all points of view, but often have no clearly defined ideas of their own. To influence generalists, you must recognise the balanced and even-handed nature of their motivation.

How to influence people with different patterns

The essence of influencing other people is to recognise that although they may think and behave differently from you, IN THEIR OWN MINDS THEY BELIEVE THEY ARE JUST AS RIGHT AS YOU ARE. Once the world is divided up into various degrees of helper, activist and thinker, and the various pattern blends that occur, then it is possible to see what influencing styles will have most and least effect. Think of it in terms of using an appropriate language for the listener. The data and the concept we wish to influence stays the same in all cases, but you try to speak French to a French speaker, German to a German speaker, etc. In our view using helper, activist or thinker language appropriate to the listener is very similar to choosing French, German or Italian depending on the needs of the listener.

Putting influencing into practice

Say you are trying to get funds to design and launch a new kind of computer game for eight to twelve year-olds. Your concept is an educational game, as opposed to the classic shoot-the-baddies type. How would you persuade the helpers, activists and thinkers at the meeting?

First, *helpers* will be attracted by the educational aspect of the game. They probably have children who spend too long playing 'useless' games, so they will value the educational component. There may also be a chance of putting together a company design team that links, say, the educational people with the software specialists. Helpers will like the idea of creating linkages across the organisation.

The *activists* in the group will see this as an opportunity to gain market share from your competitors. They will be keenly aware of what the competition did recently to outsell your own company in the market, and will seize on your idea as a way of getting their own back. They will be impatient of long development time-scales and less than clear objectives. They will want to know what needs to be done *now*, and how quickly proto-type software can be produced.

The *thinkers* will want to know about the available data, so make sure you have got market research information, neatly tabulated, with as much data as possible about market potential in this age group. Demonstrate with graphs parental concern at the negative effects of conventional computer games. Show how there is a logically identified gap in the market which you are aiming to fill with this new product.

Demonstrate to *generalists* how this product, by linking strengths in the organisation, will be a good way of developing the entire organisation. Generalists often act as 'translators' in an organisation, so involve them in helping you to deal with the other groups.

The example above shows how different facets of the same idea can be revealed so that each listener feels you are talking his or her language.

KNOW YOURSELF

While it is important to know the person or people you are trying to influence, it is just as important to be aware of your own styles of influencing, your own strengths, your own weaknesses. You yourself will have a tendency towards helper, activist, thinker or generalist, and you may need to adapt your normal style in order to influence someone with different tendencies.

This section examines ways of assessing your own strengths and weaknesses and how these can effect your ability to influence others. Some of the concepts used by William Schutz can help in understanding one's strengths and weaknesses in influencing. Schutz suggests that each of us has three fundamental orientations:

1. inclusion
2. control
3. affection/openness

Inclusion

Inclusion means how much you involve others in what you do, and how much you want to be involved by them.

Someone who uses a lot of inclusion behaviour spends much time with others, and can often draw a crowd – even at the coffee machine. The social situation is one of their favourite influencing methods. On the other hand, people with low levels of inclusion prefer to be on their own or with a small number of close associates. The complaint 'why was I the last to know?' often shows that a person wants to be included. But if they do not include others, then, generally, others do not include them.

People who don't want the world to include them often form cliques. Cliques are themselves a way of influencing people. If you would like to be part of a clique, then you will want to adopt the styles and beliefs of that clique. At meetings, the clique can be a sort of inner cabinet.

High-inclusion people will sometimes influence a meeting by using their (often considerable) social skills to encourage others to 'join' their way of tackling a problem. Part of the attraction is the social nature of working together. (See *participation* and *trust style*, later in this Chapter.)

Control

People who need to control seek opportunities to do just that. They like to be in charge. They often find it hard to delegate effectively. They find it difficult to trust anyone else to do the work as well as they believe they can do it themselves. Sometimes in a meeting the chairperson is a strong controller, and won't let the meeting debate the significant issues or offer alternative solutions to the problems being discussed. The strong controller will want to push his own ideas and decisions through the meeting.

On the other hand, some people like to be told what to do and want others to control them. A chairperson like this will fail to give direction and the meeting will easily lose its way. Whoever talks fastest or loudest will be allowed to do so. Chairing a meeting requires some control to achieve the fine balance between allowing people their head and preventing them from contributing effectively.

Some people don't want to control or be controlled. They take the view that if you give them broad aims and objectives they will get on with it, without you needing to look over their shoulder. At meetings they will tend to contribute in short bursts on areas where they feel they have a direct impact, but otherwise won't get involved in the politics and power-mongering (see Chapter 12 on hidden agendas.)

Such people seldom try to influence others except in areas of direct concern to themselves. They are also harder to influence unless they agree with the proposal being made. They operate independently of the meeting, yet they may have useful data to contribute. They will make one or two attempts to speak, and if they fail to be heard they will probably stay quiet for the rest of the time.

Affection/openness

Inclusion is about social relationships; affection is about individual relationships. A person can show low inclusion behaviour but high affection behaviour, and vice versa. Affection means being prepared to form deeper and longer lasting relationships with individuals. At a party people with high affection needs will want to have one intense conversation rather than 10 shallow ones. People with high levels of affection/openness generate individual personal warmth; even brief conversations with them have a positive effect. In many cases if a leader is described as charismatic, it is his or her high affection and openness that is being commented on.

People with low affection needs tend to be very selective about whom they form close relationships with and often wish the other person to break the ice. At a meeting the people skilled in using affection behaviour will be enhancing their one-to-one relationships. They will use that direct personal contact as a way of influencing and recruiting people to their own ideas and causes.

Thus a person may, depending on his or her personality, use social (inclusion), power (control), and personal (affection) methods to influence others. Which of these methods work most effectively will depend on the circumstances, the organisation in which they are operating, and the comfort and skill with which the individual uses these styles.

Exercise

Think about the way you prefer to behave:

1. Do you use social, power or personal methods to influence people?
2. Which methods work best in your organisation?
3. Could you use more of any these methods?

Which of the methods could you develop and use more effectively?

KNOW THE CIRCUMSTANCES AND THE NEED

In order to choose the right influencing style, you will need to study the circumstances first. They include the culture and norms of the organisation, the stage of the project, the amount of power (or lack of it) you have and the urgency and importance of the task.

Roger Harrison has developed a useful way of identifying different types of influencing. There are four main approaches; two are 'push' styles and two are 'pull' styles. People tend to use one or two of these styles more often than others. This is partly because of the type of organisation, and partly personal preference.

First, let's look at 'pull' styles.

Common vision

This is a way of presenting an idea that is still in the future. It takes other people's opinions and beliefs into account and offers a view of what *could* be. It implies that through individual and collective effort a common vision can be achieved. The managing director might express such a vision as in: 'I see this organisation as becoming one of the top three chains of retailers of children's toys in Europe, giving unparalleled service to parents, and an enjoyable and educational experience to children on every visit.'

This style collects and mobilises other people's energy and resources by appealing to their hopes, values and expectations. It is an emotional style because it offers hope for the future.

Not surprisingly the common vision style of influencing has been used extensively by great leaders who were launching their followers on difficult journeys towards a far-off goal. Martin Luther King had a dream of black and white being equal, Jack Kennedy wanted to put a man on the Moon by the end of the decade, Churchill promised blood sweat and tears, and Hitler offered 1000 years of the Third Reich. This technique demands energy, enthusiasm and charisma, and works best for large and long-term common goals. Detailed plans need not be laid out at the same time. It is quite normal for the common vision style to include a first step which may be of symbolic rather than practical value. However, the influencer must also have an effective and detailed plan of how to *start* on the road to the common vision, although if the style is successful it is unlikely that followers will ask detailed questions.

This is one of two 'pull' styles that attract people and recruit them to a cause they believe in. The other 'pull' style is:

Participation and trust

This involves making an individual want to join an existing group, or the workforce to join you in doing interesting or attractive work. Participation and trust means influencing people by involving them in the decision-making process. It is very good for decisions and strategies that will have a long-term impact on a team and help keep them involved. It is less appropriate for quick decisions.

What's important is identification with colleagues in the team, or in the meeting. An atmosphere of mutual trust and co-operation has to be created, and then people will go along with the decisions (and sometimes emotions) of the group. Participation is encouraged by receptivity, understanding and openness and will not work well if competition or overt control is being used.

In training its SAS soldiers, the British army moves away from the usual military rewards and punishments style (described next). It sets up four-man groups that encourage a strong sense of participation and trust. These men will be relying on each other for their lives, therefore considerable commitment and trust needs to be developed between the four of them.

This is in direct contrast to the needs of the regular army where one soldier issues a command and hundreds of other soldiers obey it instinctively. This is the first of the 'push' styles of influencing:

Reward and punishment

In this style pressure and rewards are used to control the behaviour of others. Rewards are offered and given for compliance, and punishment is threatened and imposed for non-compliance. This style is clearly in contrast to the previous two 'pull' styles. This is a 'push' style where the individual being influenced does not need to agree, indeed may not agree, with the influencer. If the influencer has greater power, as in the military, then the influencer can force the other person to do what has to be done.

In companies, rewards and punishments are applied somewhat more subtly. Rewards are called 'incentives' and 'motivators'. Giving praise, giving pay increases above the norm, are examples of organisational rewards. In meetings, there are many ways a contributor or the chairperson can give rewards or punishments. This style includes identifying what is 'right', and what is 'wrong'. People are told that their behaviour is good or bad, correct or incorrect. This is in contrast to the second 'push' style.

Assertive persuasion

This style relies on logic and data and clearly expressed opinions to persuade others. People who use this style present the facts and the arguments as lucidly and as unemotionally as possible. They also say what the consequences will be of following their advice, or of failing to follow it. This may sound somewhat like rewards and punishments, but there is far less emotion involved in the assertive persuasion style. People using it are persistent and energetic, but instead of telling people they are right or wrong, the influencer may say they have 'understood' or 'failed to understand' the data. People who use this style effectively will be articulate and good in discussion and arguments. They enjoy the debate even if they are defending what seems to be an inferior position; they will still argue with great vigour. It is a style used in many public sector organisations.

Using different styles

At the beginning of a new project, the 'common vision' style may be appropriate in order to catch attention and give a long-term focus. It may also distract people from their present problems. Once the project is underway, participation and trust can keep the group together, and one of the push styles may emerge. If there's a strong and powerful leader, then the reward and punishment style is likely to be used more frequently. People are rewarded for helping the leader and punished for hindering. If no strong leader emerges, but a number of committed people work together, it is likely that assertive persuasion will be the chosen method of influencing, since everything will depend on the quality of the data.

In influencing effectively, whether before, during, or after the meeting, it is important to take into account the kind of person you are trying to influence, your own strengths, weaknesses and preferences, and the circumstances in which you are influencing.

We will now look at the notion of 'ownership' in meetings and discuss how to get people to take responsibility for issues, problems and solutions.

Ownership

By the combined use of power, trickery, shame and threat it is possible to get someone at a meeting to do what you want. But the job is far more likely to be done well if the person feels some 'ownership' for the work, and this ownership was recognised at the meeting when the task was allocated. None of the influencing approaches described in this chapter are guaranteed to generate ownership on the part of the person being influenced. They are all concerned with ensuring that the need for the task, and the methods to be used on the task are communicated effectively. But this may only produce acceptance that the work needs to be done, ownership does not always follow.

The Ownership Spiral

How do you get someone to own a problem? We have developed what we call the ownership spiral, which helps in plotting the course to ownership. It is viewed from the point of view of the person who eventually takes ownership, and it goes through eight stages.

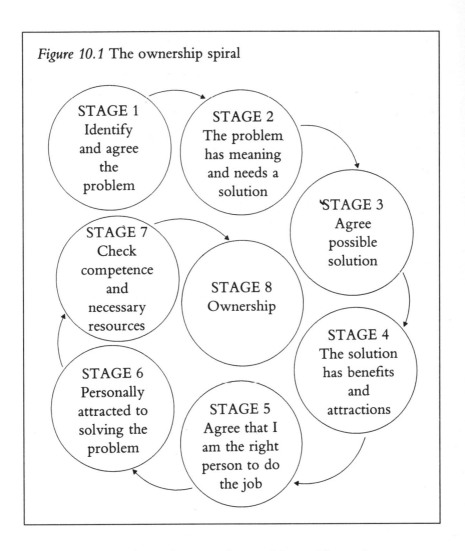

Figure 10.1 The ownership spiral

STAGE 1
Identify
and agree
the
problem

STAGE 2
The problem
has meaning
and needs a
solution

STAGE 3
Agree
possible
solution

STAGE 7
Check
competence
and
necessary
resources

STAGE 8
Ownership

STAGE 4
The solution
has benefits
and
attractions

STAGE 6
Personally
attracted to
solving the
problem

STAGE 5
Agree that I
am the right
person to do
the job

Stage 1. **Identify and agree the problem.** If you do not agree that the problem exists or regard it as a problem, then you are hardly likely to take ownership of it: 'If the problem only affects purchasing, then why should those of us in finance have to help solve it?'

Stage 2. **The problem has meaning and needs a solution.** You accept that it is a real problem, and you have sympathy with those who are suffering from it: 'I agree that something must be done, but I don't see how it involves my department.'

Stage 3. **Agree possible solutions.** The problem needs to be dealt with and the solutions being suggested are not going to cause you or your department any difficulties. You may even contribute to an appropriate solution during discussion: 'That solution seems to be the most efficient, although it is not going to be the fastest option.'

Stage 4. **The solution has benefits or attractions.** In most organisations, any action is in fact part of a chain reaction. Few tasks can occur in isolation. A solution may have some spin-off benefits for you, or it may accord with your values: 'Although in personnel we aren't directly concerned, I agree with the decision to make maximum use of recycled materials in the new packaging.'

Stage 5. **Agree that you are the right person to do the job.** If you feel that someone else could or should have taken on the task, then you are less likely to accept full ownership. It is important at this stage that other options for solving the problem are talked through and eliminated. 'Yes, I can see that given the time-scales, it would not be possible to train up anyone else to rewrite this particular software.'

Stage 6. **You are personally attracted to solving the problem.** When you become genuinely interested and actively want to solve it, you are very close to full ownership. You have to ensure at the next stage that you have the necessary competence and resources. 'I very much want to take on the quality issue, but I'm not sure that I will have the time to do it justice.'

Stage 7. **Check competence and necessary resources.** You may want to tackle the problem, but if you do not believe that you have the personal competence or if you do not feel supported by the necessary resources, then you will still not quite own the problem. Before you leave the meeting you must ensure that all those present who may be able to provide resources, or to release you from other projects that may be competing for your time, have made the necessary commitments: 'So we have agreed that if I pull out of Susan's project, and can make use of two of Bill's people, then I will take on the urgent rewrite of the quality package.'

Stage 8. **Ownership.** You think the job is important, you want to do it, you feel competent and confident to do it, and you feel supported by your colleagues. So DO IT!

SUMMARY

In order to influence people at meetings it is necessary to know three things:

a) The person or people that you are trying to influence, and what style is likely to have the greatest impact. Identifying the people as *helpers*, *activists*, *thinkers* or *generalists*, or some combination of these, will help you choose the right language and style.

b) Yourself and your own strengths and weaknesses in influencing people. What style do you naturally prefer to use? The *inclusion*, *control*, *affection* format will help you to find the most effective approach.

c) The need, and the circumstances in which that need is to be met. Choose 'push' or 'pull' styles of influencing as appropriate to the situation. In the short-term, use push methods like reward and punishment, in the longer term use pull methods such as common vision.

Finally, if you are asking someone to do a task, or take on a problem, use the Ownership Spiral to check whether they will assume ownership of that project rather than simply carry it out.

The checklist on the following page will help you to monitor the influencing style you choose.

CHECKLIST – INFLUENCING A MEETING

1. Are you *influencing* or using *power*? (If it's power, go to Chapter 12).
2. Who precisely are you trying to influence?
3. What exactly do you want?
   a) Is it their help and support? (*Helper style.*)
   b) Is it their power, energy or competitive ability? (*Activist style.*)
   c) Is it their ability to analyse and their knowledge of the data? (*Thinker style.*)
   d) Is it their all-round ability to work with others, and see all sides of a problem? (*Generalist style.*)
4. How will you try to influence them?
   a) By socialising with them and involving them in more of what you do? (*Inclusion style.*)
   b) By using power and giving orders? (*Control style.*)
   c) By forming a close personal relationship with them at an individual level? (*Affection/Openness style.*)
5. What are the time-scales involved, and what does the organisation's culture expect as the normal style?
   a) Are you trying to convince them of your compelling view of the future when things might be much better? (*Common Vision.*)
   b) Are you asking people to join you and your group to take on who knows what kind of problems? (*Participation and Trust.*)
   c) Are you telling people what they ought to do and how they will be rewarded, and if they fail what the punishment will be? (*Reward and Punishment.*)
   d) Are you explaining with the use of data and logic exactly what will happen if this or that course of action is undertaken? (*Assertive Persuasion.*)
6. Is the person you have influenced tackling the problem because he feels forced to, or does he *own* the task?
   a) Has he agreed that the problem is real and needs a solution?
   b) Has he contributed to the solution, and does it have some benefit for him?

c) Does he accept that he is the right person to tackle the problem, and is he attracted to it?

d) Has he the competence, confidence and resources to tackle the problem?

11. Presentation Skills

A survey conducted in the United States asked people what was the thing they most feared. At the top of the list, way ahead of fire, sharks, drowning, snakes or death was . . . speaking in public.

However, if you go to meetings on a regular basis, it is fairly certain that at some time you will be asked to make a presentation.

The presentation might be anything from proposing a completely new organisational structure to a large group of senior executives, to presenting information to a few colleagues about your department's reaction to the new lunch menus.

Whatever the scale and importance of the presentation you make, there are ways of doing it well and ways of doing it badly. In this chapter we look at the various elements that can help you to make your presentation as good as it can be. There are four major steps in making a presentation effective:

- planning
- preparation
- practice
- presentation techniques

PLANNING

Good planning is essential in ensuring that your presentation will be successful. No two situations are alike so you will not be successful unless you adapt your approach to fit the occasion. There are a number of aspects to consider.

1. Who is the audience?

The people to whom you are making the presentation should have an effect on how you prepare your subject matter. But, whether it is a conference of Heads of State, a meeting of the Mothers Union, or the Monday Morning Meeting in the office, there are various factors about that audience which you need to take into consideration.

Background knowledge

How much background knowledge of the subject do they have? If they know nothing about it, then a few simple explanations giving some background detail may be needed. If they are au fait with the subject matter you may be able to use jargon which is common to you all.

Are they hostile or friendly?

Many people who fear making presentations tend to assume that the audience is the enemy. In fact, most audiences start off as sympathetic, willing to give the speaker the benefit of their attention. Of course, hostile audiences do exist, either because you are presenting an idea which they know beforehand they won't like, or because you represent in some way a group or set of ideas or ideals they disapprove of.

So there are two points here:

a) Unless you have reason to believe the contrary, regard the audience as your friends. They will be sympathetic to nervousness and the only thing that can alienate them is you. Later on in the chapter you will learn how to avoid this.

b) If your audience *is* hostile, you need to win some respect from them. The best way to do this is to acknowledge the differences between you, to acknowledge that there may be other points of view than your own. Ask for space to say what you need to and for their willingness to listen to you. By saying that you know that yours may not be a universally popular report, suggestion or decision, you are disarming your audience by showing some empathy with them.

What are their strengths and weaknesses?

It will help you to know which members of your audience are very supportive of new ideas and how many need to have things spelt out for them. Perhaps you have an audience that is likely to understand all your technical terms, or one that may be receptive and intelligent, but will not understand the technical niceties and will need to have technical ideas presented in terms they understand.

Why are they there?

Is your audience there because they want to hear what you have to say, or because they have been told to attend? Have they come specifically to hear your presentation or because they have to sit through it before they get a chance to speak? Have they come to applaud or to heckle? What benefits or threats might your ideas hold for them?

What are their expectations?

What are they expecting from you? A detailed exposition of the arguments for and against the siting of a nuclear reactor, or a brief summary of the results of the most recent public awareness campaign? Are they expecting a lecture or a question and answer session? Are they expecting you to talk for five minutes or fifty?

What are their initial perceptions of you?

What is your perceived status and how will that affect your audience's perceptions of you? What power do you have apart from status – information, almost certainly, expertise or charisma perhaps? If you have power that directly affects your audience they may have a different attitude to you than if you do not. We deal with power in more detail in Chapter 12.

What impression do you want to create?

First impressions are very important. It has been established that most interview decisions are made in the first few minutes of the interview – based almost entirely on first impressions. The same principle applies to meetings. One of the first impressions you make on your audience will be your appearance. This may not matter for the Monday Meeting, but if you are presenting material to an audience that does not know you, think carefully about the impression you wish to create and then dress accordingly (more about this later on in the chapter.)

The other parts of the impression you create will be to do with how nervous you appear and how much preparation you appear to have carried out. If you do not seem to be well prepared, you give the impression of thinking that your subject is not very important.

What approach should you use?

Is your aim to startle and surprise, or is it to make use of any common ground between you and your audience? You need to think through all aspects of your ideas and decide how they will make most impact on the audience. Identify the approach that will appeal to them. Think through the points you wish to emphasise. Think about the sort of objections that may be raised and how you might answer them.

PREPARATION

'If a man sits down to think, he is immediately asked if he has the headache,' said Emerson in 1833 and things haven't changed much since. Thinking time is one of the essentials of preparation but there are also a number of other essentials.

Collect the necessary information

Having decided what it is you want or need to present, collect all the information required to do the job. This might mean collecting facts and figures from company or personnel records, checking back over the records of previous meetings, gathering information from various people or doing some research in a library or other source of information. Much of the information may already be in your mind. Write it all down and do check that you have *all* the information you require.

Arrange it in a logical order

Be systematic when presenting your information. Think of your presentation as a string of pearls (of wisdom) strung together with a logical thread. It's up to you to decide what is logical, but remember that almost any system of organisation is better than a succession of clumps of unconnected facts or thoughts.

If you put the various aspects of your presentation into a logical sequence it makes it much simpler for your audience to listen and to absorb. It also makes it a lot easier for you to remember.

Enough and no more

Ensure that you have enough detail in your presentation to make it clear and easy to understand, but do not overload it with detail so that it has the effect of baffling or boring your audience rather than informing them. Gaps in the information present problems. If people cannot follow you they will continue to think about the part they did not quite grasp, rather than paying attention to your present point. Do not be repetitive and cover the same ground more than once. This is boring, time-wasting and distracts people from what you are actually saying.

Know what you are talking about

Don't try to present a subject unless you are thoroughly familiar with it. If you are expert in only part of a subject, try to stick to the part you know. Everyone is more confident when they are speaking about familiar subject matter as they have all the necessary information instantly available for recall. If you are speaking about a subject you are familiar with you will be able to field the awkward questions comfortably and expand or contract your talk as necessary even while on your feet.

If you know your subject you will be less nervous, more enthusiastic and more self assured. If you are not completely familiar with your subject how can you persuade your audience to be interested? If you are not enthusiastic, how can you expect them to be?

Opening and closing

'Tell them what you're going to tell them, tell them, then tell them what you told them'. Everyone who has done any instructing will have heard that maxim. But don't knock it, it works.

Opening

The opening of your presentation needs to:

- get the attention of your audience
- tell them briefly what you are going to talk about
- give them an indication of what you want from them

An opening statement that really grabs the attention of the audience can get your presentation off to a flying start. Of course, you have to be able to follow up the brilliant start with good material, but grabbing the attention of your audience is the first problem.

Having done that, tell them briefly what you are going to talk about, how long it will take and whether or not they will have the opportunity to ask questions.

In many meetings, you are making a presentation in order to gain a specific outcome, i.e. you want budget approval for research into a new processing method; or you want to find out how many departments would support the introduction of an electronic mail system; or you want to bring forward by three months the release of phase III of the advertising schedule. So in your introduction tell your audience briefly what outcome you are expecting from the presentation.

> The personnel manager of a public company wanted to install a com-
> pany-wide system of management development training. He spoke at
> the main board meeting and got one of the regional MDs to explain
> what she had been doing. The aim was to use the regional MD as an
> example of what could be done. Unfortunately, the personnel manager
> didn't explain that he wanted the meeting to develop its own training
> plans rather than slavishly copying the regional MD. The regional
> MD's plans were most appropriate to her own region and less relevant

to most of the others present, who wasted no time in saying so. They also resented having the regional MD's ideas foisted upon them – and they said that strongly too. Result: bad tempered meeting with little progress. All because the personnel manager didn't explain what he wanted from the participants.

Closing

The best presentations end with a bang, not a whimper. All too many presenters, having said their piece, don't know how to finish off and peter out pathetically, with a murmured 'Thank you'.

The ending of a presentation is perhaps the most important part of it because that is the part people will go away remembering. Because of this, it is worth putting some effort into ensuring that you do not fade away at the end of your presentation but end on a positive and upbeat note.

Finish your presentation with a short summary of the main points covered, emphasising the positive aspects if necessary. Then, if at all possible, link your ending back to the beginning. Remind people of the brilliant start you made by finishing just as brilliantly. If you want or need an outcome from your presentation, this is the place to be *very clear* about what you want from your listeners.

PRACTISE

If you are learning to play the violin or make leak-proof plumbing joints, the more you practise the better you will become. Some people may have more of a talent for presenting, playing the violin or plumbing than others, but even virtuosi violinists and master plumbers only got there because they practised. The same principle applies to making presentations. The more often you do it the better you will become. Maybe you have heard some really awful speakers who are long-standing presenters? Don't forget, they have been practising their bad habits for a long time in order to become as awful as they are.

Rehearsal

The amount of rehearsal you need will depend on your own confidence, the complexity of the subject, and the type of audience you will be speaking to. Rehearse enough to know your presentation thoroughly, but don't overdo it and risk sounding stale. Beware of learning speeches parrot-fashion – the more you depend on your memory, the harder it will be to think on your feet. An unexpected question, even a cough, could throw you out of gear and you may find it difficult to resume.

Timing

One of the most crucial things to get right is the timing. If you are given a five minute slot at a team meeting, or a 20 minute slot at a conference, you need to be able to tailor your material to fit that slot. It is embarrassing to finish too early and frustrating for other people if you take too long. The cumulative effect of a number of speakers over-running their timeslot even slightly can mean a very long and tedious meeting.

When you rehearse your timing you may find that you over-run or under-run at first, so you need to adjust the amount of material you include or the speed of your delivery. Remember to allow time for summing up, questions and for the fact that you may well speak more quickly to the mirror than to a real live audience.

Be yourself

Present the material in terms that make sense to you. You will have your own individual style and approach to the subject, so make the most of your raw material in your own style rather than trying to imitate someone else's too closely. By being yourself you will let your own natural style develop and you will learn through experience how to deal with different subjects and different audiences.

PRESENTATION TECHNIQUES

Attitude

It may seem an odd thing to include 'attitude' as a technique. Yet your attitude to your subject and your audience can make all the difference between the success and failure of your presentation.

Have you ever been with someone who had a fit of laughing, and found that you couldn't help joining in? Just as laughter can be infectious, so can enthusiasm. If you really believe in what you are saying and enjoy it, you have a good chance of instilling the same feeling in the listener. If, however, you are talking about something which doesn't interest you, your audience will notice immediately.

Enthusiasm, sincerity and commitment are obvious not just in what you say, but most of all in the tone of voice and other non-verbal signals you use. If you are genuinely enthusiastic, that will show through if you allow it to, so don't dampen your approach because you are afraid it won't be appropriate. If your audience can see and hear that you are sincere and keen about what you are saying they will respect your point of view even if they don't agree with it.

Build rapport

It is much easier to build rapport with one person than with 10 or 50, so when you are talking to a meeting of 12 people you would not expect the same level of rapport as if you were talking to them one at a time. However, it is possible to build some rapport even with a large group. To do this you need to make them feel that you are talking *to* them, not *at* them.

Earlier on, we talked about the importance of knowing some-thing about your audience so that you could make the subject matter appropriate for them. Talking to the audience at the right level is one important way of building rapport – after all it's difficult to feel rapport with someone who is patronising you or baffling you completely.

Another way is eye contact. While it is not possible to maintain eye contact with each and every member of your audience, you can look around the group, making sure that you turn towards each section and give your attention to them. Don't let your eyes wander from floor to ceiling or from side to side of the room without glancing at people's faces and their eyes in particular. People like to feel that you are talking especially to them and eye contact rein-forces that feeling. It also helps you to tell whether they are follow-ing you and are interested.

Avoid two temptations. One is to look at the most influential person present and address him or her exclusively. By doing this you are excluding the others, which is not only impolite but will not make them feel as much sympathy for what you are saying.

The other temptation is to look at something more comforting than your audience. It might be one friendly face (which incidentally will begin to feel embarrassed if you look at and talk to that person all the time). It might be your notes, which will make you appear uncertain and unenthusiastic. It has been known for presenters to use their flip chart as a comfort blanket. Having shown their diagram or bullet list to the group, they then talk earnestly to the flip chart, with their backs turned to the audience.

Appearance

Appearance can be used to say something about yourself. Most people use their appearance, consciously or unconsciously, to send messages about themselves. If you are at home relaxing for the weekend, you will dress differently than you do when meeting an important client.

Our appearance can have an important effect on our self-confidence. If we feel we are dressed for the part, then we tend to feel more comfortable playing that part. Sometimes, the dressing up can be the thing that gives us the confidence to play the part. For many men whose uniform at work is a suit, dressing up may be less obvious, though still important as the examples below show. Women perhaps need to be most aware of the effect that dress can have on the impression they want to create.

When 'power dressing' was first identified, it was easy to send the signals you wanted because everyone knew what the rules were – important people wore smart, formal clothes and less important people wore more casual clothes. Now that the rules have become blurred it may take a little more research to gauge what style of dress sends the right message to the people who are going to be at your meeting.

A colleague of ours went to address the main board of a major financial services company during a weekend workshop. Without checking and because he thought of these people as bankers, he went in his most formal suit. He was met by the MD in sweatshirt and jeans. Our colleague felt overdressed and embarrassed. He said it took him much longer than usual to establish rapport with his audience.

On the other hand, sometimes you have to suffer for your art.

Another colleague was consulting the chief executive of the state petroleum company of a country in the tropics. Although many of the staff wore short-sleeved open-neck shirts and shorts, he learned that the chief executive was a formal person and expected full business rig. So that was what he got, even though there was no air-conditioning and the temperature was over 100°F.

Voice
The way you use your voice is crucial.

Volume
The volume at which you speak will depend on the size of the group and the size of the room. Obviously if you are speaking to a group of people, your voice needs to be louder than if you were speaking to an individual. Human bodies absorb sound and some of the group are going to be further away from you than if you were having a conversation on a one-to-one basis.

If you are speaking to a large group, and 'need to be heard at the back', speak in a voice that sounds a bit too loud to you – this will be just right for your audience. You don't have to shout. Shouting takes more breath, wears out your throat and means that you are unable to use tone and pitch effectively.

Tone
Few things are more boring than speaking in a monotone. Use the tone of your voice for emphasis, to show your enthusiasm. Many people have naturally musical voices and use tone a lot to emphasise what they say, whereas others have to work at it a little more.

Pitch
Fact one: the pitch of our voices tends to rise as we become nervous. Fact two: most people find low-pitched voices more attractive than high-pitched ones. This is rather hard on those who become nervous when faced with making a presentation. The trick? Start your presentation by using a slightly deeper voice than would be normal for you. You will find if you do so that your voice comes out at its normal pitch.

You can vary the pitch of your voice to make an impact during your presentation. A key point emphasised by a change in pitch, higher or lower, can have a dramatic effect.

One particular danger when making presentations is that some people allow the pitch of their voice to drop at the end of sentences and particularly at the end of the talk. It's usually a sign of relief, but it has a very bad effect. Dropping the pitch at the end of a sentence makes the presentation sound very boring, even if the subject matter isn't. Dropping the pitch at the end of the talk means ending with a whimper. Watch out for this. If you do practise, use a tape recorder. Suffer the agony of hearing your own voice and listen in particular to see if your voice drops away at the end of sentences, paragraphs or the conclusion.

Speed

When you are making a presentation you should speak more slowly than normal (though not so slowly as to make everyone anticipate what your next word or sentence is likely to be).

Unfortunately, nervousness often has the effect of making you speak more quickly than normal. So you'll need to slow down your delivery deliberately. One reason for speaking fairly slowly is that your audience may well be unfamiliar with the subject and need more time to absorb it than you think.

Use pauses. When you come to the end of a sentence do not immediately rush on to the next; pause, breathe, then speak again. Pauses give time for people to absorb what you have just said. They are also extremely useful for emphasis. Any great speakers, or speeches, real or fictional, all use pauses to give meaning and emphasis to their words. Imagine Julius Caesar saying 'I came, I saw, I conquered' without any pauses between the words.

Breathing

Breathing can often get you in a tangle when making a presentation. Someone who has clear memories of reading aloud in church as a child remembers finding halfway through the reading that she had breathed in but omitted to breathe out, so that she had to stop for a great exhalation of breath before being able to continue. This is not an uncommon event as you do breathe more quickly and less deeply when nervous. Quick and shallow breathing can make you feel so full up with air that you can hardly speak.

The answer is to breathe deeply from the diaphram, making sure that the whole front of your torso, down as far as your waist, is moving in and out as you breathe. Don't forget to breathe out. Remember that pauses are an extremely effective way of adding emphasis and you can use the pause to breathe.

If you want to study voice, tone, pitch, speed and breathing, pay close attention to radio announcers and newsreaders. They are the professionals and they know that without any visual assistance they have to convey the content of a message as well as hold the attention of the audience. This is particularly hard for relatively standardised information such as shipping forecasts and stock exchange numbers. Notice how good intonation, pitch and speed can make even these difficult subjects easier to listen to.

Using your face and body

Face

Your face is what most of your audience will be looking at. If you look particularly grim, miserable or bored, then they will observe that and take their cue from it. If you have a serious message to put across you will probably look serious. If at all possible, let your feelings about the information you are presenting show in your face. A deadpan expression is perhaps the most offputting of all.

Try to remember to smile at the group. It brings a warmth to the presentation and helps to create a friendly atmosphere. Even if the subject matter you are presenting is bad news, there is no reason why you should not smile at your audience before you start to speak. After all, they themselves are not the bad news (usually). You can smile at them to help establish rapport, then when starting your presentation, use your words and your face to put over the sense of the message whether it is serious, exciting, alarming or whatever.

Body

There are a few very basic points here:

- You look and sound as if you have more authority when you stand up than when you sit down. Sales trainers teach salespeople to make telephone cold calls standing up so that they feel and sound more powerful.
- Hold your head up, not nose down in the notes. Your voice will be clearer and stronger and you will be able to look at your audience. Opera singers know that an upright posture produces a better, stronger sound.
- Don't fiddle. The key jangler and spectacles-polisher are spectres that stalk the corridors of meeting rooms.
- Don't prowl. Move by all means, but don't try to wear a path in the carpet with the beat of your feet. It can make the audience feel as if they are watching a slow motion tennis match.

Words

The words you use are very important. Say what you want to say in clear simple English, without trying to impress your audience with the extent of your vocabulary. Spoken English is very different from most written English, so if you have written a lot of your presentation, think about how it will sound when it is spoken. As a general rule of thumb, we use shorter, simpler words and sentence constructions when we speak. Look at these examples and think about which would go down better when spoken to a group of people.

'I regret to inform you that owing to a slight indisposition, Charles Joseph will be unable to be present this evening.'

'I'm sorry to tell you that Charles Joseph won't be able to come this evening because he is not well.'

'The new site will be formally opened by the Member of Parliament who will then proceed to an inspection of the production line.'

'The MP will formally open the new site then go on to inspect the production line.'

Paint pictures with your words. Visual aids are important but you can also use words to create vivid pictures in the minds of your audience. If you want to do this, use words such as 'Imagine . . .', 'Picture . . .' 'In your mind's eye . . .'

Link complex issues to simple ideas that the group can relate to. Illustrate them with examples that your audience will understand. A very simple example would be explaining to your audience that Concorde flies at Mach 2 – i.e. approximately 1,400 miles per hour. This is so fast that it does not mean much to most people. If you put it in everyday terms, it is one mile every four seconds, or 60 miles in less than the time it takes you to boil an egg. Most people have boiled an egg and have a clear concept of 60 miles. Even better if you say from here to (a well known local place) . . . in the time it takes, etc.

As we discussed earlier, don't use jargon unless you know that your audience will understand it. The trouble is that we become so familiar with the jargon of everyday life that we cease to think of it as jargon. Do use active rather than passive verbs. Look at the following examples and decide which would have more impact:

- 'We decided to implement the new system straight away'
- 'It was decided that the new plan should be implemented straight away'
- 'The staff worked overtime every day'
- 'Overtime was worked by staff every day'

Examples a) and c) use active language and have much more impact than examples b) and d).

Notes

Memory is an unreliable tool, so don't try to remember what you want to say without any form of notes. The notes you use will depend on your own personal preference. Some people like to use index cards with a heading plus sub-headings on each card, others like to use A4 paper with headings and sub-headings spread out over the page. Sometimes it depends on your surroundings, and whether you are standing at the front of an audience or sitting around the table in a much smaller group.

Whatever system you use for your notes, make sure they are *notes* and not a written script. A written script is fine as a rehearsal tool, but by the time you come to present it, you should know your subject well enough to talk about it without having your head in your papers.

Small chunks

The secret is small chunks. Break your subject matter down into headings and sub-headings, so that you can talk about each small chunk with confidence and without needing to read anything. Then all you need to do is write down your headings and your small chunk sub-headings in largish, bold letters so that you can see them at a glance. Your talk will appear much more natural and spontaneous than if you were reading from a script.

Visual Aids

Many people think of visual aids only in training rooms or when giving a presentation to a large audience. Simple visual aids can also be of huge value when presenting material to a very small audience – we take in far more information through our eyes than through our ears.

Visual aids should be an aid to communication. To do this they need to be relevant, simple and bold. They also need to be large enough to enable everyone in the room to see them clearly. A visual aid is not much good if it isn't visible! A skilfully used visual aid can arouse interest, show things that are difficult to describe verbally, focus interest and regain lost attention.

So what sort of visual aids should you use? The visual aids most commonly used in meetings are flip charts and overhead projectors, with occasional use of slides. All this equipment is fairly easily portable. Blackboards, whiteboards and films are more often used in training rooms than in meetings. Perhaps the best sort of visual aid is a real object that illustrates a point you are trying to make.

Flip charts and overhead projector transparencies can be pre-prepared. If you do this make sure that you only put a few points on each chart or transparency, as a cluttered, full display is more likely to confuse than aid understanding. The head of one training organisation used to be the despair of his staff as he would insist on having overhead projector transparencies made up of typed A4 pages which he would then display to an audience of 100 or more. They were totally impossible to read for anyone sitting further back than the third row.

If you use visual aids make clear reference to them in your own notes. Don't just write 'production forecast'; write 'flip chart (or 'overhead') to show forecast for line A production next year'.

If you want to write as you talk, the flip chart is your best friend. The same rules apply as for pre-prepared charts – don't try to squeeze too much on. Flip charts are often used at meetings for events such as brainstorms and they can be a very valuable way of ensuring that ideas and decisions don't get lost.

Questions

Always leave time for questions to allow people to clarify points they don't understand, or to ask for more information on the material you presented. You may wish to allow people to ask questions as you go along, or to keep questions to the end – it will probably depend on the formality and size of the meeting. Whichever way you choose to deal with questions, make sure that you tell your audience at the beginning of the presentation, so that they know whether to butt in, or to make a note and hang on to their question until the end.

If you are really familiar with your subject, then answering questions may be the easiest bit of the whole presentation. If you don't know your stuff, it may be the sticky part. Here are a few pointers for answering questions to help you keep your credibility and integrity as a presenter:

1. Treat all questions as real and answer them as straightforwardly as possible. You may think that someone is asking a particular question in order to wind you up, but maybe their mind wandered during that part of your presentation, and they really *do* want to know what you said about spring washers.

2. Don't treat questioners as stupid or frivolous. The answer may be obvious to you, but then you know an awful lot about the subject.

3. Don't avoid the question by talking about something else. The

questioner and the rest of the audience are unlikely to be fooled or satisfied by this trick.

4. If you are asked a question to which you don't know the answer, be honest about it. If you are presenting material to a regular meeting you can offer to find out the information for next time. If it is a one-off affair you may need to refer people to the place or book where they are most likely to find the answer. If you do decide to flannel your way out of the situation and get the wrong answer, Murphy's law dictates that there is bound to be somebody in your audience who knows the right one. Once you have lost credibility you may never regain it.

SUMMARY

You may well be asked to make a presentation to a meeting at one time or another. The meeting could be large and frightening or small and cosy. Whatever the size and type of meeting you address, your presentation can be made more effective by the planning, preparation, and practise you put in beforehand and the presentation techniques you use on the day.

Planning involves doing some research about the audience; who they are, why they are there, what they expect from you. Preparation involves dealing with the material you are going to present; collecting the information, putting it in a logical order, deciding how to open and close, and most of all, ensuring that you know exactly what you are talking about. Practise involves rehearsal and getting the timing right, plus ensuring that you sound like yourself, not a stuffed windbag.

The presentation techniques you use can make a great deal of difference to how well your material is received. Demonstrate your enthusiasm and sincerity in the way you put across your point. Build rapport with your audience by talking at their level, looking at them, and by ensuring that your personal appearance fits in with their expectations. Use volume, tone, pitch and pauses to make your voice expressive and interesting. Be nice to your audience –

smile at them and they will think you more pleasant than if you scowl at them.

Use simple words and active verbs to make your presentation easy to listen to; use words to paint pictures and give examples to make your points come alive. Visual aids add interest and can make it easier to explain complex information. Make it clear to the other people at the meeting whether you expect to answer questions as you go along or at the end. When you do answer questions, treat them straightforwardly, but do not flannel if you are not sure of the answer.

Use the following checklist to ensure that you do as much as you can to make your presentations effective.

CHECKLIST – PRESENTATION SKILLS

PLANNING
1. Do you know as much as you need about your audience?
   a) Who are they?
   b) How much background knowledge do they have?
   c) Are they hostile or friendly?
   d) What are their strengths and weaknesses?
   e) Why are they there?
   f) What are their expectations?
   g) What are their initial perceptions of you?
2. What impression do you want to create?
3. What approach are you going to use?

PREPARATION
4. Have you thoroughly prepared your material?
   a) Collected all necessary information?
   b) Put it into a logical order?
   c) Is it the right length?
   d) Are you thoroughly familiar with it?
5. Have you prepared a punchy opening?
   a) Will it grab the attention of the audience?
   b) Does it give them a clear idea what to expect?
   c) Does it tell them what you want from them?
6. Will you finish on a positive, upbeat note? Have you
   a) summarised all main points?
   b) reminded the audience of the outcome you expect?

PRACTICE
7. Have you rehearsed your presentation?
8. Have you checked that it runs for the right amount of time?

PRESENTATION TECHNIQUES
9. Are you enthusiastic about, or at least committed to, your subject matter?
10. How are you going to build rapport with your audience?
    a) Talk to them at the right level?

    b) Make eye contact with them?

    c) Checked that your clothes will fit the occasion?

11. Are you using your voice effectively?

    a) Is it loud enough?

    b) Do you add interest and impact with tone and pitch?

    c) Do you talk at the right speed and use pauses for effect?

    d) Are you breathing from the diaphragm?

12. Do you remember to smile at your audience?

13. Are you using your body to help create the right impression?

    a) Holding head up?

    b) No prowling?

    c) No fiddling?

14. Have you got the language right?

    a) Is the vocabulary clear and simple?

    b) Have you eliminated unnecessary jargon?

    c) Are your verbs active not passive?

    d) Can you use words to paint pictures for the audience?

    e) Have you given as many examples as possible?

15. What do your notes look like?

    a) Are they in note form rather than a written script?

    b) Do they use sub-headings to remind you of small chunks of information?

16. Are you going to use visual aids?

    a) Are they large and bold?

    b) Will they make an impact?

    c) Have you made clear reference to them in your notes?

17. When will you deal with questions from the audience – during the presentation or at the end?

12 . Politics and Power

A senior local government official is talking about a council meeting at which the majority political party and the opposition party are present.

> 'Of course the only people who didn't actually know what the outcome would be were the most junior officers. Both political parties had got together beforehand to work out their strategy. The ruling party would cope with dissidents by doing trade-offs – for instance, "I'll vote down that planning permission if you let through money on my proposal". The opposition party will have put their heads together in order to work out when they would make a fuss, when they would threaten to walk out, when they would shout and so on. We senior officers had been called in by the ruling party beforehand to brief them on the true state of affairs, we knew exactly what would then be happening.'

The official who was speaking came from a local authority in England. It sounds extreme but it probably happens every day in most parts of most political systems. It nods its head at democracy, since the public is allowed to be present during the meeting, but it gives a false impression that the meeting is called to *decide* something. All the important decisions are kept as far away from that meeting as possible.

In this chapter we shall be looking at the politics (non-party) which go on in meetings within all organisations, whether they are a multi-million turnover conglomerate, or the local Gilbert and Sullivan society. Politics are closely related to power, and to people's perceptions of that power and how it can be used or abused.

Some people are better at political activity than others; some use politics for their own ends, others use politics for the organisation's ends. The hidden agendas brought to meetings by many of the people who attend them are a manifestation of how the participants feel they need to manipulate events in order to get their own way. The main aspects of the use of politics and power dealt with in this chapter are:

- lobbying
- different kinds of power
- how you use power
- how politically skilled you are
- hidden agendas
- personal weaknesses
- using an appropriate style
- meetings as theatre
- how to wreck meetings

LOBBYING

The technique of keeping all the important business away from the meeting is one which will be familiar to most managers. It arises from the expectation on the part of the proposers of an idea that they will be opposed. The easiest way to deal with that opposition is not to fight it out directly, but to take whatever precautions are possible beforehand, in order to maximise the chance of getting the proposal through. A quote from a senior manager in one of Britain's larger industries:

> 'Of course anything significant was decided before we got to the main board meeting. The board was there to inform lesser beings what was going on, and to make sure that no one felt they hadn't had the chance to voice their views. However, if the subject was important enough we would have spent a lot of hours lobbying and generally smoothing the path so that the idea would be actioned without serious opposition'.

So in these circumstances what are meetings really about? Clearly in many cases there is a component of display or public visibility that needs to be acknowledged. An issue needs to be seen to be debated, or at least raised, in public. There will be public minutes or some other public record of the meeting, and occasionally not everything is fixed beforehand and a decision gets changed or modified beyond the expectations of the proposer.

In some cases meetings are called to spread the risk by making everyone responsible, and therefore to blame, if something goes wrong. Meetings can also be used to signal that a person has power and status. Not everyone has the power to call a meeting.

What can be done in these situations since a huge amount of time is wasted in meetings that are often little more than the acting out of a pre-prepared script? Opinions differ since it depends on whether you feel the system overall should be completely revised or whether your aim is to manipulate the existing system to your own advantage. The first option is really beyond the scope of a book such as this, but in order to find your way through the maze of politics (with a big and a small p) we would like to look at some of the ways of coping with a highly political system of meetings.

USES OF POWER

Power is a fact of life. We all have various kinds of power and we all respond to the use of power by other people. We use our power as consumers when we return faulty goods, our power as parents to give or withhold pocket money, our power as the only one who knows how to use a piece of software to get respect from our colleagues.

It is therefore important to know what kinds of power are available to be used for and against you.

KINDS OF POWER

John French and Bertram Raven in a classic study identified five main bases of power:

Reward power
A person has reward power if they can reward others for compliance with their instructions. In an organisation these rewards

might include promotion, monetary rewards, involvement with interesting work, increased responsibilities, new equipment or support for some project. It might also simply mean giving public praise. The user of reward power can also make promises about rewards which he or she can offer in future.

Coercive power

Coercive power is almost the reverse of reward power. It is the ability to punish. Kinds of punishment may include withdrawal of favours, humiliation, withdrawal of friendship or emotional support, reallocation of work to less desirable tasks, reduction of promotion or promotion chances, delayed pay rises, etc.

In both the above cases it is the receiver's perception of reward or coercion that gives the power its strength. In practice, the individual wielding the power may not really have very much direct influence. But it is the perception of that influence that counts, and this can, of course, be considerably greater than the reality. For instance, if you think that a person has some influence on whether or not you will be promoted, then that is quite enough for you to perceive that he has coercive power, since you recognise the possibility that he could use his influence against you.

Referent power

This is also called power through charisma and it is where people will follow an individual because they believe that that person has characteristics that are desirable and should be copied. People therefore identify themselves with that individual. It depends directly on the personality of the individual. With a man like Ghandi, his lack of other forms of power (his powerless-ness) was itself attractive to many of his followers. There is a link here between charismatic power and the use of the common vision style described in Chapter 10.

Legitimate power

In many organisations there is a hierarchy that gives people power simply by virtue of their position. Generals have more power than privates. Position power can sometimes rest purely on the person's title. Think of the respect that is normally given to people wearing a white coat with the title 'doctor'. It is also tempting for others to expect power and ability beyond the person's title. The chairman of the company is not necessarily the best person to chair a meeting.

Expert power

We live in an age of experts. If we believe someone has specific and specialist knowledge that is relevant to the task being considered, then we consider them to have expert power.

Expert power can be very potent, expecially in technical areas that are mysterious to most people. Computers, statistics and tax law seem to be three commonly quoted areas of mystery in the business world. On the other hand, it is much harder to have expert power in areas like personnel because it is about people and everyone feels they know something about people.

The problem is which expert do you believe? In so many cases, expertise gained a few years ago is now inappropriate and may be downright wrong for dealing with the present situation. People who believe themselves to be experts, even when they are not, are a problem in any meeting. So incidentally are the true experts who are too quiet about their expertise. We dealt with some of those issues in the Belbin behaviours described in Chapter 7.

In addition to the five types of power identified above there is a sixth type called connection power.

Connection power

This is particularly significant in the political kinds of meetings that we have been discussing. It has to do with a person's connections, who she knows and what she knows about them that makes her important. It was said of J Edgar Hoover that he had a private file on every politician in Washington. Because of the fear of what was *perceived* to be in those files, Hoover was never sacked from office, even though in his extraordinary career he had major disagreements with almost every American leader. Everyone understood him to be a very powerful man because of what he knew and who he knew.

In slightly less dramatic form, many meetings can be strongly

225

influenced by people exercising previous social and emotional ties. It used to be said of the City of London that it was not what you knew, it was who you knew, and particularly who you had been to school with. And who has not appreciated, at some time in their career, the value of being on good terms with the managing director's secretary as a crucial way of getting a late item onto a board agenda?

HOW YOU USE POWER

Before we go on you may like to take a few moments to jot down the major meetings you attend, and to assess how you use power at those meetings. Are you a person who relies mainly on expertise, or do you rely on being on good terms socially with the key people at the meeting? Perhaps, instead, you have the ability to reward, or to punish? Which of these do you use? Bear in mind that you can use coercive or reward power upwards as well as downwards. If you have the ability to make life tougher or easier for your boss, then you can use coercive or reward power upwards too.

Having looked at your own use of power this might be a good moment to think about a recent meeting you attended, and consider how some of the other main contributors were operating. What kinds of power were they exercising? And how appropriate were those power types to the situation? Here is an example from a local authority. The politics involved in this example could have occurred in any business meeting and are not related to the political nature of local government.

> 'There were something like 16 or 17 chief officers and when we all met it was usually clear that some deals had been done in advance. There were about four of us who were the main budget holders and spenders – social services, education, etc. We had most of the money and most of the employees and therefore we agreed on the way something should be done; the other much smaller departments really had no choice but to get on with it. Even if a decision makes life very difficult, when you are a director of a department with only 15 or 16 staff and a trivial budget, there really isn't much you can do against the millions being spent by one of the larger employing departments. Your only course of action

would be to get alongside one of the big players before the meeting and influence them down a path that met their needs, but also met your own department's needs.'

Obviously successful influencing at a meeting in these circumstances starts before the meeting takes place. It is important to anticipate a trend, and if you are a small player, to align yourself with one of the larger players and influence them directly. Understanding needs is therefore a key skill in working effectively in these kinds of meetings.

HOW POLITICALLY SKILLED ARE YOU?

How good are you at reading the politics of a situation, and how do you use your skills to your own or your organisation's benefit? We have found that the four types of political orientation that Baddeley and James have identified are a useful guide to appreciating how you are likely to operate in a meeting that is clearly political. There are two scales:

1. politically skilled — politically unskilled
2. concerned with — concerned with
   own needs organisation's needs

The donkey
The inept donkey is politically unskilled and concerned with his own needs. He has not got the sensitivity to anticipate who are the major power players and therefore tends to be unaligned and unable to influence the direction of the discussion. The donkey is the sort of person whose attempts to manipulate are as subtle as a half-brick. Everyone can see the donkey trying to get his own way, and for most people it is easy to anticipate and sidestep. The donkey tends to resort to stubbornness and blocking behaviour whenever things don't go his way. People regard the inept donkey as something to be worked around.

The sheep
The innocent sheep is politically unskilled, and is concerned with the needs of the organisation. She tends to be pushed and pulled by

the greater forces that are in play. She certainly has very little influence and is disregarded by those who are exerting power. Many sheep are unaware of the subtleties of play going on around them. Others may understand that political manoeuvres are taking place, but decide not to get involved.

The fox
The clever fox is politically skilled and is concerned with his own needs. These people are always perceived to have an ulterior motive. They are masters of the hidden agenda. No one quite trusts them, but everyone slightly fears them since they are difficult to read and rarely reveal their entire game plan.

The owl
Finally, the wise owl is concerned about the organisation but also has a high level of political skill. Wise owls are recognised for their understanding of the geography of power, and are well respected by those who wish to use power for their own ends. They can be very influential, but tend to use that influence for the good of the organisation.

These divisions are of course very crude, but you might like to consider which of the four categories you spend most of your time in at each of the key meetings you chair and attend as a contributor. The other important question to ask yourself is how you treat the sheep, donkeys, foxes and owls around the meeting table.

THE HIDDEN AGENDA

In Chapters 3 and 5 we put great emphasis on the need to clarify and communicate the agenda of a meeting. If the declared purpose of a meeting is well understood, then there is a good chance that the meeting will produce useful and effective outcomes. However, in some cases members of the meeting may declare their purpose to be one thing, while actually having a different, additional or even alternative purpose in mind. This broad range of concealed hopes and feelings are referred to as the hidden agenda.

Hidden agendas generally arise from one of two emotions. The first is fear that the result of the meeting may lead to some unpleasant consequence. If the other participants cannot be persuaded to change their minds, then the only way to prevent the unpleasant consequence is to undermine the meeting itself. The second emotion is to do with subterfuge and deception. It occurs when people believe that if their true aims were revealed, it would produce considerable opposition, or would reveal some secret that would make the furtherance of these aims difficult or impossible.

Fear

Sir Graham Day has, in his time, taken over and turned around British Shipbuilders, the Rover car group, and, at the time of writing, is chairman of British Aerospace. He says that when he takes over an organisation he makes as thorough an assessment as he can of the business and the top management team. Then he decides who he wants to keep and who he wants to let go. He has a night of the long knives. But he says he does it once and once only. When certain top managers have gone, he can then assure the rest of the workforce from top to bottom that there will be no further cuts initiated by him in the turnaround of the business. Sir Graham argues that fear is a very defeating emotion to have rampant in an organisation. While in the short-term fear produces instant obedience and action, in the long-term it creates defensive and avoiding actions that will not help build the business.

Identifying and dealing with the hidden agenda caused by fear usually starts with the suspicion that something is not right. This example was seen by us recently:

> A meeting was called by three divisions to launch a project in which two managers from each division would be involved. The divisions were finance, new business development and personnel. The declared aim of the project suited the needs of the three divisions and was seen as a high status project in the company. It therefore also appeared to be quite an attractive prospect for each of the individual participants. On the surface everyone was very positive and supportive. However, as the first meeting went on, it became clear that one member of the finance division was showing a clear pattern of opposition to the suggestions

and ideas put forward by the two participants from the new business division. This systematic blocking and lack of co-operation emerged over a period of about an hour or more. Whichever way the new business division people turned, the finance man would find a reason for opposing their approach. It seemed as if he were trying to exclude them from involvement in one part of the project. After the meeting, in private conversation, the finance man was asked what the problem was.

At first he denied that there was a problem, but with further encouragement and assurance of confidentiality he then explained that he felt his particular skills and expertise in financial analysis were being threatened by the people from new business. He had been known in the company as the sole user of this particular set of skills, and now these upstarts were invading his territory and might even show him up as less competent than he believed he was. With yet more encouragement, it also turned out that he had applied for the same job in new business now held by one of the members of the project meeting. Our man was worried that having beaten him for the same job, his 'colleague' would now try to prove her superiority in financial analysis as well.

Some shuttle diplomacy followed, resulting in a second meeting where both parties agreed to talk about their true concerns and explained what they felt they could gain or lose by the project going ahead. It turned out that all three divisions, and all six people, could lose something if the others chose to be difficult, but happily all three divisions and all six people could gain something if they worked positively together and trusted each other. It wasn't easy, and it took some time, but eventually all six managed to achieve their objective of working together positively.

Without bringing that hidden agenda to the surface, several meetings would have foundered because of the finance man's need to stall some of the decisions on the project for as long as possible. When you don't believe you can trust the other members of the meeting you cannot reveal your worst fears to them, particularly if you believe they may be competing with you.

Although it is probably the chairperson who is in the best position to spot a hidden agenda, any member of a meeting can raise the possibility that the participants are not talking about the most important issues. Bear in mind that the hunt for a hidden agenda can easily be perceived as a witch hunt, and needs to be conducted with the utmost tact. This is especially true if it is the chairperson who is suspected of bringing the hidden agendas.

Subterfuge

When fear is causing the hidden agenda, the removal of the fear or the cause of the fear will usually remove the hidden agenda. When subterfuge, (i.e. secrecy aimed at gaining more for one person in the meeting than for the others) is the main motivation it is far harder to bring it out in the open. The whole point of subterfuge is that it is not discovered, and people will sometimes go to considerable lengths to avoid detection.

In his book *Getting Past No*, William Ury suggests that there are three broad tactics for subterfuge. The first is acting as a stone wall and refusing to budge. The person will argue that he has no choice but to do what he has to do. There will be much delay, many offers to get back to you which don't happen, and anything that you suggest is generally met with a refusal. The second kind of tactic is attack. The people who use this tactic attack everything. They attack you, they attack your status, they generally insult and bully you, hoping that they will push you by force of noise until they get their way. The third tactic is to use tricks and games, to try and trick you into giving some concession that you would not otherwise do.

Ury argues that the best way to neutralise any tactic is to recognise it. And to make that recognition clear to the person who is using the tactic. The point is that because you are showing that you know this tactic too, your opponent will cease to use it on you.

Paranoia rules

There is a difficult balance between being on the look-out for tricks and being suspicious of everyone. If you end up being overly suspicious, you bring your own hidden agendas to every meeting. If you are not alert enough you join the ranks of the innocent sheep or the inept donkeys.

Recognising personal weaknesses

If you suspect some of the meeting participants of wanting to play dirty, then it is wise to recognise what weaknesses you have personally and what vulnerabilities your agenda items have. If you react badly to a style, a form of words, or even just a subject, then anyone who wishes to use that as a tactic will have a major advantage. All of us have these 'hot-buttons' and it is useful, if sometimes painful, to acknowledge them in ourselves.

> *At his weekly staff meeting Don regularly used to find himself driven up the wall by George, one of his more junior members of staff. 'It's the whining approach he always uses that really gets my goat', Don used to complain. So we got Don to talk about why George had this effect on him. The problem turned out to be that Don didn't realise that George was winding him up until Don was ready to blow. By then it was too late and he had already achieved lift-off and was pressed hard against the ceiling. What could be done? A signal was needed to let Don know that George was getting to him again.*
>
> *We arranged for one of Don's assistants, who sat near him at the meeting and who was clearly aware when Don was beginning to fume, to lean across the table and move one of the pencils in front of the note pad. Don recognised the signal immediately, inspected his internal temperature, and set off his own internal fire control system. It only took two meetings of conditioning practice for Don to recognise when he was getting too heated and then finding his own way to control the situation. From that point on George was never able to wind up Don again.*

Have you thought what your hot buttons might be in a meeting, and therefore what your vulnerabilities might be to a deliberate tactic of winding you up?

Using an appropriate style

The use of power in organisations makes things happen, and frequently gets the user noticed higher up the power ladder. Sometimes people forget that they are recognised for what they do, not for the way they use power.

A parable of power

> Alan was a very effective salesman, and was promoted to district manager. He was in charge of a group of sales people and other staff who were felt by the company to need a lot of kicking. Alan duly did the kicking and was rewarded by bonuses and commendations from his managers when they came down from head office to visit him. 'These people only understand tough management', said his boss on one of his visits. 'You show them who's in charge and keep producing the results.'
>
> Alan carried on in this way and was promoted to regional manager. Here he was in charge of some districts like the one he had come from and others that were better motivated. His abrasive style was less well appreciated in these other districts, but the region was still a long way from head office and overall he thrived and was much congratulated. One day The Great Call came: 'You are to be a regional director. Come to head office, work with my senior managers and join the board.'
>
> At board level, Alan was frequently in meetings with senior managers in the company. As an, albeit junior, member of the board he was now asked to make presentatiions and help decide strategy with managers who had a lot more experience than himself. Now bear in mind that Alan had spent some 15 years learning to be more and more abrasive with his staff, and generally being rewarded for his performance by the top management. Imagine his concern and surprise when he found himself being shunned by members of the board. What was wrong?

The simple answer is easy to appreciate when Alan is seen through the eyes of one of the existing divisional directors. 'It's all very well Alan being tough and abrasive when he is 300 miles away from here,' said the divisional director, 'but when the man is sitting next to you at a board meeting and still uses the same style on you and your colleagues, it is another matter.' Clearly Alan had failed to recognise that styles and techniques that are effective in the regions do not work in the board room. He had not changed his style simply because he thought he was being rewarded for being abrasive. Actually he was rewarded for being effective; it was his style that had to alter.

No two meetings can be treated in quite the same way. This is especially true when they are conducted at different levels by different kinds of people. A certain agreed style is used at each meeting. If like Alan you come from being successful with a style in one meeting to a different kind of meeting which has already created a style for itself, then be sure to pay some attention to the new style of the meeting you are joining.

MEETINGS AS THEATRE

'Sometimes at a full council meeting we would have what we called a "dirty-suits meeting". This was where members of the public would bring in eggs and flour to the public gallery and when they felt that the meeting was going the wrong way they would hurl these weapons at the speaker who offended them most. It didn't seem to matter whether the speaker was an elected politician, or a paid employee of the council. Those of us who used to have to go to these meetings on a regular basis always kept one suit aside to wear especially on these occasions. Dirty-suit meetings were quite fun really, as long as you were fast on your feet. It livened up what was often a very tedious event. However, it seemed to me that nothing of any value ever got decided at these meetings. They were set piece affairs where even the members of the public were taking part almost to a script. I wouldn't be surprised if some of the press representatives were able to write up the proceedings before they even saw them. Such was the predictability of what happened.'

Of course not all formal meetings involve the throwing of flour and eggs! But most formal meetings are in part a piece of public theatre. The public has a right to see decisions being taken and to acknowledge them. Outside the public political arena, in many organisations there are certain 'public' meetings which are designed to allow everyone in the organisation to feel as if they have taken part in discussions and decisions. Annual general meetings, share-holders, meetings, political meetings, proceedings of law courts – these are all examples of public meetings which to a greater or lesser extent are public theatre, and as part of their effectiveness need to make their proceedings open to people other than the direct participants.

If it is your job to attend and prepare for meetings with a theatrical component, then you must discover beforehand just what areas of procedure are already decided upon, and what leeway you have for influencing decisions and the operation of the meeting itself. Some very formalised meetings will have a very clear procedure and pattern. There is little point in expecting to operate outside that pattern. In these cases your only chance of influencing the outcome probably occurs sometime before the meeting itself. The lobbying approach which we mentioned at the beginning of the chapter is one that is widespread in influencing political outcomes. An annual general meeting is rarely troubled with the need to make original decisions. Almost everything has been organised and decided before-hand. The purpose of the meeting is to make public a series of statements to comply with the various legal requirements. Occasio-nally at shareholders' meetings questions from the floor have a significant impact, but for the most part the aim of a meeting organiser is to minimise the risk that something original and unique might happen. Compare that with the aim of someone organising a brain-storming meeting where the whole point is to generate some-thing unique and significant.

When a meeting has a major theatrical element be aware of your own performance and performance abilities. You may be expected to make a speech, which you should certainly have rehearsed. You may be expected to give an impromptu speech which you should also have rehearsed. It is usually possible to find someone who has been around for some while and understands the format of these meetings. Get him or her to give you advice on who does what and when, and the acceptable ways of presenting yourself. Formal meet-ings like those in the Houses of Parliament have extensive rules, regulations and codes of conduct. The same will apply to your shareholders' meetings and annual general meetings etc.

HOW TO WRECK MEETINGS

In this chapter we have looked at a whole range of possible ways
that meetings can go wrong, not by mistake but because someone
wanted to sabotage them. The wrecker's aim is to make the meeting
fail in order that it does not reach its likely conclusion. We should
add at this point that in our view many more meetings go wrong
because of cock-ups rather than conspiracies. While it is tempting to
believe that the world and its partner are plotting against you (see
paranoia earlier in this chapter), in meetings there is far more
incompetence than scheming.

That said, it is interesting to look at the ways that meetings *can* be
wrecked, so that those of you who wish to spot the tactic being
used can take these methods into account. The following list is by
no means exhaustive. So many of the words start with D that we
decided to call it the eleven D's to DEFEAT the meeting.

1. *Distract and disrupt.* Make a loud noise, talk about anything off
    the point, bring in subjects that are irrelevant, generally offer
    advice where it is not needed.
2. *Disagree.* Beg to differ, perhaps politely, but find ways of falling
    out with the main thrusts of everyone else's argument. Disagree
    on principle, disagree on fact, disagree with emotion.
3. *Defend and attack.* Related to number 2 is the use of defence and
    attack. Attack the people with whom you disagree and when
    they attack back defend even more vigorously. If you have the
    skill, introduce a hint of paranoia – that always seems to attract a
    decent crowd.
4. *Dominate.* Push your own points at the expense of others. If
    you have a powerful voice use it, if not wave your arms about,
    shuffle your papers, lean over and point at someone else's
    papers, but generally impose yourself on the meeting and ensure
    that no one else gets the same degree of time and space as you.
5. *Deviate.* Take things off the point and down alley-ways that are
    of interest to you. Refer back to previous meetings when you
    did not get your way and say why you feel you should be
    recompensed. Tell people that this situation reminds you of that

time back in '86 when you were Head of Public Relations for . . . and if your reminiscences don't work, try to get someone else reminiscing – preferably the oldest and most sentimental participant at the meeting.

6. *Divide.* Ensure that you have spoken to each of the different lobby groups before the meeting and said different things to each one. Try to set one lobby against another and then sit back and watch the fun develop.
7. *Deride.* Generally imply that one or other member of the meeting is not quite telling the honest truth. Lines such as, 'but we all know what can be done with statistics like these,' or 'but have we heard what *really* caused the production manager to want to buy the Mark IV modification?', will cause enough of a stir. The waverers at the meeting will sense that there is too much smoke for there not to be a fire somewhere. With incompetent chairing they will probably not notice that it is you who is providing most of the smoke.
8. *Dubious data.* This is a particulary effective way of ruining a meeting with scientists and engineers. They tend to like data and factual arguments. So give them data and facts, but don't worry about whether any of them are accurate or not. Wave statistics, graphs and charts around with gay abandon. When challenged, imply that these are early provisional results and that a more detailed survey is being carried out. That should delay things by several months.
9. *Damn with faint praise.* Often used in conjunction with no 7. If someone uses the 'dubious data technique' on you then apply a serious and knowing eye to ripping the data apart. Say that the data they are quoting comes from material that was of use 10 years ago but things have changed now. Doubt the credibility of the people who collected the data, doubt the sanity of the people who added it up.

In looking for D's we found two other d-words that are not well known but seem to apply very appropriately to certain kinds of wrecking techniques. The first is:

10. *Decrepitate*, which means to heat a substance until it admits a crackling sound. Otherwise known as baiting, or the corporate

wind-up, this is when marketing gets back at personnel for all those appraisals, or production gets back at finance for all those forms, or just about anyone gets back at corporate planning. How many of us have been at meetings where decrepitation has occurred on a massive scale?

The other word that attracted our attention was:

11. *De-flocculate*, which means to disperse, forming a suspension. One of the best ways of wrecking a meeting is to reach no further conclusion and leave everything in suspense. De-flocculation is a favourite method of appearing to act but actually deciding nothing.

These descriptions of wrecking techniques are meant as a guide to what *not* to do. But even if your intentions are truly dishonourable, we hope that by exposing them, we have weakened their impact. None of these techniques will work in meetings that are well chaired and have competent and knowledgeable contributors.

SUMMARY

Politics are found in meetings in most types of organisation. Preventing the important business reaching the meeting by lobbying or holding pre-meeting meetings are frequently used tactics.

Power is often associated with politics. The six kinds of power: *Reward, Referent, Coercive, Legitimate, Expert* and *Connection*, are all seen in meetings. The important thing is to know what power you and your colleagues are using, and whether it is appropriate.

Some people have political skill, others do not. The donkey, sheep, fox, owl model helps to decide your own and other people's relationship to the meeting.

People often bring hidden agendas to meetings. Can you spot a hidden agenda, and more important, can you do something about it? Removing the fear or identifying and neutralising the subterfuge are the ways of dealing with hidden agendas. Being aware of your own 'hot-buttons' is a way of guarding against weaknesses that others might use against you.

The appropriate and flexible use of power in the right circumstances will avoid the problem that Alan faced in our example. He did not appreciate that he was being rewarded for his results, not his particular use of power.

Meetings are often a kind of public theatre. If you are involved in this kind of meeting, then be sure you are clear on what formalities you need to respond to and what customs are practised.

Finally, use the 11–D list to anticipate meeting-wrecking techniques and use the checklist on the following page to check your own and other people's use of politics and power in your meetings.

CHECKLIST – POLITICS AND POWER

1. Where is the important business decided, in the meeting or elsewhere?
2. Who needs to be lobbied before the meeting starts?
3. What kind of power do you use at your meeting?
   a) Reward
   b) Coercive
   c) Referent
   d) Legitimate
   e) Expert
   f) Connection
4. What kinds of power do others use on you at meetings?
5. How politically skilled are you, and how do you use those skills? Are you a:
   a) donkey?
   b) sheep?
   c) fox?
   d) owl?
6. Do your meetings have hidden agendas?
7. Are they caused by fear, or by subterfuge?
8 What are you doing to identify the fear and neutralise the subterfuge?
9. Are you aware of your own 'hot-buttons', so that they cannot be used against you?
10. Are you keeping paranoia at bay by balancing your alertness for hidden agendas with trust for your colleagues?
11. How flexible is your use of power? Can you adapt your methods to the needs and style of the meeting?
12. What preparation have you done for a 'theatrical' meeting? Do you know what the formalities are, and what part you have to play in them?
13. Can you identify and stop a wrecker? If you use these wrecking tactics, could you find an approach that is more positive.

13. Follow-Up and Follow-Through

Manager 1: *'Whatever happened to the idea for an internal news-paper we discussed at the Divisional Heads Meeting six months ago?'*

Manager 2: *'I don't know, I suppose not enough people supported it after the meeting. Come to think of it, weren't we supposed to send in possible contributions and nominate one of our staff as the supplier of local gossip?'*

Manager 1: *'Yes, I believe we were. Still, no one followed it up and I got distracted by the Japanese competition. Pity, it was a good idea and would have been worth doing.'*

Although some meetings have a life of their own and exist in a timewarp that takes no account of the real world, most can only be judged by what happens after they have finished. If there has been no discernible change in any direction after a meeting, then what was the point of having it?

In the meeting referred to above, our two managers and their colleagues spent nearly an hour discussing the MD's idea of the introduction of an informal company newsletter. Unfortunately, the level of commitment was not clearly established and, worse, no one was given personal responsibility to follow the MD's idea through. As a result, the original enthusiasm was swamped by other more pressing work needs.

This chapter looks at what should happen *after* the meeting; at what steps should be taken to ensure that decisions and actions are carried out and information is communicated. Sometimes decisions can be implemented by one person who was present at the meeting and who can undertake the action alone. At other times a number of people need to be involved to get the thing done. Sometimes information has to be passed to one or two people, at other times the whole workforce may need to know.

COMMUNICATION

Meetings deal in information. Some exist only to impart it, others discuss information to solve a problem or decide on action. Whatever the meeting, there is usually some information to be communicated at the end of it. The way this information is communicated will depend on a number of factors such as the culture of the organisation, the nature of the information itself – its complexity or importance – the managment style of the communicators, the need for speed and many more. When you have to communicate information after a meeting, you may wish to ask yourself:

- what needs to be communicated
- to whom
- how
- when

Usually you need to choose between written and spoken communication.

Written communication

Minutes
Minutes serve an extremely useful, though limited, purpose. They are a record of the meeting, so they need to be seen by certain people for specific reaons (these are covered more fully in Chapter 5). Minutes can play an invaluable part in helping implementation. They can:

- remind people of what was agreed and the action they need to take

- help to increase motivation to put a plan into action
- strengthen resolve to implement a task

Circulating the minutes is not the best way to communicate the decisions of a meeting to large numbers of people. There may be individuals or departments who need to know just some of the decisions made, i.e. those that affect them directly or indirectly. The way you communicate information from a meeting depends on the number of people who need to know, the nature of the information and the conventions used by your own organisation. Let us look at some of the other methods.

Memos

Informal, even handwritten, memos can be used to communicate a small amount of information to a few people. Alternatively, they can convey a specific piece of information to the whole staff – for example, a security announcement to alert everyone to the dangers of unknown and unclaimed packages. Memos are fairly public so should not be used for information that is politically sensitive, secret or controversial.

Letters

Letters can contain more sensitive and secret information, but they are not always the best way to break news of a startling or unpleasant nature to people. They are best used to confirm facts that people knew or suspected. For example, if you need to inform someone that they are to be made redundant, it is perfectly reasonable to do it by letter provided they already knew this was likely to happen. If it's a bolt from the blue it can cause a great deal of unnecessary stress and will not lead to good relations with the remaining staff.

Reports

Some meetings take such major decisions that it is necessary to write and send out a report. Obviously, the circulation list will depend on the content. Perhaps the full report would go to senior staff or those directly involved, but it may be necessary to send a potted version to all staff.

Directives
Sometimes as the result of a meeting, it is necessary to send a directive to all staff. This is usually done by letter or memo.

Newsletters
Some organisations have a newsletter system that distributes all major decisions and other company news on a regular basis. This is an effective way of ensuring that all staff are kept up to date, but only if the information is not urgent, since newsletters are often distributed on a monthly or bi-monthly basis.

Get the sequence right
When you send out your memos, letters, reports, or newsletters to a large number of people, ensure that they are sent in the right sequence. Politically, it is sensible to ensure that people of high status within the organisation receive their copy of the report at the same time as the people who attended the meeting, if they are of lower status. It is not a good idea for the chief executive to accidently find out about something which everyone else has known for a week.

Spoken communication
If a manager's staff allocation needs to be cut by three in order to remain within the budget next year she is unlikely to be delighted however she hears about it. But there are ways of softening the blow. One is to tell her in person. Face-to-face communication allows the person giving the bad news to empathise with the reaction of the person receiving it. It also allows the listener to ask questions to ensure they understand the reasons behind a decision.

Even if a large number of people need to be told of a change of plan or direction, it can be more effective to hold a briefing session than to write to them – especially if the information is complex (see Chapter 4, *Planning a meeting*). If it is, follow up the briefing with written confirmation. Thus the manager losing her three staff has it confirmed in writing after the face-to-face interview. This means that the information becomes official, is recorded and filed.

IMPLEMENTING DECISIONS

To be effective, this process should start before the meeting begins, should be considered during the meeting, and continue after the meeting has finished.

Before the meeting

People are likely to be an organisation's most expensive resource, so even before you bring them together, it makes sense to check that they are going to be able to operate without too many obstacles. Some of the obstacles that need to be considered are:

- financial restraints
- resource restraints
- political restraints

Financial restraints

These are a fact of life. Budgets never seem to be just right – either you are not able to spend what you want because you would go over the limit, or you have plenty in the budget for technology, but nothing for extra people.

Unless the people who are meeting have done their homework and are aware of any financial restraints that might affect their decision, they will have problems trying to implement it.

Resource restraints

You must also make sure that the resources that might be needed to implement a plan are not only financially available, but *physically* available. Are there enough people in the organisation willing to work on Sundays? Is there actually enough space to extend the workshop at Basingstoke?

Political Restraints

These need to be taken into account for every major decision made at a meeting. Before they decide to close a branch, open a helpline, or make 100 people redundant, the participants must be absolutely clear about the precise limits of the meeting's authority. They may have a wonderful idea and the enthusiasm and drive to carry it through, but unless they also have the authority to do so, they are wasting their time.

They must also check that any agreed outcome is politically acceptable. Will it upset good relations between management and union? Will it deeply offend the sales department? Is the managing director opposed on principle to anything that smacks of cosseting the workforce? These and other such questions need to be asked before coming to a decision.

Think carefully about the political implications of decisions, preferably before the meeting occurs. It's an awful waste of time and money to come up with a good plan, only to bin it because it's not politically acceptable.

Taking the example given at the beginning of this chapter about the company newsletter, some of the restraints that should have been taken into account were: *budget:* whose budget would it come out of? and *resource/politics.* Resource is the restraint most likely to apply because if the MD wants it, it's politically OK. The resource restraints include the time needed to edit it and the availability of contributors. Would someone need to take it on as part of their job? This might be politically sensitive as it could be seen either as kudos to have responsibility for an internal newsletter or a problem to have to find time to do it.

At the meeting
The factors affecting implementation that need to be considered at the meeting are:

- attending to detail
- clear delegation
- the people factor

Attending to detail
Taking our earlier example, it's easy enough for a group of managers to decide to have a company newsletter, but unless they consider the details they will not know what the major constraints are. Who will decide how contributions will be encouraged, what

sort of contributions are wanted, how often the newsletter will be brought out, how it will be distributed, etc? Unless the major problems have been anticipated by the meeting, the chances of that newsletter actually being produced successfully are fairly low. Many more great events have been planned than have happened, because the vision was there but the detailed planning was not.

When something is decided at a meeting the details should include: what is to happen, to whom, when, where, by whom, with what, how. So that, for example, at a meeting of the pensions department about the Christmas party, it is not enough to decide to have one. If a Christmas party is to take place the detail needs to be filled in. For instance:

- the type of event it will be
- whether or not partners are invited
- the date
- the place
- the time
- how much it will cost and who pays
- how long it will last, etc.

Not forgetting, of course, one of the most crucial details of all: who is to organise it. Which leads us on to:

Allocating responsibility
Failing to allocate responsibility is one of the most common reasons for lack of action after a meeting. There must be very few people who have not been involved in the sort of conversation that goes:
'Can we have your report on the xyz then, Josephine?'
'Oh, Sally was doing that.'
'No I wasn't, you were supposed to.'
'I'm sure we agreed that you were going to do it, Sally' and so on.

The responsibility for action must be allocated to a particular person or persons so that everyone is crystal clear about who is responsible for what, and who needs to liaise with whom.

If one person is responsible for some action, he or she needs to know exactly what is expected of them, when and to whom they need to report and what are the deadlines and the constraints. If a number of people are involved, they must be absolutely clear who is doing what, and what co-operation and consultation is needed between them.

Going back to the example of the Christmas party, if Anthea agrees to approach a band, she needs to know the date they are wanted. This may depend on the available slots at the local Palais de Dance which Gary has agreed to sort out. Anthea and Gary obviously need to get together.

The people factor

The meeting must also consider how an agreed plan or decision might affect people within the organisation. It might be a much better use of resources to replace Nellie the tea lady with drinks machines on each floor. It might be more convenient, allowing people to have a drink when they want it, rather than waiting for Nellie to make her slow and arthritic way around the building. It might also be cheaper and allow greater choice. However, the staff like Nellie and her trolley. They enjoy the ritual of queueing up with their mugs and having a joke and a gossip. They enjoy the crusty rolls with cheese spread and the rather nasty coffee that Nellie sells in the morning, not to mention the excitement of wondering whether she will have sticky buns with the even nastier tea in the afternoon.

So the decision to replace Nellie, taken for the sensible pragmatic reasons of cost and convenience, might cause deep resentment among the staff. The outcome would depend on the depth of staff feeling, the level at which the decision was taken and how important getting rid of Nellie was in terms of time and cost saved. It is just a small example of the problems that can occur when the reactions of the people who will be affected by the decision are not taken into account.

After the meeting

After the meeting, implementation is affected not only by what is done, but by the way it is done. The factors that can affect implementation after the meeting are:

- the way the decision or information is communicated to people
- the motivation and commitment of the people who are to carry out the plan
- monitoring and evaluation procedures

The way in which the information is communicated
The people who are going to implement the decision must be told in the appropriate way. Their motivation and commitment can be crucially affected.

The office of a construction company was badly in need of refurbishment and more up-to-date technology. The staff knew that a meeting was to be held to decide on these two points.

At the meeting, two decisions were made:

1. *not to go ahead with the refurbishment plan at the moment because cash was a bit tight*
2. *to review the decision in three months time if cash flow improved*

The managers at the meeting also agreed that cash flow was likely to improve because of the increased number of orders in the pipeline.

The staff were told that the refurbishment plan would not go ahead, but not that it was merely postponed. They were told of the decision by memo, which meant that they had no chance to ask questions. As a result, they became very demotivated.

As we said earlier, information of a sensitive or controversial nature should be communicated face-to-face. Whether or not people are given reasons for decisions can also affect how they feel about implementing a decision.

Motivation and commitment
Perfect plans don't work unless the people who are going to be affected by them or carry them out also think they are perfect – or at least pretty good.

The success of the plan obviously depends on the people who are chosen (or who volunteer) to implement it. The enthusiasm and willingness they feel depends on:

- the degree of ownership they feel for the project
- the perceived need for carrying out the project
- the recognition they feel they are receiving
- the support they feel they are getting

Ownership

Imagine that you are a member of a squash club committee. Membership is growing very quickly and it is becoming more and more difficult to book a court when you want one. You are part of the team that decides to build an extension to the club that will include three new courts and enlarge the bar.

Because you have been part of the decision-making process, you are much more likely to feel committed to achieve the plan than a casual member who plays on a Saturday morning. Ideally people who are going to execute a plan should be present at the meeting that discusses it, but in this far from ideal world it is not always possible. But if the person who has to implement a plan is not present when it is decided on, he or she needs to be given the chance to take ownership of the task somehow. Only the people who feel ownership of the plan will have the drive and enthusiasm to put it into execution.

To feel ownership an individual needs the opportunity to get involved in the vision behind the plan as well as the practical details. Thorough briefing and an opportunity to ask questions is one way of achieving this. If a number of individuals are involved, it is better to brief them together: when colleagues ask questions and discuss outcomes, everyone becomes personally involved and begins to feel a joint ownership. (For more on ownership, see the Ownership Spiral, Chapter 9.)

Perceived need

Going back to the squash club example, the committee clearly perceive the need for new courts and will start fund-raising projects.

The Saturday morning player will support these projects if he sees that there is a need for the extension. If on the other hand, he has never had any trouble getting a court when he wants one and can always find a place to sit at the bar, he is less likely to support fund-raising events which cost him hard-earned cash.

People must see the need for a decision or project, especially if it involves change. Many people resist change but this resistance is strengthened if they do not understand the reason for the change. If someone is to be involved in implementing a plan, he or she needs to understand the reasoning behind that plan and the necessity for it to happen.

Recognition
Many of the classic theories of motivation agree that one of the major motivators is recognition. If you write a really good report and you know it is good because you have really pulled out all the stops, is it enough to know that you've done it well? Or would it be better if your boss told you so? When you do a good job, you get some intrinsic satisfaction from the feeling that you have performed well, but praise and recognition that you have done well is more likely to motivate you to perform well again.

> *At management seminars we sometimes ask two questions concerning praise and recognition. The first is: 'Do you praise your staff enough.' Usually, more than half the participants put their hand up. Then we ask: 'Do other people praise you enough?' Usually, the number of hands drops by half. Yet we have asked the question of managers ranging from very senior to very junior. The proportions vary very little. We have formulated what we call the law of Praise Recognition: 'People feel that they praise others more than others praise them.'*

So if you are responsible for the implementation of a plan or decision agreed at a meeting and you need to involve other people, make sure that you give them recognition for their efforts.

If you are chairing the meeting, don't forget to recognise the work carried out by the people there, which might include implementing action, providing information, or presenting a report.

Recognition of their efforts and achievements will help to ensure their continuing support.

Support

When people go away to take some action after a meeting make sure they are not abandoned without any form of support network. Such a network can be very informal and can be set up at the meeting. Depending on the importance and complexity of the task, support can be provided by one person whom the implementor knows he can turn to, or by a group who communicate regularly.

Monitoring

This is the continuous process of checking that things are progressing as they should, that time-scales are being kept, that people understand what has happened so far, that it is clear what should happen next and so on. It may involve:

- follow-up meetings
- interim reports
- day-to-day checks

Follow-up meetings

If the action involves several people they may need regular meetings to ensure that everyone keeps up-to-date. Sometimes an individual needs to report back to and consult a group that made the original decision, or has some expertise in the matter. Follow-up meetings do not usually mean reconvening the original meeting, but involve only those who are concerned with a particular decision or action.

Interim reports

If an action is proceeding as planned and the only reason for a follow-up meeting would be to give information, it may be sufficient to send a written report or memo to those concerned. This keeps everyone up-to-date without incurring the time and expense of a meeting.

Day-to-day checks

This is an area of dual responsibility. The person responsible for the action should liaise with key implementors on a regular, possibly day-to-day basis, keeping up with what they are doing, and providing them with encouragement and recognition. The person actually carrying out the work should report any problems or changes of plan to the person with overall responsibility.

Evaluating

Evaluation occurs less frequently than monitoring and will make more judgements about whether or not the action is successful or the decision was right. In order to evaluate, the original meeting should have set some criteria for success. How would you measure whether or not a decision to set up a scheme for internally advertising vacant posts was successful? Would it be successful if it advertised some posts? If some departments used it? If it eventually got off the ground in a year's time? Having criteria for success involve setting standards of performance:

- quality – e.g., accuracy, consistency
- quantity – e.g., number produced
- time – meeting deadlines
- cost – within budget

Evaluation may also involve follow-up meetings, or even reconvening the original meeting if monitoring shows that it is difficult for one reason or another to implement the original decision.

Sadly, human beings spend more time looking at what went wrong than at what went right. Only too often, meetings are called to evaluate decisions that are *not* going according to plan. Wouldn't it be nice now and again to have a meeting to celebrate plans that went well?

SUMMARY

All meetings should have some sort of outcome and that outcome needs to be communicated or implemented. It makes sense to think about who the information should be communicated to and choose the best way of doing it. Some information is best disseminated by written means, some face-to-face. When decisions need to be implemented, aspects such as financial, political and resource restraints should be considered before the meeting. Details should be checked and responsibility allocated at the meeting, which should also take into account the likely reactions to any decision. After the meeting, motivation and commitment can be enhanced by ownership, perceived need, recognition and support. Any action should be monitored on a regular basis and have its success evaluated.

CHECKLIST – FOLLOW-UP AND FOLLOW-THROUGH

1. Do you have a clear idea of what needs to be communicated, to whom, and by when?
2. How private, sensitive or startling is the information? What is the best way to communicate it?
   Minutes?
   Memo?
   Letter?
   Report?
   Directive?
   Newsletter?
3. Have you sent it to, or told the right people in the right sequence?
4. Have you considered all the restraints that might affect implementation?
   a) financial restraints
   b) political restraints
   c) resource restraints
5. Have you attended to all the details, such as who needs to do what, dates, times, places, costs etc?
6. Have you allocated responsibility for actions?
7. Have you taken into account the likely reaction of people outside the meeting who might be involved or affected?
8. Have you made sure that any decision or course of action is communicated in such a way that those affected will be prepared to accept it?
9. Do the people who are going to implement the action feel motivated and committed to do so?
   a) Do they feel ownership for the project?
   b) Do they understand the need for carrying out the project?
   c) Are they receiving the recognition and praise they deserve?
   d) Do they have the right kind of support?
10. Have you monitored the implementation of the decision with follow-up meetings, interim reports or day-to-day checks?
11. Have you evaluated the action by measuring it against standards of quality, quantity, time and cost?

14. Other Kinds of Meetings

So far we have concentrated mainly on planned meetings in businesses and other organisations. However, there are many other kinds of meetings, and the purpose of this chapter is to discuss any significant differences they may require in our behaviour. We have divided the chapter into five categories:

1. formal meetings and ceremonies
2. meetings with experts
3. informal meetings
4. meetings with food
5. meetings using technology

FORMAL MEETINGS AND CEREMONIES

Some meetings are very formally structured. For instance, a court of law has clearly defined roles for the major participants. The AGM of a company, a charity, a society or any other organisation usually has a very clear and strict agenda. A shareholders' meeting or an extraordinary general meeting will very often have, at least to start with, a formal structure.

All these meetings combine practical business with an element of ceremony or ritual. Meetings like speech days, weddings or funerals, military honours and other ceremonial meetings, have ritual as their main purpose rather than the transacting of business.

The crucial point is to know the agenda and formula by which these meetings work and to be clear on your part in it. A court of law is a good example of a very clear and rigid formula that involves the transacting of business specific to each individual.

As with all meetings, the essential ingredient is good preparation. It is important to anticipate the kinds of questions that may be asked, or the data that may be needed. Over and above this obvious point, you may have the additional pressure of publicity, stress and emotional involvement with the outcome of the meeting. Being a witness in court is in essence no different than being, say, an expert at a business meeting. However, the pressure of cross examination make it hard to give effective and useful evidence. In the same way, a media interview may unnerve someone wishing to contribute to a debate on a subject of importance to them.

The best advice we can give is to be as thorough in your preparation as you would be for any ordinary meeting, and to give yourself as much practice in the unusual circumstances as you can. In other words, practise being interviewed on television, rehearse being cross-examined by a lawyer, plan what you will say when you accept an award, go through the marriage lines before you say them to your betrothed. No one can guarantee success, but familiarity with the ordeal will reduce stress levels to some extent.

MEETINGS WITH EXPERTS

We live in an age where experts and specialists abound. They may be information technologists, lawyers, doctors, accountants or providers of specialist services. Part of the problem with experts is that because they are expert they don't appreciate when they are talking clearly and when they are talking jargon. (An expert has been defined as a person who doesn't know that he is speaking jargon.)

We referred in Chapter 7 to the Belbin approach to dealing with specialists. Here is an additional idea to help clarify how much progress you are making (see figure 14.1 overleaf). The left side of the matrix shows what the expert knows about your problem and what the expert does not know about your problem. Along the top of the matrix is what you know and what you don't know about the problem.

Figure 14.1 Meetings with specialists and experts

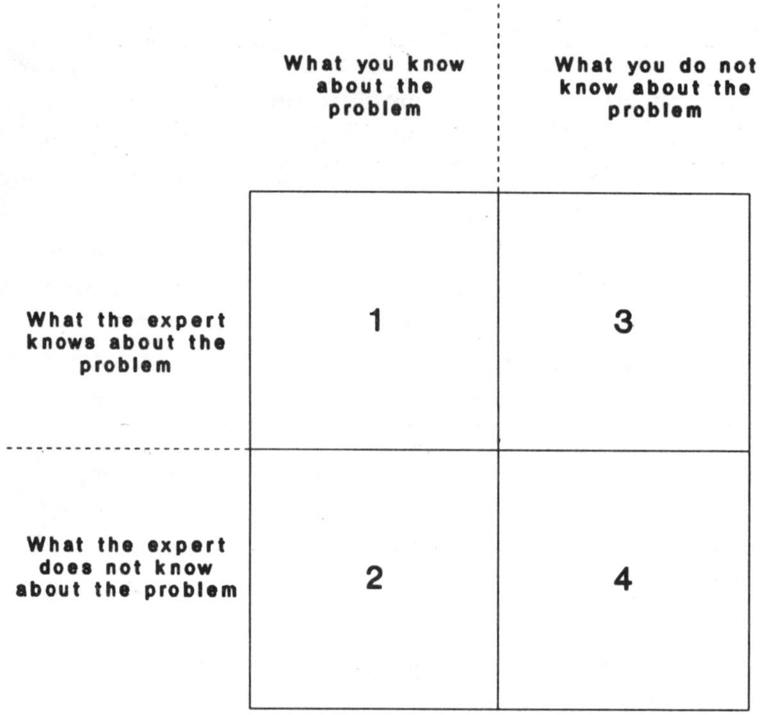

	What you know about the problem	What you do not know about the problem
What the expert knows about the problem	1	3
What the expert does not know about the problem	2	4

We recommend that in dealing with any expert you should proceed from box one through to box four in the way indicated. Resist the temptation to jump straight to box three and ask the expert to solve your problem from her existing knowledge. She may then make a snap judgment based on an insufficient grasp of your particular problem. Unfortunately some experts jump straight to box three because they feel they know exactly what is wrong and what has to be done to put it right. Ideally, go through the following four stages.

Stage One

Meet the expert and brief him or her on the problem. Start with what you both understand about it, including the language you will use to communicate the various aspects of the problem. You may need to learn some of the expert's jargon before you can describe precisely what your own problem is.

Stage Two

Elaborate on the areas of the problem the expert is unaware of. Explain about other influences on the problem outside the specific expertise you are asking for. You go beyond the expert's speciality because it is very likely there are vital things he or she really needs to know. For instance, in discussing a new computer system, you need to mention that you are planning to move offices in 18 months time so that the expert can take this into account in thinking through the implementation of the new system.

Stage Three

Now the expert quizzes you about the problem using his or her view of what has been described so far. This is where you discover aspects of your problem that you had not expected or had not thought about. For instance, with the computer example, it might be that the expert wants to know to what degree your managers would be prepared to learn keyboard skills in order to make use of electronic mail, sending their own faxes, accessing centralised data, etc. In this part of the discussion the expert is putting forward possibilities and refining ideas with you to check what is possible and what would be appropriate to your own needs.

Stage Four

The final stage is to explore a solution that would be most appropriate to your needs. Stage Four should be new for both parties. If it is not new for you, then ask yourself why you are employing an expert. If it is not new for the expert, ask yourself if the expert is genuinely tailoring a solution to your specific needs. After all, every problem is slightly different.

In talking to experts it is very easy to be overwhelmed by their confidence and the dreaded jargon. How many of us in meetings with doctors, lawyers and other authority figures have felt pressured to accept their advice without ever getting into stages two or four?

We suggest that when an expert is invited to join the meeting, it must be the joint responsibility of the expert and the other participants to ensure that everyone understands what is said. The Emperor's New Clothes Syndrome of accepting jargon without challenging it is a recipe for disaster. If you find yourself having to translate to your colleagues what the expert said, then something is going wrong. Make sure the expert speaks in plain language in the first place.

INFORMAL MEETINGS

Many meetings simply happen because we bump into people – in corridors, by the coffee machine, in toilets, in the car park – and if we need to talk we take the opportunity. Meetings held in corridors are just the same as other business meetings with two important differences. First, neither of you has had the chance to prepare. Second, there is no one officially taking notes. If your chance meeting with Fred is to be of value, and not rebound badly, there are two things you need to do:

1. When you see Fred ask him if he has time to talk about the export problem. If he says yes, watch and listen very carefully. He may be being polite or he may be feeling guilty that he ought to be able to speak about it but genuinely isn't ready. You are wasting your time having a meeting under these circumstances.

2. Let us assume that Fred is ready to talk about the export problem and you go ahead. The most important thing to do now is to summarise what you have agreed and write it down immediately. You can write it on anything you like but make sure that no more than 30 seconds go by before writing something down. When you get back to your office take the extra precaution of sending Fred a brief note – handwritten will do – of what you have agreed, any time deadlines and any other people who need to be involved. Copy them in as well. At a normal meeting you will have minutes as a written record. The danger of corridor meetings is that you both go away believing something slightly different about the outcome.

Some people argue that to get the best out of certain kinds of meetings you have to choose the appropriate place. There is probably a lot of truth in the joke that many board meetings are fixed in the toilet before and afterwards, while the formal meeting in the boardroom is just for show. In the same way it is argued that some meetings around tables need a more relaxed setting if the business is to be properly conducted. Many sales meetings are held in restaurants, at the theatre or wherever the atmosphere is convivial.

MEETINGS WITH FOOD

Breakfast meetings, lunch meetings, dinner meetings, meetings with beer and sandwiches – all have the extra complication of food and drink. One selection technique for young officers used by certain British regiments was to invite them to dinner and watch how they conducted themselves during the meal. This was considered just as important as the more formal interviews and tests. A major oil company still has a formal dinner with senior managers as part of the selection procedure for graduates. If you are going to mix meeting with eating, then a few precautions are worth taking.

At a restaurant table you will never have a large note-pad, lots of papers, a flip chart and all the other paraphernalia of normal meetings. So, ensure that any note-taking that has to be done won't knock all the plates on to the floor and tip over wine glasses. A narrow pad is useful because a normal A4 pad is often too large.

Bear in mind that people don't talk quite as freely when their mouths are full. Influencing a meeting often means breaking into the conversation at pauses in the discussion. If the pause comes when you are just about to swallow the meat and potatoes, you are going to have more difficulty in speaking, let alone influencing. We have attended many breakfast meetings where at least half the participants ate nothing at all. If the breakfast meeting is significant and you intend to say a lot, always eat beforehand, is our advice.

Alcohol is a hindrance to clear thinking and memory. If the wine has been flowing freely, it may blur memories of the decisions taken. Past masters of dinner meetings always reduce decisions to a very simple yes or no and numbers. These can be written down on a napkin or a shirt cuff and kept for the next day to resolve any arguments. They also try to ensure that both parties exchange notes on what they have agreed at the time. There is nothing like your own handwriting to convince you that you actually said something.

MEETINGS USING TECHNOLOGY

With telephone and video conferencing we can now hold meetings without the participants being physically present. Video conferencing especially is used by companies with multi-site headquarters spread around one or more countries. The initial set-up costs may be high, but for regular meetings it's a lot cheaper than flying people from New York and Aberdeen to London.

The major points to remember when telephone or video conferencing are these. First, there is often a slight delay between you speaking and the person in Scotland or Sweden receiving the sound and vision and replying. You must pause before following up any comment you make, since you may find yourself talking over another participant. In telephone conferencing, always indicate if you want a particular person to speak and announce who you are if your voice does not make that obvious. As we discussed in Chapter 8, body language adds to the meaning of the message you are sending. In the absence of these visual clues, you have to convey information by sound alone.

A video conference does allow visual aids, but only those that can be seen on camera. Sometimes a member of a video conference will have an adviser off-camera, and it can be very irritating for participants at the other end of the line to see their colleague continually whispering to an unseen party. Much better to bring him or her into the meeting.

Another use of technology is for simultaneous translation. Again this normally happens in a conference room where you can see the other participants. One has to get used to the slight delay in hearing the translation.

Sometimes gestures in one culture are perceived differently in another. It can be disconcerting to a westerner to hear the translator through the ear-phone saying broadly, yes, when the speaker (from the east) is shaking his head!

CONFERENCES

We have included conferences in this chapter because they combine all five of the categories already mentioned. A useful definition of a conference is 'A series or collection of planned and unplanned meetings'. The word normally refers to a fairly large, set-piece gathering of people for a specific purpose.

The formal agenda of a conference is often concerned with the speeches made by a smallish number of keynote speakers and sometimes with formal discussion groups. Occasionally these may involve specialists or use technology. The ceremonial or even ritual aspect of conferences is more marked in some organisations than others, but almost all conferences have some sort of ritual, or after-dinner speakers if nothing else.

The informal agenda of the conference is the opportunity for many people to meet, sometimes with people they do not see very often, or have not met before. There are opportunities for renewing old acquaintances and making new ones. Deals are done and contacts are made; networks are enlarged. These informal meetings take place in corridors, over food or waiting to get into the conference room.

To get the most from the formal aspect of a conference, you need to be well aware of what is on the agenda, the value and meaning it has for you, and how you can best influence it. To do this you need to have done some homework.

To get the most from the informal side, find out who might be there that you would like to influence in some way, and take advantage of the opportunity to meet people who may only be a name on a sheet of paper or a voice on the other end of the phone. Don't forget a notebook to record what went on.

SUMMARY

Meetings come in endless shapes and sizes. They vary from the formality of a court of law to the informal meeting in the loo. Some will be very carefully thought out and planned, others spontaneous. Formal and ceremonial meetings need to be planned and rehearsed.

Meetings in odd places such as corridors need a check for readiness to discuss the issue and a record of what was discussed. Meetings with experts need to be well thought through, with much information passing back and forth before a solution is suggested. Meetings with food need thought and preparation, too – and if you don't spare the wine you may spoil the winning. If you use technology in your meetings, be patient and especially careful to ensure that you understand and are understood. Conferences have many uses, both formal and informal. Use them to influence and extend your networks.

CHECKLIST – OTHER KINDS OF MEETINGS

FORMAL MEETINGS AND CEREMONIES
1. Are you aware of the agenda and formula and your own part in it?
2. Have you prepared as thoroughly as you can to lessen the stress caused by the formal or ceremonial aspect?
3. Have you practised?

MEETING WITH EXPERTS
4. Have you briefed the expert on the problem as you see it?
5. Have you learned some of the expert's jargon?
6. Have you expanded on the problem to give the expert a wider picture?
7. Has the expert questioned you in detail about the problem?
8. Has the solution illuminated something new for you and for the expert?

INFORMAL MEETINGS
9. Are you sure the person you have bumped into is ready and willing to talk about the subject you wish to raise?
10. Have you written down a summary of what was agreed and given a copy to the other person?

MEETINGS WITH FOOD
11. If the meeting is really important, are you prepared to forego the food and drink?
12. Do you have a suitable-sized pad for notes and do you ask other people to write down what they think was agreed?

MEETINGS USING TECHNOLOGY
13. Are you prepared for the slight stiltedness of meetings using telephone and video conferencing?
14. Have you remembered that the discussion will not be as spontaneous and that non-verbal clues will not be as good?

CONFERENCES

15. Conferences marry all of the above aspects of meetings. Are you prepared to get the most from them, both formally and informally?

15. Developing a Talent for Meetings

> *On 13th January 1982 at approximately 15.30 hours, Air Florida flight 90 was due to take off from Washington DC's National airport. The temperature was several degrees below freezing and it had taken the crew nearly half an hour to taxi into position for take-off. During that period the (junior) first officer said several times how concerned he was about the bad weather. On take-off he said that the speed indicated did not look right but he was overruled by the captain. When the aeroplane stalled, it crashed into the barrier wall of the 14th street bridge and fell into the icy waters of the Potomac River. It was just one mile from the runway. Because of the conditions only four passengers and one crew member of the original 79 on board survived.*
>
> *Although the first officer had repeatedly questioned the wisdom of taking off without further de-icing procedures, the captain had overruled him with disastrous consequences.*

This tragedy helped to convince airline managers that there was a considerable need to change air crew procedures on the flight deck. Analysis of accident statistics suggests that human errors are the major cause of about 70 per cent of aircraft accidents. Further analysis shows that more than 50 per cent of accidents occur either on take-off or landing, when air crews have the most tasks to complete, and the greatest need to co-ordinate their actions. During take-off and landing the captain, first officer and flight engineer are all required to cross-check their decisions in order that the flight can proceed safely. The quality of their interventions is therefore of enormous importance.

We do not normally think of flight crews having meetings while managing a flight but all the elements are the same as at any business meeting. The major difference is that they are making decisions and taking actions that, as flight 90 showed, can have life or death consequences.

In this chapter we look at ways in which organisations can develop better meetings. First, the company itself. What it can do is to create the right circumstances to encourage people to go on looking for better ways to conduct their meetings and implement the decisions.

There are a number of ways it can do this:

1. putting learning on the agenda
2. improving the quality of leadership in meetings
3. understanding how meetings can be developed
4. systematic evaluation of meetings
5. using a meetings coach
6. mentors at meetings
7. action learning
8. developing a learning organisation

PUTTING LEARNING ON THE AGENDA

Nothing in organisational life stands still. So why should you assume that the type of meeting that worked well last year will be equally effective this year? You improve your production, processing and delivery technologies, you upgrade your computers, so why not regard your meetings as a kind of soft technology that needs to be continuously developed?

One reason why we do not do this is a general reluctance to change. Wille and Hodgson, in their book *Making Change Work*, discuss the logical and emotional barriers that we erect against change. The four-stage model of learning they quote helps explain why changing an existing set of skills, like the way we run a meeting, is often so hard.

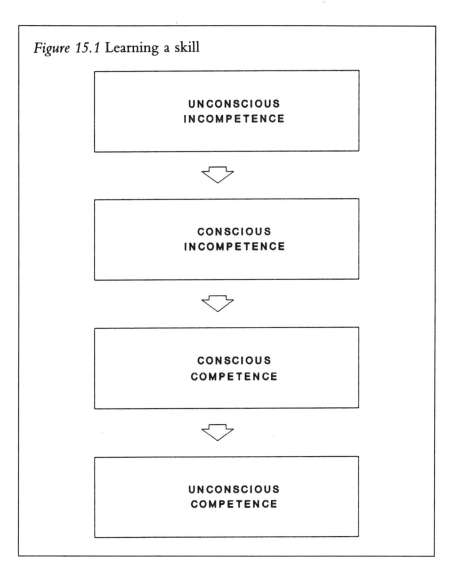

Figure 15.1 Learning a skill

UNCONSCIOUS INCOMPETENCE

CONSCIOUS INCOMPETENCE

CONSCIOUS COMPETENCE

UNCONSCIOUS COMPETENCE

Unsconscious incompetence
When you don't even known how hard the skill is. Ice skating looks easy until you first put skate to ice. Then you are at the second stage.

Conscious incompetence
Now you know how hard it is, and this knowledge can be discouraging. The first time you try to chair a meeting of strong willed

'shapers' or 'activists', you may be tempted to blame them for the fact that the meeting overran, and only covered half the agenda. Actually, it might be because of your own lack of skill . . . which brings us to the third stage.

Conscious competence
By now, with effort and concentration, you can use the skill reasonably effectively. When learning to drive a car it is usually at this stage that you take your driving test. It is nerve-racking partly because you know that any distraction will impair your performance. You need to keep up your concentration. The final stage is:

Unconscious competence
When you have thoroughly learned the skill and are running on a kind of auto pilot. You use active listening techniques automatically, without having to think about them or even concentrate very hard.

This model describes how we learned every skill since speech and walking. Generally speaking, if you are learning the skill for the first time, the progression from one level to the next can be great fun. The problem comes when you try to improve a skill.

Change often involves changing the way you use existing skills, rather than learning new ones. To make these changes you have to go back to the conscious incompetence stage. For instance, I am adjusting to a new keyboard that has a new position for the function, delete, and arrow keys. I am continually making mistakes (I am conscious of my incompetence) which I know I would not have made on the old keyboard. It is not encouraging. I would love to ditch the new keyboard and go back to the old one. Instead, I blame the manufacturer and, in the short-term, regret the decision to buy the new machine.

Reviewing your meetings so that you learn from them will probably involve becoming conscious of your incompetence. Facing up to an area of incompetence is the only way to improve, but it is frequently not very enjoyable. A voice in your head tells you that you have learned this skill once already in your life and why should you have to learn it again. So before you put learning on the agenda, be aware that this kind of learning is not without discomfort.

IMPROVING THE QUALITY OF LEADERSHIP IN MEETINGS

Returning to the airline example, it is easy to see that the flight crew want to do everything in their power to ensure the safety of their plane. But before the detailed analysis of the cause of crashes was carried out it was widely believed that nothing could be done. Accidents were put down to 'pilot error' and filed, when they should have been put down to 'meetings error'. Some captains were not always receptive to the idea that they were conducting meetings on the flight deck, and that it was the meetings that needed to improve, rather than the flying skills.

Many airline captains operating in the 20 years before the Air Florida disaster gained their original training in a military setting. In the military, a single-seat fighter is likely to be the final training ground of the pilot. Here he has a rather different job than a commercial pilot. The work is dangerous but it is also romantic. There is a large reserve of ground-based advisers to help get him in and out of the combat situation as fast as possible. The attitude for combat flying is quite different to the co-ordination required for flying an airliner in peacetime.

The heroic leader
The military pilot is very often attracted by the individual heroism of flying a combat aircraft. And it is that heroism that he takes with him into a civilian job.

Although your weekly production meeting may seem a long way from the flight deck of a modern airliner the same principles are to be found there. We are all attracted to heros. We have grown up on books and films peopled with magnificent creatures who always triumphed before the end of the story. They succeeded by taking on all responsibilities themselves, and by a mixture of sheer technical brilliance and intellectual insight they were able to defeat the opposition, solve the problem, beat the earthquake, put out the fire, right the wrong or whatever.

David Bradford and Allan Cohen have identified two kinds of heroic leader: the manager as a master technician, and the manager as conductor. These two concepts also help to explain why meetings do not develop as effectively as they could, and why sometimes everything is left to one person. Bradford and Cohen identify what they call the post heroic leader, or the manager acting as developer. We will examine this approach later, but let us first look at the two heroic styles.

The master technician approach to meetings

If you know your subject well enough, you should be able to answer any questions on it, and be better at it than any of your subordinates. Managers who have grown through a technical speciality are often loath to give up their technical expertise. Managers of accountants still try to be better than their staff at tick and bash, IT managers still aim to write better software, engineers to do better drawings, etc.

Meetings dominated by a master technician will soon be subordinated to the expertise he brings with him. He sees the meeting as a kind of solo act with the grateful audience showing its appreciation from time-to-time as complex tricks are pulled off before their eyes. This compares with the flight deck where, of the three people employed, only the captain was engaged in solving the problem. It goes without saying that the more complex and difficult a task, the more important it is to get as many brains around it as possible. Technicians, whether acting as the chairperson or a major contributor, always tend to pull all the data and the decision-making to themselves. Without meaning to the master technician excludes others from having any real part to play.

There will also be an increased focus on technical rather than managerial aspects. Data suddenly assumes considerable importance, or at least the data the technician regards as significant. Other data may not get considered at all. This style can be effective when there is little need for interaction between the members of the meeting; it will be largely resolved on the basis of technical knowledge and expertise. It is a kind of management by numbers and for those people who like numbers it can be very comforting. It is only those other people who can see the wider implications who recognise what may be going badly wrong.

Manager as conductor

Whereas the technician prefers to do everything himself, the manager as conductor wants everyone else to do the work. Conductors are skilled at this and are aware of how much they depend on others to make things happen. Conductors position themselves at the centre of the decision-making web. They like to see the complete picture and they see themselves as integrators of tasks. Very often they will use their considerable inter-personal skills to encourage others to get the work done. They will also be very concerned to set up the performance measures to ensure they know how the work is progressing.

Management by objectives, critical path analysis and other management information systems will be the stock-in-trade of the conductor. Conductors believe they alone can see the complete score. They spend a lot of time and energy making sure that each of their staff is playing the right part. When their control is threatened, conductors feel reassured to know that nobody else has all the musical notes written out in front of them.

The conductor-style works best in large and complex meetings. Co-ordination of subordinates to do sub-tasks is an important part of this leader's meeting method. Inside knowledge and a wide range of contacts are an important part of the conductor's armoury. Compared to her, most of the staff at the meeting are not very skilled or experienced.

The conductor-style does not work where subordinates are going to be asked to take direct responsibility for their own work and to bring their own inventiveness to bear on a problem.

The problem with heroic styles is that they focus most of a meeting's attention on the hero. Strong control is a feature of both styles, and there are many occasions where meetings do not need strong control, expecially when innovation and creativity are required. However, it is very tempting to slip into one of the heroic styles from time-to-time. They are strong and clear styles with which we are all familiar. But many meetings would increase their overall effectiveness if the amount of heroism was reduced, and the amount of development was increased.

Let us now look at the developmental style as it can be applied to meetings.

UNDERSTANDING HOW MEETINGS CAN BE DEVELOPED

Leader as developer

The alternative for the leader who does not want to adopt either of the heroic styles is to be a 'developer'. The developer does not tell others what to do but works alongside them to help develop their abilities. They develop *through* the job rather than off the job. The work of the meeting must continue, so the problem is how to develop the meeting while it is in progress and still achieve the tasks it was set up to do.

> A group of five managers were set a simple task: to produce a revised budget. They knew they were being recorded on closed-circuit television for a de-briefing session later that day. Peter had been given the job of chairing the group. He knew very little about the technical aspects of the work but he drove the group as hard as he could, diving in with appropriate or inappropriate technical suggestions whenever he had the opportunity. Seen from the observation room, it looked as if he wanted to support the whole group with his efforts and energy alone. Although it contained two people who were quite financially fluent, the group was getting in a muddle. No one was quite sure of the true objective of the meeting since only Peter had the full brief. It was clear they were not going to meet their deadline.
>
> After the meeting had come close to stalling on several occasions, Peter was asked to step out of the group and to hand over his briefing notes to the meeting. The group fell on the notes and read them avidly. Peter came to watch the meeting from the observation room. To his amazement, horror and eventual embarrassment, the meeting carried on better without him and solved the problem in a matter of 15 minutes. It

was a painful but salutary lesson for him. With all his effort and energy he had actually been slowing the meeting down. The group had worked better without him, and if Peter had wished to act as a developer, then one of his major contributions would have been to remain silent.

Compare Peter's failed heroic approach with the developmental style used by Suzanne in the next example.

Suzanne is chairing a meeting to design and produce a recruitment brochure for school leavers. None of her team has done this before. Mary asks what should go on the cover. Instead of saying what she thinks, Suzanne asks the rest of the group for ideas. She asks who is going to see the cover, and what message it is trying to convey. From the discussion that follows, three good ideas emerge – all from other members of the meeting. David asks how long the brochure needs to be. Again Suzanne turns the question around by asking how much the prospective reader might want to read before making contact with the personnel department.

What Suzanne is doing is getting the other members of the meeting to think through the necessary details of the brochure for themselves. If they get stuck, or go badly wrong, she will tell them and offer ideas of her own. But as far as possible she encourages them to develop their own proposals. At a later stage she even takes a risk by inviting Neema to put a rough sketch together and take it directly to the personnel manager rather than check with the meeting first. As the meeting progresses, Suzanne asks the others how they are doing as a project group, and if there is anything missing. Paul challenges everyone's assumptions about the printing deadlines they have to work to and comes back triumphant from the phone to say that they have four days more than they thought. And so on.

Suzanne works as a developer by creating the opportunities for all the participants at the meeting to learn and progress. She takes risks but she learns too. Her meetings get better and better.

Many managers probably have the same effect as Peter in our first example. It is so easy to *tell* and much harder to *ask*. Yet Suzanne's way of asking questions generates a meeting that is learning and developing. Suzanne also praises everything that is done well so that participants appreciate that they are learning too. In the next section we look at ways of systematically reviewing the learning of the meeting.

SYSTEMATIC EVALUATION OF MEETINGS

If the participants at a meeting wish to develop they need to allocate some time to a review of their performance at the meeting. It can be quite painful to hear that an item you thought was unanimously decided was perceived by others to have been pushed through too fast. When conducting these reviews, it is tempting to re-open items from earlier on the agenda and sometimes that becomes necessary. For this reason, it may be advisable to review really difficult meetings at a different time, and not get the review tangled up with the work that the meeting was originally called to discuss.

If you are going to improve your meetings you will need to know about people's thoughts and feelings before the meeting.

Avoid post-mortems and witch-hunts
Very few people think of evaluating their meetings in a formal way. A post-mortem over lunch is often the best that happens. This frequently descends into a character assassination of the chairperson or other prominent participants. It will also dwell more on the negative, although there is no guarantee that anything will be changed or improved. This type of informal discussion could be more effective if conducted in a more structured way, with some positive analysis of the bad and *good* points of the meeting, together with some recommendations on what to do in future.

Structured evaluation and feedback
We use a lot of structured methods to evaluate decisions – investment analysis, performance appraisals, advertising impact and so on. Yet it does not come naturally to use the same approach with meetings. As with all evaluation systems, simplicity is best. The learning triangle in figure 15.2 represents a very simple structure that we find works well.

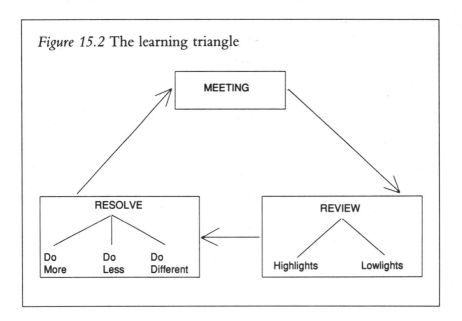

Figure 15.2 The learning triangle

1. Review the positive aspects of the meeting (the highlights) and acknowledge and praise where appropriate.
2. Identify the parts of the meeting that did not go so well (the lowlights) and analyse as precisely as possible what was wrong.
3. Agree on the type of behaviour that is lacking. Be as specific as possible. If you are going to do more of something then either you will need more time or you will need to do less of something else.
4. Identify what behaviour you or others should be avoiding to make the meeting work better. In the example above, Peter could have helped by asking more and saying less. If possible, highlight the parts of the meeting or behaviour of participants that others found irritating and explore how to reduce this. Also look out for time-wasters in the meeting, people, behaviour, agenda items and any other points that appeared to serve no useful purpose.
5. Was the meeting as efficient as possible? Are there any components that could be modified to improve it?
6. Agree what changes are to be made by whom and ensure that they are reviewed after the next meeting.

Formal feedback
For more formal meetings, some kind of questionnaire survey may be more appropriate. You could devise an evaluation form that asks participants their opinion of the meeting. Questions like:

- whether they received the agenda in sufficient time
- whether the agenda items contained enough detail
- how clear the objectives of the meeting were
- how helpful the chairperson was in giving the meeting structure (but be careful to check that the chairperson is ready to hear the truth!)

A questionnaire like this can be tremendously useful, but it can also prove to be political dynamite if the motives behind it are not made clear. Try to phrase questions in an unbiased way so that you are not accused of trying to bend the data.

Yes/no questions may not give you the range of meaning you feel you want. Have a look at the example below:

To what extent do you feel the objectives of the meeting were achieved?
Not at all   1   2   3   4   5   6   7   Completely

You may not wish to have as much as a seven-point scale, a five or even three point scale may be enough. Do not go above seven points, as evidence suggests that five to seven points is as many as most people can cope with. Summarising the response data will produce some statistics that can be fed back to the meeting. Bar charts of results can preserve anonymity, while clearly showing problem areas.

You may also wish to ask open-ended questions such as:
What in your opinion were the major problems which prevented the meeting from being more effective?
Since each answer will be different, you won't be able to produce statistics from the results. However, it may be more beneficial to have people's individual opinions tailored to the meeting you held.

USING A MEETINGS COACH

An additional way of developing meetings is to take a tip from athletes, artists and even managers: employ a coach. A meetings coach will come and sit quietly in a corner and watch the meeting while making notes and possibly diagrams. After the meeting the coach reviews with the members of the meeting how they got on, what they contributed, what opportunities they used and what opportunities they missed. A meetings coach is probably best at asking questions rather than making statements. Sometimes members of the meeting may have got so wrapped up in the content of the meeting that they will have forgotten what they said or how they said it. So the meetings coach may need to use other recording methods such as closed-circuit television. However, in our experience as coaches in a variety of meetings, if you can quote back a few words of what the person said, their memory will supply the rest quite naturally.

The meetings coach can live an exciting and dangerous life, especially if not all members of the meeting are fully convinced that:

- they need to develop
- that their need is equally as great as other members of the meeting!

There has to be a commitment on the part of all members of the meeting to want to improve and to develop. The meetings coach can identify which aspects of the meeting are ineffective, and can work out with the participants how to make them more effective, but those solutions will only be put into practice if the members of the meeting wish to do so.

At the meeting it is perfectly feasible for individuals other than the coach to tell each other how a meeting is going and whether they find contributions helpful or not. Feedback can be very powerful, and works best when an atmosphere of trust has already been created. For feedback to be effective, it needs to be given using a considerable degree of skill.

MENTORS AT MEETINGS

A meetings coach will be helping the meeting as a whole, and therefore each member of the meeting is of equal significance; a meetings mentor will be concerned with only one member.

Meetings mentors can be internal managers, the existing mentor to a participant at the meeting, or an external consultant. The technique the mentor will use is to review the meeting with the participant. He or she will go through how the participant contributed, or failed to contribute, to the meeting and discuss what actions and behaviour might need to be changed. Perhaps the participant will be perceived as being too aggressive, too forceful, too pushy and will have produced a negative reaction in other members of the meeting. They may have closed ranks to prevent the participant getting his ideas through.

In other cases the participant may not be assertive enough, and may have failed to win points that he should have won, or to contribute data that was significant. In our experience, acting as a mentor to a participant forces the person to look at himself and his attitude as well as the skills he brings to the meeting (we often find that although the skills may need to be polished, they are not really the main problem). Until the person shifts his attitude towards the value of the meeting, or the value that he himself can contribute to that meeting, the shift in skills is unlikely to follow.

ACTION LEARNING

This phase usually describes a group of people who get together either to do a job or to review tasks that their individual members have attempted to accomplish. The purpose of the meeting is to help others learn how to improve in whatever tasks or objectives they are setting themselves. Thus this meeting really puts learning at the top of the agenda and sets it as the task that all the other members of the meeting are committed to. Very often a facilitator will act as observer, coach and mentor rolled into one. His or her role is to challenge and support individuals as they struggle to learn from what they have done.

We find that a detailed, critical review of past and proposed actions is a very fruitful, but sometimes rather uncomfortable, form of learning. We mention it here because any group that wants to continuously develop its ability to meet more effectively will need to adopt some of the components of action learning while reviewing their own meetings.

Competitive advantage from continuous learning

Action learning works best when the participants are prepared to trust each other to give useful and appropriate feedback, and to act on that feedback and adjust the way they work accordingly. In turn, the recognition that your contribution is of genuine value to one of your colleagues acts as an enormous incentive to continue supporting that colleague as he or she attempts to modify her behaviour. Adult learning at this level is not easy, and often takes time to carry out. Nevertheless, in our view, it is one of the best ways for organisations to develop. Competitive advantage only comes from the ability to learn better and faster than your competitors. Since most businesses devote a considerable amount of time to holding meetings, it is patently obvious that even a small improvement in the effectiveness of meetings will result in competitive advantage for that organisation. Better meetings must eventually have an effect on the bottom line.

DEVELOPING A LEARNING ORGANISATION

When many parts of an organisation start to review how they operate, and actively seek to improve and develop, then it would seem reasonable to describe that as a learning organisation. The strategic importance of learning at an organisational level is only just being appreciated. At the same time, if your organisation has to cope with increasingly rapid change, then learning will become of growing importance as well.

As we illustrated above, developing the learning habit in meetings can also encourage learning throughout the organisation. We can anticipate the day when it will be normal behaviour in organisations not just to train their staff in the technical, supervisory and managerial aspects of their work but also to train them to pass on learning that has been gained from the review of meetings. While outside meetings coaches and mentors may be necessary to kick-start the process, in the end the organisation should seek to incorporate that behaviour as part of its normal routine. 'Learning is what we do, products are what we make' may well become the motto for many organisations in the future.

SUMMARY

Continuous development of meetings as a pro-active process should be the goal of all organisations. Taking remedial action with a particular meeting is a first step, but it is still fire-fighting. Making meetings a natural home for development can be achieved in a number of ways.

Put learning on the agenda of each meeting by including some kind of review. Encourage participants to give and receive practical feedback on how the meeting could be improved.

Carry out systematic, and if necessary formal evaluations of the meeting. Do not stop after the meeting content and decisions summary, but go on to review how the meeting has improved so far and how it could improve in future.

Use a meetings coach to provide an outside perspective, and perhaps to challenge habits that the meeting has become too comfortable with. For individual development, a meetings mentor might be more appropriate.

Review the style of leadership that is shown at meetings and the assumptions behind those styles. Heroic styles may be attractive but in many instances will not lead the meeting to learn and develop. Developmental styles may be harder to get going at first but will result in much more progress.

CHECKLIST – OTHER KINDS OF MEETINGS

1. How often do you discuss how the meeting went?
2. How often do you follow up that discussion with action lists and commitments to change?
3. Are you and your colleagues prepared to face some discomfort in reviewing your meetings? Will you risk facing up to your incompetencies?
4. What leadership style do you and others bring to your meetings? What is the proportion of *heroes* to *developers*?
5. How are you encouraging more developmental leadership?
6. What systematic forms of meetings evaluation do you use?
7. Are you taking precautions to ensure that evaluation isn't seen as a witch-hunt?
8. Do some of your meetings require formal evaluation? Can you circulate a questionnaire?
9. Do you use the learning triangle as a guide for evaluation and follow up?
10. Do all the members of a meeting agree on what needs to be changed? Do they all agree on the need to improve?
11. Will you review progress at the next meeting as part of the agenda?
12. Does your meeting need an external meetings coach?
13. Could one of the meeting participants use a meetings mentor?
14. Is is part of your organisation's strategy to encourage continuous learning, and the development of a learning organisation?

16. Meetings as a Management Tool

Meetings are the life blood of an organisation. Without them it would not be able to function efficiently. In any case, even if meetings are not planned, they happen – people bump into each other and discuss things. So meetings cannot and should not be avoided. What can and should be avoided are unproductive, time-wasting, frustrating meetings – the sort that give meetings a bad name.

In this book, we have looked at a number of ways to make the meetings you attend even more productive and useful than they already are. We have examined how to diagnose the problems of meetings, how to plan them, how to use procedures such as agendas and minutes to get the most out of them. We have suggested how you can improve meetings by the way you behave when chairing or contributing to them. We have looked at the way groups work, how to influence and how to make the best use of politics and power. Finally we explained how to develop a talent for meetings within the organisation.

So think about how meetings can be used as a management tool. What can you actually do to make your use of them a positive force for change? How can you ensure that after having had a meeting something has improved – even if the improvement is only a clearer perception of the problem? How can you make your meetings stimulating and exciting rather than tedious and frustrating? Why should you?

In Chapter 2, we discussed the cost of meetings and how cutting the time spent at them could save the organisation a great deal of money. Not only a saving of the time wasted in unnecessary or poorly run meetings, but in the opportunity cost – i.e. what those people could be doing if they weren't at the meeting. Think how much more productive you and your department could be if the meetings you held and attended were always productive. Not only would you be achieving better results in a shorter time but you would be using the extra time for something else – perhaps spending longer to get a report absolutely right, ring an extra client and gain some business, or even arrive home in time to see the children before they go to bed.

If meetings are stimulating and exciting, the participants will go away enthusiastic about decisions that have been made or action that needs to be taken. This enthusiasm and excitement will affect the rest of their work. If people feel that they are doing well they are likely to approach things more positively, which means that they will probably do them to the best of their ability. Conversely, if people come away from a meeting thinking 'Thank goodness that's over, what a waste of time', their negative frame of mind may well cause them to be less optimistic and positive about any other challenges they encounter that day, and not meet those challenges as well as they might.

So as a manager, part of whose job is to motivate staff and encourage them to produce the best they are capable of, it is in your interest to make the meetings they attend as productive and stimulating as possible.

A final checklist
If we have convinced you that it is important to improve the quality of meetings, then make use of this final checklist.

Make a Meetings Improvement Plan (MIP)
Plan how you could improve the quality of your meetings. Use the MIP on the next page for each of the meetings you chair or attend.

MEETINGS IMPROVEMENT PLAN

1. What is the purpose of the meeting?
2. Has a notice of the meeting been sent out?
3. Have the right people been invited?
4. Have pre-meeting papers been prepared and circulated?
5. Has a suitable location been selected?
6. Have you ensured that participants will be as comfortable as possible and eliminated any obvious distractions?
7. Are you using the best layout for the purpose of this particular meeting?
8. What *needs* to be on the agenda? Are all unnecessary items eliminated and necessary ones included? Have you consulted everyone you need to?
9. Have you chosen someone to make a record of the meeting? Do they have the necessary skills and sufficient knowledge of the subject matter?
10. How skilled is the chairperson? Is he or she clear about the purpose of the meeting? Have they a suitable leadership style? Have they enough skill to facilitate discussion that leads to decisions? Would any of them benefit from training?
11. How well does the group work together? Do you have the right balance between allowing the group free range, and exerting controlled leadership for the task the meeting is trying to achieve. If not, what can you change?
12. How good are the contributors? Do they make concise and useful contributions to meetings. Are they encouraged to do so? Do any of them need training to become more effective?
13. If anyone is trying to influence someone else at the meeting, is he or she going about it the right way? Have they taken into account the personalities, circumstances and needs involved? Could they learn better ways of influencing?
14. What sort of politicing goes on in your meetings? Is it useful or destructive? Is there anyone who attends with persistent hidden agendas? What can you do about these? Is power being used appropriately or inappropriately? What can you do about it?
15. What happens after the meeting? Are minutes sent out

promptly? Is all information passed on to those who need it in the most appropriate way? Are the decisions made and actions agreed always implemented to standards of quality, quantity, time and cost? Is everyone involved in implementation committed to it and motivated to do it? If not, why not? What can you do about it?

16. How can you develop meetings to be more useful and beneficial to the organisation? Should you improve the quality of the leadership? Would your meetings benefit from being formally evaluated and requesting feedback? Do you need a meetings coach?

POSTCRIPT

About a year before we wrote this book we carried out some research on high performance among senior managers. One manager we interviewed said that he regularly got into work at least an hour before anyone else. We asked why. He said 'That is when I can get some real work done.'

We asked what he did during the rest of the working day. 'Oh, mainly meetings' was the reply.

We have met a lot of managers who take that view – that meetings may be unavoidable, but they are not where the *real* work gets done. This saddens us because their attitude will inevitably lead to a self-fulfilling prophecy.

We hope that in this book we have done more than show you how meetings can be improved. We hope that we have encouraged you to feel that meetings can be effective. We would like to think that with the development of some skills and procedures, unlike our senior manager above, you will find that meetings *are* where the *real* work gets done.

BIBLIOGRAPHY

ARGYLE, M. (1972) *The Psychology of Interpersonal Behaviour*, London: Penguin.

ARGYLE, M. et al (1970) *The communication of inferior and superior attitudes by verbal and nonverbal signals*, Brit. J Social Clinical Psychology.

BADDELEY, S. & JAMES, K. (1987) *Owl, Fox, Donkey or Sheep: Political Skills for Managers*, Management Education and Development Vol. 18 Part 1 1987.

BACK, K. & K. (1982) *Assertiveness at work*, Maidenhead: McGraw-Hill.

BELBIN, M.R. (1981) *Management Teams: Why they succeed or fail*, London: Heinemann.

BENNIS, W.G. (1984) *Transformative power and leadership* (in SERGIOVANNI, T.J. & CORBALLY, J.E. eds (1984) *Leadership and Organisational Culture*, Urbana: University of Illinois Press.

BENNIS, W. & NANUS, B. (1985) *Leaders*, New York: Harper & Row.

BERNE, E. (1964) *Games People Play*, London: Penguin.

BRADFORD, D. & COHEN, A. (1984) *Managing for Excellence*, Chichester: Wiley.

CHAUDHRY-LAWTON, R., LAWTON, R., TERRY, A. & MURPHY, K. (1992) *Quality: Change through Teamwork*, London: Century Business.

FRENCH, J. & RAVEN, B. (1959) *The Bases of Social Power* in CARTWRIGHT, D. ed. *Studies in Social Power*, Ann Arbor: Institute for Social Research of the University of Michigan.

GRANDJEAN, E. (1986) *Fitting the Task to the Man*, London: Taylor and Francis.

GREEN, W.A. & LAZARUS, H. *Are today's executives meeting with success?*

HARRISON, R. (1987) in PLANT, R. *Managing Change and Making it Stick*, London: Fontana Paperbacks.

KANTER, R.M. (1977) *Men and Women of the Corporation*, Basic Books.

LEIGH, A. (1988) *Effective Change*, Institute of Personnel Management.

MARGERISON, C., DAVIES, R. & McCANN, D. (1986) *Team Management on the Flight Deck*, Leadership and Organisational Development Journal, Vol 7 1986.

MAUDE, B. 1975 *Managing Meetings*, London: Business Books.

RACKHAM, N., HONEY, P. & COLBERT, M. (1971) *Developing Interactive Skills*, Wellens.

PARKINSON, N.C. (1958) *Parkinson's Law or The Pursuit of Progress*, London: John Murray.

SCHUTZ, W. *The Interpersonal Underworld*, Consulting Psychologists Press.

URY, W (1991) *Getting Past No*, London: Business Books.

WARR, P. (1987) *Psychology at Work*, London: Penguin.

WILLE, E. & HODGSON, P. (1991) *Making Change Work*, London: Mercury.

Index